CIRCLE OF PROTEST

RONALD D. SCHWARTZ

Circle of Protest

Political Ritual in the Tibetan Uprising

Columbia University Press
New York

Columbia University Press

New York

Copyright © 1994 Ronald David Schwartz

Library of Congress Cataloging-in-Publication Data

Schwartz, Ronald David, 1947–
   Circle of protest: political ritual in the Tibetan uprising,
1987–92/Ronald David Schwartz.
      p.   cm.
   Includes bibliographical references and index.
   ISBN 0–231–10094–9 (alk. paper). — ISBN 0–231–10095–7 (pbk.
alk. paper)
   1. Tibet (China) — Politics and government — 1951– 2. China–
Politics and government — 1976– 3. Human rights — China — Tibet–
Religious aspects — Buddhism.   I. Title.
DS786.S347   1994
320.9515 — dc20   94–5522
                                                                  CIP

∞

Printed and bound in Hong Kong

c 10 9 8 7 6 5 4 3 2 1
p 10 9 8 7 6 5 4 3 2 1

This book is dedicated to
Geshe Konchok Tsering of Ganden Shartse Monastery
and to a new generation of Tibetans

ACKNOWLEDGEMENTS

Many people have contributed to the information and ideas that have taken form in this book. However, this book would not have been possible without the unfailing assistance of Robbie Barnett and the London-based Tibet Information Network. During the writing of this book Robbie has put the resources of TIN at my disposal. Equally important, he has been a constant source of inspiration and insight as we pondered together the implications of political developments inside Tibet and the shifting currents of Chinese policy. I am also indebted to Tsering Shakya and Lhamo Tsering for their help in translating the interviews. I have a special debt to Christa Meindersma, with whom I witnessed some of the events described in this book. I also owe a debt of gratitude to Nicholas Howen. There are others whom I wish to thank but am unable to name for fear it may compromise their continuing work on behalf of Tibet.

Pema Bum and Tashi Tsering provided advice on translating some of the material in the appendixes. Over the years I have benefited from many exchanges with Jamyang Norbu and Lhasang Tsering. These four Tibetan intellectuals are now associated with the Amnye Machen Institute in Dharamsala, India.

Tenzin Atisha of the Office of Information and International Relations of the Tibetan government-in-exile in India has facilitated my research and graciously helped me in manifold ways during my visits to Dharamsala. Others associated with the Tibetan Government who have aided my research and shared their thoughts with me are Tashi Wangdu, Tenzin Gyeche Tethong, and Lodi Gyari. I am grateful to His Holiness the Dalai Lama, who, as events have unfolded in Tibet, has found time on several occasions to discuss the situation there with me.

Over the years my colleagues at Memorial University have shown enthusiasm, and offered encouragement, for my Asian research endeavors. I am especially grateful to Elliott Leyton, Robert Paine, and Victor Zaslavsky for reading and commenting on portions of this book. Zygmunt Bauman has also been a source of inspiration and critical comment, encouraging me to bring political and cultural developments in Tibet in line with the insights of comparative sociology. I am also grateful to Judy Adler, Peter Baehr, Jean Briggs, Rick Johnstone, Volker Meja, George Park and Adrian Tanner for sharing ideas and experiences from many areas of research. Collectively, they have made Memorial University an ideal environment for reflection and writing.

I wish to thank Memorial University and particularly Michael Staveley, the Dean of Arts, for extending me sabbatical and research leave during 1987–8 and again in 1992–3, without which the research and writing of this book would not have been possible. A special note of thanks must go to Judi Smith, Secretary of the Department of Sociology, Memorial University, who, far beyond the call of duty, has never failed to meet my needs, forwarding mail and materials, even when I am calling from the top of a mountain on the other side of the world. Christophe Besuchet kindly prepared the maps.

The writing for this book was completed while I was an Honorary Research Fellow with the Centre of Asian Studies of the University of Hong Kong during the academic year 1992–3. I wish to thank Professor Edward Chen, Director of the Centre, and Coonoor Kripalani–Thadani, Assistant to the Director, for providing me with the facilities of the Centre during the final stage of writing. Hong Kong proved to be an ideal location from which to gauge the direction of current Chinese policies, and I benefited immensely from participating in the seminars offered by the Centre.

No amount of thanks is sufficient to acknowledge the help and support of Julie Brittain, formerly of Tibet University, my fellow conspirator and constant companion on the yellow brick road. She has been a part of every stage in the completion of this book.

Finally, I wish to express my gratitude for the help and trust of many Tibetans inside Tibet, who must of necessity remain nameless.

St John's, Newfoundland   R.D.S
January 1994

CONTENTS

MAPS

PHOTOGRAPHS

Between pages 112 and 113

NOTE ON THE TRANSCRIPTION
OF TIBETAN WORDS

Tibetan names and other Tibetan words that appear in the body of the text have been spelled phonetically to correspond approximately to the pronunciation of English speakers. The problem of spelling Tibetan names in English is complicated by the fact that there is no single system agreed on by all writers. The same Tibetan name will often appear with several variant spellings in different works. I have tried to make my own usage as consistent as possible, while, at the same time, sometimes conforming to the more common spellings of Tibetan names that appear elsewhere. The result is admittedly a compromise, and not rigorously phonetic, but it may aid the reader in recognizing Tibetan names.

I have followed the Wylie system of romanization for Tibetan equivalents for specific terms, inserting these parenthetically into the text, as well as for Tibetan appearing in footnotes and references. However, a number of Chinese words, particularly administrative and political terms, have been incorporated phonetically into Tibetan-language material produced inside Tibet. Here I use the Wylie system of romanization to transcribe Tibetan spellings of Chinese words rather than the more familiar pinyin. Thus, the word for "China" in Tibetan, as it appears in newspapers and official documents, is borrowed from Chinese and spelled *krung go* (Chinese pinyin spelling: zhongguo). Some terms are hybrid Tibetan–Chinese — e.g. *spyi bde cus* for Public Security Bureau (Chinese: gong an ju). In some cases in the text I have provided in parentheses the Chinese equivalent for administrative terms — e.g. Tibetan *shang* (Chinese: xiang). In addition, Chinese pinyin romanizations of Tibetan names sometimes occur in quoted material in English. I have left these as they appear — e.g. Jiangcun Luobo for Gyaltsen Norbu.

In general, where there is a Sanskrit word for a Buddhist religious term, I have used it in the text — e.g. Vinaya for "discipline", or Avalokiteśvara for the deity referred to by Tibetans as *spyan ras gzigs*. This follows the practice of Buddhist scholars, on the assumption that the Sanskrit terms are more familiar and more accessible to Western readers.

MAPS

Tibet

SCALE 1:11 000 000

KILOMETRES
0 50 100   200   300   400   500

STATUTE MILES
0   50   100   150   200   250

© Atelier Golok, 1994

Tibet Autonomous Region (TAR)

Areas with Tibetan autonomous status under Qinghai, Gansu, Sichuan and Yunnan provinces

Disputed territories between India and China

LHASA CITY

SCALE 1 : 33 000

KILOMETRE
0   0.25   0.5   1.0

STATUTE MILE
0   0.25   0.5   1.0

To Shungseb Nunnery and Ratö Monastery ↓

To Garu Nunnery ↑

☐ Chubsang Nunnery ↑

Sera Monastery

Drepung Monastery

Nechung Monastery

Sangyip Prison Nr.1

Sangyip Prison Nr.4

Sangyip Prison Nr.5

Michungri Nunnery

Drapchi Prison

To Gurtsa Prison ↑

Enlarged area

People's Hospital

Potala Palace

Ramoche Monastery

Jokhang Temple

Public Security Bureau

University of Tibet

To Ganden Monastery (40 km) ↑

Drib Military Camp

Public Security Bureau

TAR Government Offices

Police Headquarters

Hotel

Holiday Inn

Norbulingka

Enlarged area (inset)

To Shungseb Nunnery and Ratö Monastery ↓

Ramoche Monastery

Tsomonling

Shide Dratsang

Gyume Dratsang

Moru Dratsang

Tengyeling

Dekyi Sharlam

Remnin Lu

Jokhang Temple

Police Station

Police Station

Tibetan Hospital

Lhasa District Government Offices

Public Security Bureau

Mosque

Barkhor

Ani Tsangkhung

Mosque

Lhasa Government Offices

Jokhang Square

Women's and Children's Hospital

Military Camp

xv

1

INTRODUCTION

This is a book about demonstrations. It examines the emergence of non-violent forms of protest in Tibet since 1987. These demonstrations, led by young monks and nuns, have initiated a new phase of protest against Chinese rule in Tibet that has continued to the present. New terms have also entered the Tibetan political vocabulary, and Tibetans now associate their struggle for independence with demands for democracy and human rights. The book covers a five-year period, from the autumn of 1987 through 1992 — a significant one in both Tibetan and Chinese history. The outbreak of protest in 1987 exposed the underlying weaknesses in the Chinese strategy, launched in the early 1980s, of securing political control in Tibet through economic reforms. Martial law was declared in Lhasa on 8 March 1989, following two years of protest. Just three months later, on 4 June, demonstrations for democracy by Chinese students in Tiananmen Square were brutally suppressed, and a round-up of dissidents throughout China began. Subsequent events in both China and Tibet indicate the extent to which political repression remains an enduring feature of the Chinese political system. The apparatus of control in Tibet is the same as that throughout China. The Chinese response to protest in Tibet thus offers an opportunity to study in microcosm the limits of tolerance within the Chinese political system as well as its ability to contain dissidence.

Tibetans have been able to sustain, at considerable cost to themselves, an on-going level of protest that confounds Chinese efforts at suppression. During the period from 1987 through 1992 some 140 demonstrations by Tibetans have taken place, countless leaflets and posters demanding independence have been distributed, and many hundreds of Tibetans have been arrested. Protest has spread from Lhasa to other cities and to the countryside. The basis for Tibetan resistance lies in religion and culture, the revival of which was encouraged by Chinese policy during the 1980s, but which has had consequences unanticipated by the architects of reform. Chinese cultural and religious policy in Tibet has aimed to control and manage expressions of religion and culture and make these serve the interests of the Chinese state. Clearly the policy has not worked. This book will examine the reasons why.

1

Tibetan political aspirations pose a direct challenge to the Chinese state and the communist political system. Furthermore, the revitalization of a Tibetan national identity, which has accompanied the revival of religion and culture, has happened in spite of every effort by the Chinese to thwart it. In fact I argue that this process of revitalization is to a considerable extent sustained and reinforced by the instruments of political control designed to suppress it. Whether they take the form of conciliatory gestures or simply heavy-handed repression, Chinese policies are conditioned by the system that implements them. This book examines the apparatus of Communist Party power and its response to expressions of discontent as a necessary context for understanding Tibetan protest.

I should explain how I became involved in the study of contemporary Tibetan protest, since the circumstances were unusual. I arrived in Lhasa as a tourist on 12 October 1987. In the two weeks before my arrival three demonstrations had already taken place in Lhasa. Following the demonstration on 1 October, when a number of Tibetans were shot by police, flights into Lhasa had been suspended. I was on the last bus allowed to travel from Golmud for Lhasa. No new arrivals appeared over the next three months and the traveller population in Lhasa quickly thinned out as visas expired and people departed.

Many of the travellers resident in Lhasa when I arrived had witnessed the demonstrations. The event that precipitated the involvement of foreigners was the October 1 demonstration, when the demonstrators were arrested, beaten by police, and taken to a nearby police station. An angry crowd of Tibetans threw rocks at the police and burned down the police station in an attempt to free the demonstrators inside. For several hours police shot indiscriminately into the crowd, killing at least eight people and wounding many more. In the subsequent weeks a round-up of participants in the demonstrations and Tibetans with dissident views took place, with security police entering Tibetan homes at night to make arrests.

When I arrived in Lhasa a number of foreign travellers had already organized themselves into a network to collect information on arrests and imprisonment of Tibetan protestors. This information was used by journalists and human rights organizations who had been barred access to Tibet.[1] The network, which included several doctors, also provided

---

[1] For an account of how this information-gathering network operated, see Schwartz (1991).

medical treatment for Tibetans wounded in the shooting who were afraid to go to government hospitals. Since I spoke and read Tibetan, I was recruited into this network and over the next four months I was able to interview a number of Tibetans who had participated in the demonstrations or were involved in organizing protest activity. This included lay Tibetans as well as monks and nuns. It was still possible to travel freely, and I travelled throughout central Tibet, visiting monasteries and staying in villages. Though I was mainly concerned during this period with the human rights situation in Tibet, I began to consider studying the social and political background to current protest in Tibet based on material that I was collecting.

I spent the spring of 1988 in Dharamsala, India, where the Dalai Lama and the Tibetan government-in-exile are located. During this time I was able to interview new arrivals from Tibet who had escaped over the mountains into Nepal, then made their way to India to be absorbed into the refugee community. As well as young protestors, these new arrivals included many older Tibetans who had not necessarily been involved in recent protest, but who spoke movingly of their experiences in the decades since 1959, especially during the horrific decade of the Cultural Revolution in Tibet. Increasingly, however, I came to realize that current protest in Tibet needed to be understood in terms of the experiences of a younger generation of Tibetans who had grown up under Chinese rule and had no memories of Tibetan society before 1959. I was especially keen to locate young Tibetans — monks, nuns, and laypersons — who had come of age under the relatively liberal policies of the 1980s and yet still found reasons to challenge Chinese rule in Tibet.

The mood in Lhasa had changed considerably when I returned in September 1988. A new wave of arrests had followed the outbreak of protest in March of that year. The first batch of protestors who had been arrested in March were released toward the end of the summer, with accounts of widespread torture in Lhasa-area prisons. A year of political meetings, with cadres haranguing Tibetans about the dangers of "splittism" and the machinations of the "Dalai clique", had heightened Tibetan political consciousness and hardened resistance. Yet this was a heady time, with new political ideas in the air and Tibetans more and more openly voicing their dissatisfaction with the Chinese in Tibet and the communist political system. What had begun as spontaneous protest was now taking the form of more organized activism, with groups of dissidents planning and coordinating protest and distributing leaflets and posters.

My work during this second visit was much more systematic than on the first visit. I regularly met with the monks and nuns in the monasteries and nunneries around Lhasa who were organizing demonstrations. I heard first-hand accounts of prison conditions from released prisoners. My network of contacts within the dissident community touched every stratum of Tibetan society, including Tibetan cadres working within the Chinese administration, students at the university, merchants and business people, clerks and labourers. Procedures were developed to protect the identity of informants and to spirit materials out of Tibet. Though my primary focus during this period remained documentation of the human rights situation in Tibet, I was able to collect a great deal of information on the motives and aspirations of Tibetan protestors.

On 10 December 1988, International Human Rights Day, a small demonstration was organized by monks and nuns from several monasteries and nunneries in the Lhasa area. As the demonstrators proceeded into the central square they were confronted by a unit of the Chinese People's Armed Police, who without warning opened fire on the group of unarmed demonstrators as well as a crowd of Western and Tibetan onlookers. In the shooting one foreigner, Christa Meindersma, a Dutch friend of the author, was struck by a bullet. I accompanied her to the People's Hospital, where I saw other people with serious gunshot wounds brought in for medical treatment. The hospital was filled with Public Security officials. Following the shooting, I was detained by Public Security and interrogated over the course of three days, and finally expelled from Tibet on 16 December. The events of 10 December brought my research inside Tibet to an end. They also afforded me a personal encounter with the security apparatus through which China maintains its hold over Tibet.

The materials on which this book is based were collected under difficult conditions. The subjects of this study were involved in activities regarded as illegal by the Chinese government. Meetings with dissidents inside Tibet took place in secret. The clandestine nature of this research necessarily affected the variety and quality of the data that have been collected. The richest material comes from interviews with committed activists who were prepared to take the risk of speaking at length about their experiences and aspirations. I found, however, that their views were quite consistent with those expressed by many other ordinary Tibetans from different backgrounds whom I encountered in the course of my time in Tibet. Nevertheless, a study of this nature, focused as it is on protest and protestors, is selective and partial — a slice through contemporary Tibetan society from just one angle. Much information that would be relevant to a more complete study of contemporary Tibet was unavailable under the conditions of research I was forced to contend with. I was in no position to investigate the point of view of Chinese in Tibet or to approach the Chinese administration there directly. Chinese perceptions of the situation in Tibet are gleaned from statements by officials, Party and government documents, or from accounts offered by Tibetans working inside the Chinese administration.

For the events described in this book I have attempted to reconstruct the most accurate account possible. Some of these events I witnessed myself. In every case I have sifted through the testimony available to me of participants as well as Tibetan and Western eye-witnesses. Where there have been discrepancies, I have been forced to use my judgement in selecting the most reliable information. Particularly in accounts of crowd situations such as demonstrations and riots — and especially when people are under fire — there can be varying and sometimes contradictory reports of what happened. Informants may have a confused or partial view of events, and there is always a tendency to exaggeration. I hope I have erred on the conservative side. I believe that, based on all the material available to me, my reconstruction of events is substantially correct.

Since 1989, when Tibet was closed to free travel by foreigners, The Tibet Information Network (TIN), a London-based organization devoted to research and documentation of contemporary Tibet, has become the principal source of information on the current situation in Tibet. Relying on Tibetan sources inside Tibet, TIN assembles reports from Tibetans living in Tibet, and receives Party and government documents and copies of protest literature prepared by underground groups. TIN has given me privileged access to its incoming reports during the preparation of this book, as well as to original copies of both Party and government documents and material from underground Tibetan sources. Most of this material is available nowhere else. The wealth of Tibetan-language "internal circulation" material — documents restricted to Party cadres — in the possession of TIN has been an invaluable resource, providing a context for interpreting policies and public statements by officials.[2]

---

[2] This kind of material is usually referred to by its Chinese classification: *neibu*. In Tibetan it bears the designation *nang khul* ("internal") or *gsang ba* ("secret").

A comprehensive picture of the human rights situation in Tibet has emerged over the last few years, with lists of political prisoners and detailed accounts of treatment and conditions in prisons becoming available. Reports dealing with human rights abuses in Tibet have been issued by Asia Watch, Amnesty International, and others.[3] I have not focused specifically on this aspect of the situation in Tibet — describing, for instance, the treatment of political prisoners in Lhasa-area prisons only where I have thought it relevant to understanding the mechanics of interrogation and political indoctrination. In part this is because a treatment of human rights abuses in Tibet is available elsewhere. More important, however, I do not wish to portray Tibetans solely as victims. The price paid by them for dissent is high; protestors are well aware of the consequences of their actions and are prepared to risk death or imprisonment to express themselves politically. Nevertheless, within the harsh political environment of Chinese rule Tibetans have been able to restore some measure of cultural integrity and initiate a process of nation-building in spite of the obstacles. Their victory may be largely symbolic, but it is a victory none the less.

Because this study is concerned primarily with understanding recent protest in Tibet I have touched only cursorily on the larger international context of the Tibet problem — and then only to the extent that this has had an impact on events inside Tibet. The outbreak of protest in 1987 focused international attention on Tibet and provided an impetus for a range of initiatives by legislators in Europe and the United States, as well as initiatives on Tibet at the United Nations Commission on Human Rights in Geneva. One consequence of this increased concern with Tibet was the award of the 1989 Nobel Peace Prize to the Dalai Lama. Tibetans inside Tibet are aware of developments on the outside and have drawn encouragement from them. Also, a dialogue between Beijing and representatives of the Dalai Lama over starting negotiations to resolve the question of Tibet continued until 1989, when the Dalai Lama broke off contact following the declaration of martial law in Lhasa.[4] Though the history of this dialogue is beyond the scope of this

---

[3] See *Political Prisoners in Tibet*, Asia Watch and Tibet Information Network, February 1992; *People's Republic of China: Repression in Tibet, 1987–1992*, Amnesty International, May 1992; and John Ackerly and Blake Kerr, *The Suppression of a People: Accounts of Torture and Imprisonment in Tibet*, Physicians for Human Rights, November 1989.

[4] For the history of this dialogue, see Norbu (1991).

book, the prospect of it bearing fruit provides a backdrop to some of the events described here.

Since the opening of Tibet to the outside world in the early 1980s there has been a steady flow of people and information. Tibetans inside Tibet have received permission to travel to India to visit relatives among the refugee community, and Tibetan refugees have been allowed to visit Tibet. This has introduced Tibetans in Tibet to new ideas and influenced their thinking in a variety of ways. They are certainly familiar with the persistent demands of Tibetans in India and scattered throughout the world for independence for Tibet, and they have come to appreciate the respect accorded the Dalai Lama in the West.

The Chinese government has persistently claimed that protest in Tibet has been orchestrated from outside — by the "Dalai clique" and "foreign reactionaries". The question is sufficiently important to need addressing. I found no evidence that the demonstrations that have occurred in Tibet since 1987 were initiated or organized by "agents" of the exile government. Though the first demonstration by the monks of Drepung monastery on 27 September 1987 was precipitated by news of the Dalai Lama's visit to the United States, Dharamsala was as much taken by surprise by this act of protest as the Chinese government. Certainly no one, least of all the monks, anticipated the violence that followed as a result of the Chinese response to what have been essentially peaceful demonstrations. The exile government is quite right to feel that current protest in Tibet vindicates their efforts to keep the Tibet issue alive over many years. Tibetan loyalty to the Dalai Lama has been strengthened through protest. But the exile government and the Chinese government have both reacted to events. In particular, the young monks and nuns who have initiated the demonstrations come largely from rural backgrounds and are the least likely to have had contacts with Tibetans from abroad. The clandestine contact that the exile government has maintained with Tibetans inside Tibet over the years has been primarily with an older generation of Tibetans who remember pre-1959 Tibet and have personal ties with the exile community. The much more radical Dharamsala-based Tibetan Youth Congress, which sometimes advocates violence and sabotage directed at the Chinese, has a history of sporadic clandestine activity in Tibet, but appears to have played no significant role in current protest.

This is not to say that what broadly might be considered "propaganda" material has not found its way into Tibet. Tapes and videos of the Dalai Lama speaking on political as well as religious subjects are very much in demand and circulate underground among Tibetans. The Dalai Lama's message is always one of non-violence and respect for human rights and is significantly devoid of anything that might inflame hatred toward the Chinese. Publications printed by the exile government on political subjects also circulate (though these include as contraband material Tibetan language copies of the United Nations Universal Declaration of Human Rights. Simple leaflets printed in Nepal and India with independence slogans have also appeared in Lhasa. Sometimes in English as well as Tibetan, these are easily recognizable because of the quality of the printing, which is higher than that obtainable locally. Tibetans will distribute these leaflets if they have them, but they are not particularly informative, merely repeating familiar slogans. Tibetans involved in political action often told me that they were far more interested in receiving real information from the outside — in particular, news about China and the world in the Tibetan language, and non-Chinese sources on Tibetan history and culture. Perhaps the most important recent development in this regard is the establishment of a Voice of America Tibetan-language broadcast service.

In this study I have relied exclusively on material produced by Tibetans inside Tibet. These leaflets and pamphlets are generally hand-drawn and crudely reproduced on copying machines or by wood-block printing. They demonstrate the attempt by Tibetans to define their situation and grapple with the political issues that determine their fate. The authors of these materials have been singled out for the harshest punishment by the Chinese authorities and always face long prison sentences if they are caught.

The demonstrations that have taken place in Lhasa since 1987 are acts of cultural invention. Tibetans have developed a form of protest that reflects their present circumstances. There is no reason to assume, as the Chinese government has, that the demonstrations are part of a conspiracy orchestrated from abroad. Tibetans have largely improvised as events have unfolded, depending on a shared stock of experiences and cultural expectations to inform their actions. In any case, conspiracy theories do not make good sociology. Tibetans are not political dupes, easily tricked and manipulated. Their actions reflect their real feelings and experiences. If there is one thing that this book illustrates, it is the capacity for resistance — and plain stubbornness — that Tibetans continue to display in their response to Chinese political control in Tibet.

On the other hand, there has certainly been a "feedback effect" between protest inside Tibet and international endeavours on behalf of

Tibet, with each reinforcing the other. The exile government has been quick to capitalize on expressions of discontent by Tibetans inside Tibet. It has also been forced to accommodate a new influx of refugees from the unrest in Tibet, and has begun a process of political and administrative reorganization to present itself more effectively to the world as the legitimate representative of Tibetan interests (this has involved significant democratization of its own political structures). Tibetans inside Tibet, in turn, have increasingly looked to the exile government — and the Dalai Lama in particular — to represent their interests on the international stage. Nevertheless, the fact that protest continued even after foreign access to Tibet was curtailed, and has occurred in rural areas where there is no possibility of international attention, indicates that protest is generated from indigenous sources.

One of the most contentious issues regarding Tibet is establishing the boundaries of the area under discussion. When the exile government and most ordinary Tibetans refer to Tibet, they include eastern Tibetan areas, known to Tibetans as Kham and Amdo, that have been administratively incorporated into the surrounding Chinese provinces of Sichuan, Qinghai, Gansu, and Yunnan. Many of these eastern Tibetan areas came under the nominal control of the Manchu imperial government from the early eighteenth century onward, though the actual administration remained in the hands of local chieftains. The Tibetan government in Lhasa regained control of parts of Kham in the latter half of the nineteenth century by itself defeating the local powers. China attempted to establish direct control over Kham during the last decade of the Qing dynasty, launching a military expedition to subdue the fiercely independent peoples of the area. The government of the 13th Dalai Lama reaffirmed the Tibetan claim to all of these eastern Tibetan areas when it proclaimed the full independence of Tibet in 1913, following the fall of the Qing dynasty and the establishment of a republican government in China. Chinese troops were expelled from the areas under the Lhasa government's jurisdiction, and uprisings against the Chinese took place in eastern Tibetan areas. During the chaos of the decades of war and revolution in China, no government could be said to have exercised effective control in these eastern Tibetan areas.[5]

---

[5] See Goldstein (1989) and Richardson (1984) for accounts of Sino-Tibetan relations in eastern Tibet during the decades before and after the fall of the Qing dynasty and the establishment of the Chinese republic.

The Tibet Autonomous Region (TAR), an administrative entity created by the Chinese communist government, continues the Chinese administrative divisions of Tibetan-inhabited areas. The TAR more or less corresponds to the political entity over which the government of the Dalai Lama exercised political control in 1950. Nevertheless, the exile government has persisted in the historical claim of the government of the Dalai Lamas to these eastern Tibetan areas. In fact, the refugee community in India consists of Tibetans from all Tibetan-inhabited areas, and thus the demand for a return of *all* of Tibet — referred to as *chol ka gsum* (the "three provinces") or *bod chen mo* ("great Tibet") — remains a core demand of the exile government.

This is primarily a study of protest against Chinese rule as it has occurred in Lhasa and other areas of central Tibet. But there has been a considerable amount of political activity in eastern Tibetan areas as well, both in the form of protest in support of Lhasa-area demonstrators and protest in response to local conditions. Certainly the activists organizing the demonstrations in Lhasa have never spoken in any other terms than of a single united Tibet including Kham and Amdo. The expectations of Tibetans from these areas is more difficult to gauge. The relative freedom of movement during the 1980s has meant that many people from these areas have been able to visit Lhasa on pilgrimage and business or reside there. Lhasa remains the cultural and national "capital" for all Tibetans. Likewise, loyalty to the Dalai Lama, who is himself from Amdo, is as strong for Tibetans from Kham and Amdo as for any other Tibetans. On the cultural level there is clearly a strong sense of a Tibetan identity that includes all Tibetans — stronger perhaps than before the Chinese took control.

Only 2 million of the 5 million-plus Tibetans live inside the TAR.[6] Most of the others reside in so-called autonomous prefectures and counties inside Chinese provinces. Though some Chinese have always lived in these areas, the influx of settlers since 1950 has resulted in large minorities, and in some cases majorities, of Chinese settlers living in Tibetan areas in the new cities, towns, and settlements that have sprung up. Tibetans are administered by Chinese provincial administrations and subject to laws and policies formulated to meet the needs of the hundreds of millions of Chinese citizens of these large central provinces. Nevertheless, the Tibetan and Chinese communities remain separate,

---

[6] The exile government claims that in all Tibetan-inhabited areas incorporated into China, including the TAR, there are more than 6 million Tibetans.

with little integration, and with most of the benefits of Chinese economic policy flowing to Chinese settlers in these areas. The fact of being a minority in one's own land has no doubt contributed to a sense of Tibetan identity.[7]

Where I have reliable information, I occasionally refer to political developments in the eastern Tibetan areas that are incorporated into the Chinese provinces of Qinghai, Gansu, and Sichuan. I cannot answer the larger question of whether the aims of Tibetans in these areas are also those of the demonstrators in Lhasa, or what they expect in the long run from a settlement of the Tibet question. Tibetan inhabitants of these regions are at a double disadvantage: the influx of Chinese settlers has been much greater than in central Tibet, and has continued steadily since the 1950s, while political and economic decisions emanate from an administrative system centred in the capitals of large Chinese provinces. On the other hand, the political structures of the TAR have been in place more or less unchanged since its inauguration in 1965. It is the Party and government apparatus of the TAR that directly impinges on the lives of the people who are the subject of our discussion.

This book examines only the most recent phase of Tibetan protest against Chinese rule. However, Tibetans have engaged in protest and resistance in various forms ever since the arrival of PLA troops in areas inhabited by Tibetans. In the first two decades of communist Chinese rule, armed insurrection posed a constant threat to Chinese forces. Armed resistance to the occupying PLA in eastern Tibetan areas throughout the 1950s culminated in the Tibetan uprising of 1959 in which the Dalai Lama along with some 80,000 Tibetans fled Tibet for India. The "17-Point Agreement on Measures for the Peaceful Liberation of Tibet," which was signed on 23 May 1951, by representatives of the Dalai Lama's government and the new communist government in Beijing, offered assurances that the traditional political and economic system in Tibet would be allowed to continue in return for acceptance of Chinese sovereignty over Tibet. However, the areas of Kham and Amdo that came under direct Chinese administration were not covered by the agreement. Thus, the Tibetan population in these areas was not exempted from the socialist reforms underway in China and experienced the political campaigns of the 1950s, which included attacks on religion and the destruction of monasteries. The fear of similar measures being

[7] See *The Long March: Chinese Settlers and Chinese Policies in Eastern Tibet*, International Campaign for Tibet, September 1991.

introduced in central Tibet, combined with the flood of refugees fleeing Chinese measures in the east, in turn precipitated attacks on Chinese troops by a growing guerrilla army in central Tibet.

The wholesale destruction of Tibetan society and culture that took place in the years following the suppression of the 1959 uprising are well known.[8] Many thousands of Tibetans died in the uprising or were sent to prisons and labour camps. All of Tibet came under direct Chinese rule for the first time, and the same "revolutionary" methods prevalent in China were applied throughout Tibet. In the years following the uprising Tibetans were subjected to endless rounds of political education and "struggle sessions" in which "class enemies" and "reactionaries" were singled out for criticism and punishment. Participants in these meetings were required to beat, torture, and sometimes execute victims who were their neighbours, friends, and kin. During the first few years after the uprising most of the monks and nuns were sent home and the monasteries and nunneries closed. Monks and nuns were also denounced and targeted in the "struggle sessions."

The implementation of the "democratic reforms" in Tibet subjected every Tibetan household to a system of classification according to "class criteria" devised in China. Those who received unfavourable classifications had their property confiscated. The same treatment was extended to "reactionaries", i.e. those who had supported or participated in the uprising, regardless of their class standing, including their families and children. Though the initial phase of socialist reform — consisting largely of the redistribution of land and property among households and the creation of Mutual Aid Teams — might potentially have benefited ordinary rural Tibetans, this period corresponded with the Great Leap Forward in China and a time of food shortages and famine in which tens of millions of Chinese peasants died. Tibetans were no longer insulated from the economic disasters afflicting China. Much of the agricultural production in Tibet was confiscated by the Chinese government to meet its own needs. Severe rationing and famine conditions prevailed through 1963, with tens of thousands of deaths from starvation in Tibet, which historically has always been self-sufficient in food.

The inauguration of the Cultural Revolution in Tibet marked the beginning of a complete assault on Tibetan society and culture. Under the banner of destroying the "four olds" (old ideology, old culture, old

---

[8] For a description of conditions in Tibet following the 1959 uprising, and during the years of the Cultural Revolution, see Avedon (1986).

customs, old habits), Tibetans were punished for deviating even in the slightest degree from the new proletarian culture exemplified by the Red Guards (many thousands of whom were young Chinese who had come to Tibet to launch the campaign). Any display of religion was prohibited, the remaining monasteries were torn down, and all religious objects were confiscated or destroyed. The new round of "struggle sessions" and political education aimed to eradicate every vestige of Tibetan culture and identity, targeting not just former "class enemies" and "reactionaries", but virtually anyone. At the same time, the period of the Cultural Revolution signalled the beginning of a push to organize Tibetans fully into communes in accordance with the model prevalent in China. All individual property was confiscated by the commune and Tibetans became essentially forced labourers, following the orders of commune leaders as they worked to accumulate enough "work-points" to satisfy their subsistence needs. A system of unrealistic quotas and taxation produced unremitting hardship and poverty that lasted through the 1970s, with another major famine in the years 1968–73. The communes also functioned as a complete system of political control, restricting movement and subjecting every aspect of daily life to minute regulation.

In 1969 widespread armed revolt broke out in rural Tibet. Involving one-third of Tibet's sixty counties, the revolt was precipitated by the impending communalization of the countryside. The rebellion was suppressed only by the intervention of regular PLA troops. Though the details have never been made public by the Chinese government, the suppression of the revolt appears to have been particularly brutal, with mass public executions and large numbers of people being imprisoned.[9] Many young Tibetans also used the Red Guards as an opportunity to attack Chinese cadres. Tibetans who joined the ultra-leftist Revolutionary Rebels faction refused to take orders from Chinese, attacked and criticized Chinese leaders in the name of Mao, and ambushed and attacked PLA units. The history of this period has yet to be written, but it appears that a number of underground groups sprang into existence during the chaotic period of the Cultural Revolution, launching sporadic attacks on Chinese cadres and PLA soldiers. Guerrilla activity and sabotage continued through the 1970s.

The same hard conditions also persisted in Tibet throughout the

---

[9] Brief descriptions of the 1969 revolt can be found in Ngagpo (1988: 24–5) and in Goldstein and Beall (1989: 622–3).

1970s, though the intensity of persecution reached during the Cultural Revolution gradually subsided. The collectivization of the economy continued, with virtually all Tibetans organized into communes by the mid-1970s. Change only became possible after the death of Mao Zedong in 1976 and the ascendancy of the reformers within the Chinese Communist Party under Deng Xiaoping. A new strategy was defined for the United Front Work Department of the Party, which involved overtures to overseas Chinese, Taiwan, and the Dalai Lama, in an attempt to resolve outstanding issues. Propaganda vilifying the Dalai Lama was toned down. But the event which precipitated a revision of China's Tibet policy was the first visit by a delegation from the Dalai Lama to Tibet. Groundwork for the visit by the Tibetan delegation was laid through meetings between the Dalai Lama's older brother, Gyalo Thondrup, and representatives of the Chinese government in December 1978. One important consequence of the renewed contact between the Chinese government and the Dalai Lama was the release after 1978 of most of the prisoners from the 1959–79 period, many of whom were rehabilitated and returned to positions of responsibility in post-reform Tibet.

In late 1979 the first delegation from the Dalai Lama was sent to Tibet. Beijing may have believed reports from Party leaders in Tibet about the improvements in Tibetan living standards and the general satisfaction of the Tibetan people under Chinese rule. In any case, the reforms had yet to be implemented in Tibet, which had been ruled with a heavy hand since the 1959 uprising, and leftist cadres remained entrenched in the Tibetan administration. At that time the regional Party secretary, Ren Rong, a leftist opposed to Deng's reforms, was reporting that there was no support for the Dalai Lama and that Tibetans were ardent supporters of communism. Even after the delegation, which included the Dalai Lama's older brother, was besieged by thousands of enthusiastic farmers and herders as they toured Amdo, Ren remained confident that there would be no support for the Dalai Lama in Lhasa, the capital. In neighbourhood committee meetings, Lhasa residents were instructed to behave politely toward the delegation, even though its members were all "reactionaries."

The result was exactly the opposite: tens of thousands of Lhasa Tibetans mobbed the delegation in a huge display of affection and jubilation. Braving arrest, Tibetans in the crowd shouted out "Long live the Dalai Lama" and "Tibet is Independent." Subsequent visits by fact-finding delegations from the Dalai Lama provoked a similar response from the Tibetan people. The second delegation was greeted by huge crowds as they entered Lhasa. As members of the delegation addressed the crowds, Tibetans stood up, raised their fists, and shouted for independence. The visit was cut short and the delegation was unceremoniously expelled from Lhasa. The third delegation, led by the Dalai Lama's younger sister, completed its tour, but the visit of a fourth delegation, scheduled to leave in August 1980, was postponed indefinitely by the Chinese. This unexpected demonstration of support for the Dalai Lama after twenty years of communism led to the sacking of Ren Rong as Party secretary for Tibet, and prompted the fact-finding visit in May 1980 by Party general secretary Hu Yaobang and Chinese Vice Premier Wan Li.

When Hu Yaobang came to Tibet in 1980 to survey the effects of two decades of communist rule, he is said to have been shocked by what he found. Forced collectivization had left the local economy in ruins, the Tibetan people completely demoralized, and a pitifully inadequate infrastructure in the hands of Chinese administrators who were totally dependent on support from China. Hu is reported to have told Party cadres: "This reminds me of colonialism." On 30 May, while the second delegation from the Dalai Lama was on its way to Lhasa, Hu made a series of recommendations for a new policy that became the basis for the reforms in Tibet during the 1980s. His recommendations were in line with the reforms going on throughout China, but they also attempted to specifically redress the situation in Tibet. Hu's six-point reform policy for Tibet included the following directives:

1. The Tibet Autonomous Region government should fully exercise its autonomy.

2. Tibetan farmers and herders should be exempt from taxation and compulsory quota sales to the state as well as the assignment of work without pay. They should be free to negotiate prices for the sale of their products.

3. A flexible economic policy should be implemented in Tibet recognizing Tibet's special situation and tailored to Tibet's special needs.

4. Subsidies from the central government should be increased to develop the local economy.

5. Within the socialist framework, efforts should be made to revive and develop Tibetan culture, education, and science.

6. The participation of Tibetan cadres in the local administration should be increased and large numbers of Han cadres should be withdrawn from Tibet.[10]

Hu's directives recognized the uniqueness of Tibet, its special characteristics and special needs. In principle they sounded a positive note, for the first time since 1959 acknowledging that Tibet was in fact different from China. They laid the foundation for the economic and cultural developments in Tibet during the 1980s. The exemption of Tibetan farmers and herders from taxes and quota sales was obviously popular. As in China, the rural economy was decollectivized, and land and animals were distributed among commune members. Farmers and herders were allowed to keep their produce or dispose of it for their own benefit. With the exemption from taxes, the standard of living of rural Tibetans rose immediately; with control over the disposal of their surplus, they could sell it in order to purchase commodities or, as they have done with unexpected enthusiasm, use their surplus to rebuild and restaff local monasteries.

The relaxation of religious and cultural policy was also well received. On the level of daily life many of the distinctive markers of Tibetan cultural identity gradually reappeared. Tibetans once again wore traditional clothes, men grew their hair long and wore it in braids — fashions which had been banned and severely punished during the Cultural Revolution. Tibetans were no longer made to feel ashamed of their culture. Religious observances also reappeared in daily life. Tibetans set up altars in their homes, and could be seen once again praying and making offerings to deities, turning prayer wheels, and visiting holy places on pilgrimage. The customary personal rituals of Tibetan Buddhism, for which Tibetans had received harsh punishments during the Cultural Revolution, could be practised without interference from the authorities.

The largely spontaneous rebuilding of temples and monasteries throughout Tibet also marks this period. The government had allocated funds for the rebuilding of some of the more important monasteries, but the impetus for this came from local people. It was an extraordinary development, since support for the monasteries is voluntary. The monasteries do not, for instance, own estates as they did in pre-1959

---

[10] For the full text of Hu Yaobang's recommendations, see Beijing Xinhua Domestic Service in Chinese, 30 May 1980, in *FBIS*, 3 June 1980, 1 (108): Q3–Q6.

Tibetan society. Villagers decide on their own to rebuild them and staff them with their own children. Though officially sanctioned, the Chinese administration has sought in a variety of ways to curtail and control this process of monastic revitalization. The monasteries represent the reappearance of a Tibetan civil society, outside state control, that had lain submerged for two decades. The reforms opened a space in Tibetan society for the re-creation of the one cohesive institution that Tibetans are able to identify as their own. As such, the monasteries have come to signify Tibetan nationhood and survival, and thus have become the principal battleground for Tibetan resistance to the Chinese state.

Hu's demand that Chinese cadres be withdrawn from Tibet and that the government of Tibet be placed in the hands of Tibetan cadres met with only limited success. In the first place, many of the older generation of Tibetan cadres that Hu found on his visit were as opposed to Deng's reforms as their Chinese colleagues. Trained by the military or in cadre schools, this entrenched group made its way up through the Party hierarchy during the period of collectivization in Tibet, and thus it has resisted implementing any policies which it fears will erode its power. Yet they remain the one group of Tibetans whose loyalty the Party leadership can count on, and thus Hu was in no position to call for their removal. The group of old Tibetan cadres is comfortable working in Chinese and no longer identifies with Tibetans. The overseers of two decades of repression, they command no respect from ordinary Tibetans; paradoxically, they have been the principal beneficiaries of the call to Tibetanize the administration in Tibet.[11]

Some of the long-standing Chinese functionaries in Tibet returned to China between 1980 and 1984, but the policy basically met with resistance and ended in a stalemate. These Chinese cadres came to Tibet following the 1959 Tibetan uprising, often attached to the military, and stayed on to build careers in the regional Party apparatus. Few have learned Tibetan, nor do they identify with Tibet or the Tibetan people. They are represented in every Party department and government office and constitute the backbone of the Party in Tibet, with a Tibetan staff beneath them. In periods of uncertainty they reemerge as the ones who can be depended on to keep the administration working.

The head of the regional Party in Tibet has always been Chinese,

---

[11] For an analysis of factional struggles within the Party leadership in Tibet during the early 1980s, see Wangchuk (1992).

but the character of the leadership has changed with the reforms. Ren Rong, whose career as a political commissar with the Tibet Military Region goes back to 1965, was head of the regional Party from 1971 to 1980, until he was replaced on Hu's orders. His replacement was another long-time PLA political commissar in Tibet, Yin Fatang, whose career was interrupted by the Cultural Revolution. Yin continued to protect the interests of the entrenched old guard in Tibet, both Tibetan and Chinese.

In 1985 Beijing replaced Yin Fatang with an outsider and a reformer, Wu Jinghua. Wu was committed to implementing the policy of "openness and reform" in Tibet, and supported programmes to restore Tibetan culture, religion, and language. During this period Tibet opened to foreign tourism (and built half-a-dozen new luxury hotels, including a Holiday Inn in Lhasa), solicited foreign aid and development funds, and actively courted the economic participation of the exile community. Nevertheless, Wu remained a protégé of Hu Yaobang and an appointee of Beijing. He was resented by the conservative elements within the Party in Tibet, and the bureaucracy continued to resist or subvert the implementation of his programmes. Following Hu's ouster as Party secretary in January 1987, Beijing's Tibet policy was once again thrown into uncertainty.

The issue of Tibetan autonomy remained insoluble. Beijing faced in the 1980s, as it does today, the dilemma that the Tibetans whom it could trust to run Tibet remained opposed to reform or to any further Tibetanization that would undermine their power. There is a younger generation of Tibetan cadres with professional skills who have been educated in China and have come back to work in the Chinese administration in Tibet. These Tibetans are in favour of reform, but they cannot be trusted to protect Chinese rule in Tibet. Thus Beijing is forced to retain in power a group of conservative cadres who are generally discredited throughout China, while policies devised in Beijing must often be implemented without the enthusiasm of the local Party leadership. Conservatives need only bide their time until political shifts in Beijing, or instability in Tibet, once again bring them into favour. This is why politics and ideology continue to be important in Tibet. At the same time, Tibet retains enormous strategic importance for China as a border area and potential arena for conflict. Security is always a serious concern. Thus, no policies can be implemented in Tibet without the approval of the military, which retains close links to the TAR administration.

The problem of political control remains the central problem in Tibet. Tibetans have no say in making the decisions which affect their lives. The grip of the Party on power has a special significance in Tibet, since in the minds of most Tibetans the Party remains the administrative arm of an occupying power. The reforms were appreciated for the freedoms they allowed — freedoms all too easily revoked. The reforms did create an opportunity for rebuilding from the ground up the rudiments of a Tibetan civil society devastated by two decades of communism. The reformers in the Party hoped that a relaxation of Mao-era repression would placate Tibetan discontent and win acceptance of Chinese rule. But in fact it has been the relative absence of direction and control, as Party factions in Beijing and Tibet battled over policies and their implementation, that has enabled Tibetans to reclaim as much as they have of their own society. Thus the stage was set for the unrest to follow.

2

INVENTING POLITICAL RITUAL

In the short space of ten days in the autumn of 1987 three demonstrations took place in the centre of Lhasa, the Tibetan capital. The first demonstration, on 27 September, coincided with a ten-day visit by the Dalai Lama to the United States beginning on 19 September, where he met with members of the Human Rights Caucus of the US Congress. This prompted accusations of interference in "China's internal affairs" by the Chinese government and suggestions that the demonstrations had been instigated by agents of the "Dalai clique" with the intention of upsetting the progress that had been made in Tibet during the reforms of the 1980s. The second demonstration fell on 1 October, Chinese National Day, a public holiday celebrating the founding of the People's Republic of China in 1949. Its symbolic impact could not have been greater, since it was perceived by the Chinese government as a flagrant public challenge to the "unity of the motherland". There was a third demonstration on 6 October.

Out of these demonstrations in the autumn of 1987 emerged a pattern of performance that became the model for protest in Lhasa over the next five years. Thus protest became ritualized, assuming the same symbolic form every time it occurred. This chapter explores the expression of Tibetan national consciousness through these demonstrations. In choosing to characterize the form that Tibetan protest has taken as *ritual*, we ascribe two motives to it. The first is the achievement of what Victor Turner has called *communitas*.[1] Through protest Tibetans are able to overcome their objective powerlessness, and experience both solidarity and equality as they mutually acknowledge their common nationhood. At every turn, the institutions and practices of the Chinese regime in Tibet attempt to expunge the memory of that nationhood. The space of protest is very much a "liminal" space — a place of danger where one crosses a threshold and, by expressing what is forbidden, realizes a new condition of life.

Secondly, ritual is a way of solving problems, of resolving, in the form of a drama of symbols, conflicts and contradictions in social life

[1] Turner (1977).

20

that admit to no real solution. It can offer an anticipatory resolution of conflict, an imaginative prefiguring of the future that draws on the symbolic potential of the present and the past. Millenarianism, which expects supernatural intervention to right wrongs and restore the power of the powerless, is one expression of this second motive of ritual.[2] Current protest in Tibet however is not millenarian in character. Tibetans are prepared to enunciate in clear and rational terms what their political aims are. The problem is that the conditions of Chinese rule in Tibet outlaw expression of those political aims. Ritualized protest thus becomes a substitute for licensed political discourse and communication.

It must always be remembered that the Chinese system is totalitarian. The state monopolizes every legal avenue of public expression, suppressing all dissent, while it manufactures through its own organs the official version of Tibetan reality. Whenever Tibetans question Chinese rule the whole apparatus of communist domination is brought down on them — political campaigns, arrests and torture, imprisonment and executions, intimidating displays of military force. Tibetans are subjected to endless harangues in political meetings and police interrogation sessions about foreign conspiracies and agents of subversion. In spite of overwhelming forces arrayed against them, Tibetans persist in attempting to communicate their discontent.

Tibetan protest is not irrational; rather, it is an attempt symbolically to even the scales. The Chinese government cannot be the audience for Tibetan protest because the Chinese political system denies its opponents any possibility for debate. Tibetan protest is communication deferred and displaced; the "other" that it seeks to engage is a hypothetical fair arbitrator. Tibetans imagine an opportunity to argue their case before an impartial forum, confident that "truth will prevail."

To a large extent this hypothetical arbitrator is identified with the West and with international organizations such as the United Nations. Since the opening of Tibet in 1985 to large numbers of tourists, many Westerners visiting the region have had the experience of Tibetans slipping into their hands or pockets handwritten notes, often addressed to the United Nations. The notes typically proclaim the independence of Tibet, the oppression of the Tibetan people by Chinese invaders, and the loyalty of Tibetans to the exiled Dalai Lama. One such "letter to

---

[2] See Burridge (1969) for an anthropological framework for millenarianism. I return to the question of millenarianism in Tibetan politics in the last chapter.

the United Nations" smuggled out of Tibet by a tourist (written in August 1989, five months after the declaration of martial law) requests that "you assemble all the people of Lhasa, monks and lay people, including the Chinese authorities, and without discriminating between Chinese and Tibetans, give us the opportunity to talk about our true history." There may be little likelihood of this hearing ever taking place, but by demanding it Tibetans display their commitment to what they understand to be universal values.

Buddhism, the religion of Tibetans, occupies a central place in current protest. Demonstrations are led by monks and nuns, and Tibetans have come to see political protest as religiously-sanctioned action. But it is the ethical aspects of Buddhism as a religion — rather than its magical elements — that predominate in current protest. The demonstrations draw on traditional forms of Buddhist religious practice that ordinary Tibetans understand and value. Buddhism offers Tibetans assurance about ultimate religious ends as well as effective means to realize those ends through individual behaviour. Religious discourse is the one area where Tibetans retain confidence after decades of assault on their society and culture. It is not surprising, then, that political protest has come to be framed in religious idioms. The novelty of the demonstrations lies in extending the meaning of familiar cultural symbols and practices into the dangerous territory of public opposition to Chinese rule.

Three demonstrations

Sunday, 27 September 1987. Early in the morning a group of twenty-one monks from Drepung monastery gathered in a teahouse on the Barkhor across from the small market where carpets are sold. They had slipped out from the monastery before dawn and walked the eight kilometres into town one by one so they would not be noticed.

On 25 September local television in Lhasa had shown a one-minute segment of the Dalai Lama's visit to the United States for meetings with Congressional leaders. The Chinese government had condemned the Dalai Lama's visit and authorities in Tibet were suggesting that demonstrations in support of Chinese policy and against the Dalai Lama be staged. There was a great deal of discussion among ordinary Tibetans in Lhasa of the significance of the Dalai Lama's visit to the United States and speculation about whether a diplomatic breakthrough for Tibet was impending. Handprinted wall posters appeared around the Barkhor in support of the Dalai Lama.

On 24 September, at a mass sentencing rally in the sports stadium in Lhasa, eleven Tibetans received sentences for criminal offences — two of them were condemned to death. 15,000 Tibetans were compelled to attend the rally by their work units and neighbourhood committees. Leading Party officials were present, including the vice-mayor of Lhasa, who used the occasion to lecture the crowd on the need to "preserve unity and stability" and to "adhere to the four cardinal principles."[3] It may be, as many Tibetans claimed, that some of those sentenced had in fact committed political crimes. Mass sentencing rallies for convicted criminals are a frequent occurrence in Tibet (and throughout China), but the scale of this rally, combined with its harsh ideological tone, indicate that it was a reminder to Tibetans of Chinese government power timed to coincide with international interest in the Dalai Lama's mission.

In the week leading up to 27 September many lay Tibetans had visited Drepung and the other monasteries around Lhasa to make offerings of money in the temples, requesting prayers from the monks on behalf of the Dalai Lama. Some of the monks felt that reciting prayers was not enough and had been discussing for several days among themselves staging some kind of public show of support for the Dalai Lama.

Word of the plan to go down to Lhasa had spread through a network of friends, young monks in their twenties. The monks had no clear idea of what they would do when they got to Lhasa or of the consequences of their actions. They had drawn a crude version of the banned Tibetan national flag on a piece of cotton. The previous night they had taken an oath before a statue of the protector-goddess Palden Lhamo (*dpal ldan lha mo*), the patron deity of Tibet and the Dalai Lama, promising not to betray each other if caught, but to sacrifice themselves. As they walked into town they stopped at Nechung monastery to burn offerings of juniper leaves (*bsangs*), a ritual for pacifying the gods and winning their support.

At the teahouse the decision was made to stage the demonstration in the Barkhor. They left the teahouse around 9.00 a.m. and completed a circuit of the Barkhor, carrying the Tibetan flag and shouting the slogans "Tibet is Independent" (*bod rang btsan*) and "May the Dalai Lama

---

[3] Lhasa Xizang Regional Service in Mandarin, 24 September 1987, in *FBIS*, 1 October 1987: 27. The four cardinal principles are: (1) the leadership of the Communist Party, (2) the socialist road, (3) Marxism-Leninism-Mao Zedong thought, and (4) the dictatorship of the proletariat.

Live Ten Thousand Years" (*skyabs mgon d'a la'i bla ma khri lo brtan par shog*). A crowd of about 100 people from the street joined them as they marched. After completing three circuits of the Barkhor the crowd of demonstrators walked across the square in front of the Jokhang temple and continued down Renmin Lu ("People's Avenue") toward the offices of the Tibetan Autonomous Region (TAR) government. Here the demonstrators were confronted by police. The twenty-one monks along with five lay Tibetans were arrested. The crowd was dispersed without violence.

Thursday, 1 October 1987 — Chinese National Day. The demonstration on 1 October also began around 9.00 a.m. This demonstration was planned by twenty-three monks from Sera monastery (about 5 km. north of Lhasa), but included eight monks from the Jokhang temple and three from Nechung monastery (near Drepung). Like the Drepung monks on 27 September, the demonstrators proceeded around the Barkhor carrying a Tibetan flag and shouting slogans for Tibetan independence. The thirty-four monks were joined by about fifty lay Tibetans. On the fourth circuit the demonstration was quickly broken up by police, the demonstrators beaten, and the monks, along with about thirty lay people, were arrested and taken to the local police station at the southwest corner of the Jokhang square.

A crowd of from 2,000 to 3,000 Tibetans gathered in front of the police station, spilling out into the adjacent square. Stones were thrown at the police, at first by women and children. At one point a boy picked up a rifle dropped by one of the policeman and smashed it on the ground. Approximately fifty police standing in front of the police station were forced to retreat into the compound. The crowd then over-turned and set on fire a number of abandoned police vehicles in front of the police station. As fire engines and armed police reinforcements arrived, they were driven back by the crowd throwing stones. Blankets and wooden stall-tables from the market were then placed next to the wooden door of the police station and set on fire with kerosene.

A number of young monks in the crowd, led by Champa Tenzin, a monk in his forties from the Jokhang, pushed through the blazing doorway and into the compound. Champa Tenzin emerged ten minutes later from a window on the side of the building, his arms badly burned. The crowd lifted him on to their shoulders and carried him around the circuit of the Barkhor. Some of the monks held inside the police compound escaped through the doors and windows of the burning building. Three were shot dead as they ran into the crowd.

At about 11.00 a.m. the police began shooting into the crowd from the roof of the police compound, still partly in flames. The shooting was at first aimed above the heads of the crowd, but then the police fired directly into the crowd, mostly with pistols. Police reinforcements arrived at about 1.30 p.m. and cleared the alley on the south side of the police station, firing above the heads of the crowd with automatic weapons. As the reinforcements arrived, about twenty people were arrested and held in a school across from the police station. Some were beaten with rocks and rifles, but all were released after a couple of hours.

Two dead Tibetan laymen were carried on wooden boards through the crowd and into the Barkhor. The body of a fourteen-year-old boy was carried down Renmin Lu and placed on a traffic podium in front of the TAR government compound. A crowd of about 100 accompanied the body, and others joined as they stopped in front of the compound. A small group of police moved toward the crowd, then quickly retreated. The crowd then set another vehicle on fire.

The shooting continued until about 3.00 p.m., when all the police left the area around the police compound. The crowd began to loot the police station while it burned. The looting continued through the next day and thousands of police files were scattered in the street. No police were visible that day in the square around the police station, but a night-time curfew was enforced in Lhasa and police vehicles with wailing sirens patrolled the deserted streets. During the following days convoys of trucks with soldiers armed with automatic weapons and motorcycle-sidecars with tripod-mounted machine-guns paraded through the main streets surrounding the Tibetan section of Lhasa.

Tuesday, 6 October 1987. At about 2.30 p.m. a group of fifty young monks left Drepung monastery and walked into Lhasa to protest in front of the TAR government compound against the continued detention of the twenty-one Drepung monks who had staged the first demonstration on 27 September. The night before, political cadres had appeared at the monastery and put up announcements condemning the demonstrations. One Western witness to the demonstration asked the monks as they walked toward Lhasa what they planned to do when they arrived at the government compound. They answered that they didn't know. At one point, after assembling in front of the compound, the monks began shouting Tibetan independence slogans and started to walk up Renmin Lu toward the Jokhang. They turned around after going no more than 20 metres and returned to the government compound entrance, where they continued to shout and raise their fists in protest.

A few minutes later, around 4.30 p.m., 250 armed police arrived. As the monks were arrested and taken away they were viciously beaten with belts, sticks, rifles, and pieces of metal. The monks were unarmed and did not resist or throw stones at the police. They did not carry a Tibetan flag. Two days later all of them were released.

In fact a demonstration for independence had been planned by the monks of Ganden monastery, about 32 km. east of Lhasa. Since it was one of the "three seats" of the Gelugpa sect, the young monks of Ganden felt that, after Drepung and Sera, it was now their turn to stage a demonstration. However they were unable to arrange transportation into Lhasa, and the arrival of police and political cadres thwarted their plans. People in Lhasa assumed that this demonstration had only been postponed until a suitable occasion, and that the next big demonstration would be initiated by monks from Ganden. They did not get their chance until March 1988, following the Mönlam festival.

Khorra as protest

Almost all the demonstrations that have taken place in Lhasa since 1987 have had the same form. Small groups of monks — and, in later demonstrations, nuns — assemble near the Barkhor, then march around the Barkhor circumambulating the Jokhang temple, carrying the Tibetan flag as they shout independence slogans. This continues until the demonstration is halted by the arrival of security forces. In a few of the smaller demonstrations the protestors have managed to slip off into the maze of sidestreets surrounding the Barkhor and avoid immediate arrest. After completing a circuit or two of the Barkhor, the protesting monks and nuns are sometimes joined by ordinary Tibetans who fall in behind.

Circumambulation or "khorra" (*bskor ba*) has a central place in Tibetan Buddhism. It is practised universally around temples and other holy sites, and is for lay Tibetans a common means of accumulating merit (*dge ba*). It is often accompanied by religious verbalization (*mani*), the repetition of prayers counted off on the bead rosary that many Tibetans carry with them wherever they go. Khorra is just one of a variety of meritorious actions — actions performed to overcome sins committed in this and past lives with the hope of achieving a better rebirth and ultimately salvation in future lives. Merit attaches to both ethical actions (charity, acts of self-sacrifice) and ritual (prayers, prostrations, offerings at temples and monasteries).

Khorra provides Tibetans with visible and obvious evidence of the practice of religion. Unlike other practices, it is done in public and outdoors, among strangers and acquaintances alike, and can be mixed with other activities. The Barkhor circuit in Lhasa is also the central market for Tibetans and the busiest public space in Lhasa. Here khorra is combined with shopping and gossiping. Lhasa residents are accustomed to doing khorra before work in the morning and at sunset in the evening. The Jokhang temple in Lhasa is the holiest site in Tibet and khorra performed there is especially meritorious. Pilgrims come from all over Tibet to do khorra on the Barkhor.

Robert Ekvall, commenting on the ubiquity of khorra among Tibetans and the tendency of visitors to Tibet to overlook it in favour of more intricate and specialized forms of religious ritual, observes: "It is as though the travellers saw movement but never realized how ceaseless and universal it was and how, in the crowds, the same faces would recur again and again as the circuits were made."[4] Khorra literally draws the largest possible circle around Tibetans as a people and a community. It offers a religious practice without status distinctions, and thus an opportunity to recognize common features shared with other Tibetans from every background and every part of Tibet. The characteristics that Ekvall associated with khorra still describe the Barkhor today, where khorra effectively distinguishes Tibetans from Chinese, who do not practise khorra and remain visibly foreign:

Thus the Tibetan is associated with his fellows in what is essentially a group activity, performed either with the members of his own group or in the knowledge that they have engaged in, are engaged in, or will engage in the same activity. He responds to the stimuli of such association and partakes of its satisfactions. To the extent that he feels he is participating in a common endeavor, he is given a sense of oneness with his fellows, for they all, the Dalai Lama not excepted, walk the *bsKor Ba* path. This pattern of behavior gives him sure criteria for recognizing his fellows.[5]

In choosing the Barkhor as the site for protest in the first demonstration on 27 September, the Drepung monks were able to mobilize and build on the familiar meaning of khorra for Tibetans. Khorra retains its ritual significance as a means of accumulating merit; however,

---

[4] Ekvall (1964): 235.
[5] *Ibid.*: 247.

merit-making is transposed into the arena of political action and the everyday private practice of religion is transformed into public protest. Tibetan Buddhist ritual in principle is dedicated to "all sentient beings" and performed for the benefit of the community, to ensure general well-being, not exclusively for one's own benefit. By combining khorra with symbols of Tibetan nationhood — the Dalai Lama, the flag — the Drepung monks forged a link between the powerful motivation that underlies religious ritual and the national consciousness that divides Tibetans from the Chinese.

In the same way, the monks are taking the private religious verbalization that ordinarily accompanies the performance of khorra — the reciting of prayers — and transforming it into public and collective ritual by substituting the slogans of Tibetan independence. The oath taken in front of the protector-deity Palden Lhamo and the burning of *bsangs* are likewise simple familiar religious acts, performed before embarking on any dangerous or important undertaking; here they initiate protest.

The rituals that punctuate the daily life of Tibetans — khorra, prostrations, burning *bsangs*, reciting *mani* — are familiar and accessible habitual acts. They are learned and remembered through imitation. Their meaning in terms of religious ideology is thus secondary to the fact of their performance. Since Tibetans have been allowed to practise religion again, these ordinary rituals of daily life have been spontaneously recovered simply because people remember how to do them. Much of the "inscribed" specialist knowledge that interprets ritual may have been lost; habits are less easily eradicated. As Paul Connerton points out, the "performativeness" of ritual, expressed through bodily habits — postures, gestures, and movements — provides the basis for collective social memory.[6] If commemorative ceremonies, for instance, function to remind a community of its identity, they do so through performances that are habitual and, ultimately, bodily acts.[7]

Khorra as traditionally practised in fact conforms to the requirements of the current official policy on religion that allows the expression of "voluntary religious faith" (*chos dad rang mos kyi srid jus*). Throughout the Cultural Revolution any display of religion was forbidden and only in the 1980s did Tibetans begin to practise religion publicly again. Khorra — along with prostrations, turning prayer-wheels, and

---

[6] Connerton (1989).
[7] *Ibid.*: 70–1.

burning incense — is acceptable under the new policy precisely because it appears to be private and personal; religious "superstition" is tolerated as long as it does not challenge the authority of the Chinese state. The use of khorra for political protest by the monks illustrates precisely the limits of Chinese-defined religious freedom. In effect, the monks are forcing the Chinese to strike out at religion by striking out at nationalism. At the same time, they are showing ordinary Tibetans how to transform their personal practice of religion, which Chinese policy allows, into a practice which, through recovering symbols of nationhood, becomes an act of rebellion.

Conventional religious practice in Buddhism certainly favours private acts of ritual. There is a strong "antirelational" bias in the merit system of Buddhism.[8] Acts of charity, for instance, that implicate giver and recipient in a relationship of personal obligation are perceived as less desirable in religious terms than acts of giving where reciprocation is not expected. Typically, lay Buddhist practice is individualistic and voluntary. Merit-making is ideally identified with larger, universalistic and hence impersonal interests. It requires a notion of general welfare that is not delimited by, and is opposed to, particularistic social bonds.

Nationalism also fulfils this requirement. The nation in this nonparticularistic and general sense can be a medium for realizing these same religious interests. The nation is, in Benedict Anderson's words, "an imagined political community" which offers Tibetans an opportunity to recognize the "deep, horizontal comradeship" that collectively defines them over and above personal relationships and loyalties.[9] Here it is only necessary to substitute the Tibetan nation in the canonical Buddhist formula of acquiring merit by working for the welfare of all sentient beings to appreciate what the Drepung monks have accomplished by inventing a new form of protest.

Circling the Barkhor as an act of protest against Chinese rule in Tibet was only one of several possibilities. Marching down one of the long boulevards running through Lhasa and assembling in front of government buildings were two others. In the third demonstration, on 6 October, the monks assembled in front of the government compound; primarily they hoped to win the release of their comrades arrested on 27 September. They did not carry a flag and this demonstration was perceived neither by the Chinese authorities nor by Tibetans as a repeat

[8] See Ortner (1978): 37–8.
[9] Anderson (1983): 15–16.

of the previous two demonstrations around the Barkhor. The response of the government was also different; though the monks were brutally beaten as they were arrested, they were released just a few days later. Even so, there was a moment of uncertainty before the monks decided not to move on to the Barkhor for a demonstration for independence and to carry on petitioning the government.

In the demonstration on 27 September the monks were arrested after leaving the Barkhor as they proceeded down Renmin Lu toward the TAR compound. The three circuits of the Barkhor that they completed could be seen as a kind of ritual preparation for a confrontation with the government, the demonstrators gaining confidence and adding to their numbers (ritual action in Buddhism frequently follows a pattern of "threes" out of reverence for the Triple Jewel: Buddha, Dharma, Sangha). Different possibilities for protest certainly remained open at this point. But demonstrations around the Barkhor take place on the home ground of Tibetans, in the traditional old part of the city. The government compound is on Chinese territory, in the Chinese part of the city. Lhasa is really two cities: a dense Tibetan core — all that remains of pre-1959 Lhasa — and a much larger modern Chinese city that has grown to encircle the shrinking Tibetan centre. Chinese feel uncomfortable when they venture into the old part of Lhasa. With the demonstrations around the Barkhor Tibetans thus were symbolically marking out their own territory. The audience for khorra protest is the Tibetan community, not the Chinese government.

Protest in front of the government buildings might have been the kind of demonstration that the Chinese authorities expected and may have understood, but for the Tibetans it would have meant acknowledging the Chinese representation of the issues — e.g. how much and what kinds of religious freedom are to be permitted, or whether special treatment is to be accorded to minority nationalities by the Chinese state. This was in fact the case with the demonstration on 6 October, where the audience was Chinese and the context was the familiar though still illegal one of protest directed toward a government. Instead, as Khorra protest around the Barkhor has continued, it has served to sharpen the social and symbolic opposition between Tibetans and Chinese. Tibetans have thus developed a way to highlight the separation of the Tibetan and Chinese worlds, staking out and defending Tibetan territory in a manner that repels Chinese efforts at incorporation.

Violence erupted following the second demonstration on 1 October when lay people were drawn into the conflict with the arrest of the demonstrators. It is clear from many accounts that the police response on this occasion was confused and unplanned. Their orders must have been to prevent further demonstrations at all costs. Certainly it was a mistake to confine the arrested demonstrators in a police station just yards from the Jokhang (this mistake was never repeated). The shootings when they occurred were brutal and provocative; the crowd of stone-throwers outside the police station could have been easily dispersed with tear-gas using standard riot-control methods.

The flow of pedestrian traffic on the Barkhor is always in the clockwise direction. For instance, to return to a shop passed earlier on the circuit one is expected to continue all the way around (the full circuit is about 0.75 km.). Movement for more than a few feet in the reverse direction is perceived as wrong, though there are no sanctions and little public notice is taken of an individual violator. The exceptions to the rule are the Chinese, who either wilfully or from ignorance frequently walk in the reverse direction. Tibetans always perceive this as irreligious, an affront to their idea of sacred order (though, in line with Buddhist individualism, the sin rebounds only on the individual violator). The excuse that the Chinese are not engaged in religion is irrelevant; the Chinese remain trespassers on terrain whose symbolic topography is as apparent and familiar to all Tibetans as its visible features.

The Barkhor became contested territory as Chinese security forces attempted to occupy it and Tibetans attempted to reclaim it as their own through public protest. Following the second demonstration on 1 October, after the burning of the police station, the Barkhor area was free of visible security forces for a number of days as the patrols confined themselves to the main roads. From 15 October onward armed Chinese security forces began to patrol the Barkhor in the anti-clockwise and thus anti-religious direction. Whether the Chinese were aware of the symbolism of this or not, it was noticed and commented on by Tibetans. In order to suppress displays of Tibetan nationalism the Chinese were drawn into the Tibetan symbolism in a way that cast them as destroyers of religion and violators of the sacred order represented by khorra.

In fact those who perform khorra must be "actually or symbolically unarmed".[10] The monks demonstrating for Tibetan independence were always unarmed. In the second demonstration a young boy smashed a gun left behind by a retreating soldier. In all subsequent demonstrations the security forces have always moved into position to confront the

[10] Ekvall (1964): 234.

circumambulating monks and nuns by going counter-clockwise, a manoeuvre that could not but help to produce the spectacle of armed soldiers crushing unarmed demonstrators. The opposition between the armed might of the Chinese state on the one side, and the unarmed monks assembling the Tibetan nation as they circle the Jokhang temple on the other, could hardly be more vivid.

Tibetans certainly did not have a consciously elaborated plan as they initiated the current phase of protest in Lhasa in the autumn of 1987. The demonstrations around the Barkhor began as commemorative performances — ways of acknowledging events of political significance through universally understood habits and gestures. The performance of khorra provides for a ritual representation of action into which unfolding events can be incorporated. With each iteration the link connecting ritual performance and political protest becomes more compelling. Tibetans rapidly formed an idea of what protest should look like, and what motives and symbols it should mobilize.

Thus, in the second demonstration on 1 October, Champa Tenzin, the monk who rushed into the burning police station to free those arrested was carried around the Barkhor on the shoulders of the crowd. His political act was immediately assimilated into the religious symbolism of khorra — simultaneously an act of self-sacrifice, bravery, and rebellion performed for the benefit of the community. The bodies of two Tibetans shot dead were also paraded around the Barkhor (though the body of the fourteen-year-old boy was taken to the TAR government compound, suggesting that the other possibility for protest directed *toward* the government occurred to some in the crowd). In later demonstrations the bodies of the dead were always carried around the Barkhor, an act which associated their ultimate political sacrifice with religious motives of merit-making and action performed for the benefit of others.

The example of the demonstrating monks provided Tibetans with a new and powerful way to understand political protest: as action sanctioned by religion, accomplishing religious ends, and benefiting both the individual and the community. Khorra protest enables Tibetans to cross the dangerous threshold separating private religious practice from public political protest against Chinese rule.

Tibetan grievances against the Chinese occupation of their country and the depredations of Communist Party rule are long-standing. Tibetan resistance has taken a variety of forms during forty years of occupation — including acts of sabotage and periodic armed uprisings. Current protest, however, has taken the form of a symbolic opposition by Tibetans to the Chinese state in which Tibetans have been able to mobilize their own symbolic resources in a coherent challenge to Chinese hegemony. Thus, in reclaiming the Barkhor as Tibetan territory, Tibetans are reproducing as a symbolic opposition the structural (and geographical) opposition between Chinese and Tibetan communities in Lhasa. To reject protest on Chinese territory — i.e. to reject petitioning the government for a redress of grievances — is just to reiterate this opposition.

The political symbolism of ceremonial sites

The symbolic centre of Tibetan protest since 1987 has been the Jokhang temple. Tibetans have selected this site for the performance of political ritual over other historically important possibilities. The Jokhang temple evokes a multi-layered symbolism of Tibetan nationhood that has resisted Chinese efforts to represent Tibetan national history as ancillary to the power of the Chinese state.

The Jokhang temple was founded in the seventh century by Songtsen Gampo (*srong brtsan sgam po*), the king who first introduced Buddhism to Tibet. Lhasa became the political centre of Tibet under Songtsen Gampo, who is reputed to have founded a number of Lhasa temples, but the Jokhang contains the most sacred image in Tibet — Jo Rinpoche (*jo bo rin po che*), a statue of the Buddha Śākyamuni brought to Lhasa by a Tang dynasty princess who became the king's wife.

Tibetans in succeeding centuries assimilated Songtsen Gampo to the universal Buddhist paradigm of the ideal king, the Cakravartin or wheel-turning king who subdues demonic forces and establishes a polity committed to promoting Dharma or righteousness.[11] The Jokhang is

---

[11] See Tambiah (1976) for the Indian origins of the paradigm of the Cakravartin, who upholds a specifically Buddhist socio-political order, in the kingship of Aśoka Maurya. It should be noted that the elevation of Songtsen Gampo to a Cakravartin is an act of historical remembrance of Tibetan greatness by later centuries. Songtsen Gampo comes to signify a specifically Buddhist Tibetan political identity in the *Mani bKa'-'bum* literature, so-called "treasure" (*gter ma*) texts, hidden inside the Jokhang and attributed to the king, but "discovered" during the twelfth and thirteenth centuries, a period of political chaos in Tibet. In these texts Songtsen Gampo assumes the status of a bodhissattva, an incarnation of Avalokiteśvara (as are the Dalai Lamas in a later period), and Tibet is identified as a country whose people have a special collective relationship with this deity. The cult of Avalokiteśvara (*spyan ras gzigs*) is universal among Tibetans. Now identified with the Dalai Lama, his six-syllable mantra, *om mani padme hūm*, is recited by all Tibetans. See Kapstein (1992) for a discussion of the *Mani bKa'-'bum* literature and the significance of the cult of Avalokiteśvara.

the centre and origin of this feat of nation-building. Through the founding of the temple Tibet emerges as a realm ordered and regulated in accordance with the tenets of Buddhism. The subjugation in myth of the forces of the underworld, turning them from evil to good, signifies both the triumph of Buddhism and the consolidation of the polity under the governance of a righteous king.[12] Songtsen Gampo is said to have built the Jokhang over a lake where Lhasa is now situated. A popular legend has it that the lake

. . . where the first Buddhist king built his temple represented the heart of a she-demon lying on her back. The she-demon is Tibet itself, which had to be tamed before it could be inhabited and civilized. Her body already covered the whole extent of Tibet in its period of military greatness (eighth and ninth centuries). Her outspread limbs reached to the present boundaries of Tibetan settlement.[13]

Thus the Jokhang temple refers back to an earlier historical period, to the royal period that precedes the end of dynastic rule in the ninth century and the eventual establishment of a theocratic state under the Fifth Dalai Lama in the seventeenth century. Its foundation is situated exactly at the juncture in Tibetan history when the consolidation of the nation under the secular power of the ancient kings acquires a new legitimacy through religion. As an evocative symbol for Tibetan nationhood the Jokhang temple has the three terms — nation, state, and religion — ordered according to the original Buddhist paradigm. It thus provides a yardstick against which the exercise of state power (Chinese or Tibetan) can be measured and judged.

The other great landmark in Lhasa is the Potala palace, constructed in the seventeenth century by the Fifth Dalai Lama. Since that time the Potala has been the seat of the Tibetan government and the residence of the Dalai Lama. It represents a later development of the state in Tibet: the reconsolidation of Tibetan power under the Gelugpa sect in the

---

[12] Mumford (1989) discusses the link between Buddhist kingship and the underworld. This relationship is reproduced in the performance of Tibetan Buddhist rituals as well as in the founding of temples. Kapferer (1988) examines the same relationship in legends of state formation in Sri Lanka.

[13] Stein (1972): 38–9. The legend of the "supine demoness" (*srin mo*) also first appears in the *Mani bKa'-'bum*, where she is portrayed as both the living landscape of Tibet and the principal obstacle to the propagation of the Buddhist faith. Nevertheless, though "pinned" and subdued, she remains very much alive. See Gyatso (1987) for an analysis of the symbolism of the demoness and her place in Tibetan cultural and national identity.

form of a bureaucratic hierarchy in which monastic power and lay power are combined. This is the government that the Dalai Lama headed until 1959.

The Potala now lies within the Chinese part of the city, 1.5 km. from the Jokhang, and operates as a museum administered by the Chinese government, with a set route for tourists to follow through the few rooms open to the public. The Jokhang was damaged during the Cultural Revolution and remained closed till 1979, but it is now largely restored and has been able to function as a religious centre for Tibetans with its own monastic staff. The Potala escaped destruction, but is now an empty shell, its former residents absent, its secular state functions assumed by the Chinese administration in Tibet. Its absorption into Chinese Lhasa has effectively negated its potential as a site for protest.

The Chinese government in Tibet has laid claim to the Norbulingka, former summer palace of the Dalai Lama, as the site for celebrations of the secular power of the Chinese state. The Norbulingka lies on the outskirts of Lhasa about 3 km. from the centre. The 10 March 1959 uprising against nine years of Chinese occupation began at the Norbulingka; pitched battles in which hundreds of Tibetans died were fought on its grounds. It was from here that the Dalai Lama fled into exile in India. Under the post-1959 Chinese administration the Norbulingka has had the status of a public park. Within its spacious grounds, once private gardens for the Dalai Lama, Party officials give long speeches commemorating the anniversaries of the Chinese political calendar, Tibetan music and folk arts are performed under government patronage, and Tibetans are invited to celebrate traditional holidays under state supervision.

As the Sera monks marched around the Barkhor on the morning of 1 October, Party officials were leading just such a celebration of Chinese National Day at the Norbulingka, replete with performances of Tibetan music and dance. Two days earlier, on 29 September, the TAR government had sponsored a huge picnic there to mark the end of the traditional monastic summer retreat for 350 of these same monks from Sera monastery and some 3,000 of the "religiously faithful masses" (*chos dad mang tshogs*).[14] The picnic was an occasion for Tibetan

---

[14] The picnic is described in an article in the *Tibet Daily* (*bod ljongs nyin re'i tshags par*), 2 October 1987, bearing the caption "opposing splittism and protecting the unification of the motherland, flying the flag of patriotism and unity" (*mthun sgril dang rgyal gces kyi dar cha mthon por bsgrengs nas mes rgyal gyi gcig gyur srung skyong dang kha bral la ngo rgol byed pa*).

officials in the regional Party apparatus to address the monks on the danger of "splittism" (*kha bral ring lugs*). The audience included representatives of organizations responsible for implementing the Party's policy on religion — the regional Chinese People's Political Consultative Conference (CPPCC), the United Front Work Department of the Party, the local Bureau of Nationalities and Religious Affairs, and the Buddhist Association. The speeches were a warning to the monks of Sera not to repeat the mistake of the Drepung monks who had demonstrated two days before. People with "religious vocations" were instructed to condemn the protestors and strive to establish a "new socialist Tibet" by "continuously protecting the unification of the motherland, emphasizing the unity of nationalities, and opposing splittism." In exchange the leaders promised that the Party's present policy on religious tolerance would remain in place.

When the Sera monks staged their own demonstration two days later they repeated the performance of the Drepung monks. They returned to the Barkhor.

Tibet closes

At least eight Tibetans died in the shooting in front of the police station on 1 October and dozens were wounded. Many of the wounded were afraid to go to hospitals for fear of arrest and remained in hiding. The authorities made it difficult for Tibetans to reclaim the bodies of the dead from hospitals. The obstacles thrown up by the government contributed to the uncertainty and confusion in the days following the shooting. What emerges is a picture of a crackdown on dissent and an attempt to suppress the flow of information to the outside world about events in Tibet.

Here is a description by one Tibetan of his experiences following the shooting. He is a monk from the Jokhang who went to retrieve the body of another young Jokhang monk named Buchung who was killed in the confrontation at the police station. Buchung had been on the roof of the Jokhang when the conflict started, and had seized and smashed the camera of a security policeman photographing the crowd below. Buchung then went to help the monks escaping from the police station, and was shot and killed along with a Sera monk while removing iron bars from the window on the south side.

For ten days we couldn't find their bodies. We went to look everywhere. Some said they were at the hospital, but we discovered that they were not at the hospital. The Chinese said they didn't know the reason. They wouldn't tell us where the bodies were because at the time there were foreign journalists and the Chinese believed that we would take the bodies around the Barkhor. After the Chinese had ordered the journalists to leave within twenty-four hours, they said, on 11 October, that we could come and collect the bodies from the hospital. A teacher from the Jokhang, Chönpal-la, and other monks went to collect the bodies from the hospital. The faces were totally unrecognizable. We tried to look where the gun wounds were. The bullet had gone from the right shoulder through to the left shoulder. We could only recognize Buchung from the scar on his head. The Chinese said, 'We have kept this body for 11 days and we want 30 yuan per day.' They took 300 yuan. Unless you paid this the body would not be released. I wanted to argue with the Chinese, saying, 'Why do we have to pay this?' But Chönpal-la said, 'Don't worry, we'll pay out of funds at the Jokhang and take the body quickly.' We wanted to take the body back to the Jokhang, but had to take it straight to the burial site.

Sera monastery, whose monks had organized the demonstration on 1 October, was surrounded by soldiers on the night of 2 October as security police swept through the monastery arresting monks suspected of participating in the demonstration. During the next several weeks as many as 600 Tibetans were arrested, mostly at night between 11.00 p.m. and 2.00 a.m. The government announced that those who gave themselves up before 15 October would be dealt with leniently. On the afternoon of 15 October some sixty people were arrested in the Barkhor area. On the night of 24 October some 200 to 300 soldiers sealed off all the streets and alleys running into the Barkhor and broke into houses, making arrests at gunpoint. Arrests following these and subsequent demonstrations were often based on the identification of participants from film and video taken by Chinese reporters and police photographers.

Official Chinese accounts of the events surrounding the demonstrations never acknowledged either the shootings by police or the scale of the crackdown that followed. The Chinese press insisted that the injuries were caused when "rioters went so far as to snatch away guns carried by policemen and opened fire at the police and common people."[15] The sole admission by a representative of the Chinese government that the shootings did take place came four months later

---

[15] Beijing Xinhua in English, 2 October 1987, in *FBIS*, 5 October 1987: 26.

from the Panchen Lama. Responding to "complaints among the masses," he suggested that "a number of policemen fired warning shots in the air or ground" and "ricochets" injured or killed people. He also claimed that only one person had been hit and killed directly by a bullet.[16]

Chinese sources attributed the demonstrations to a coordinated attempt to "split the motherland" that had been "instigated and engineered by the Dalai clique." Reporting of the 1 October events on Chinese domestic radio was especially lurid: instigators were described inciting Tibetans to demonstrate by shouting: "Those refusing to come out and join the demonstration will have their house smashed" and "Throw stones! Six jiao for throwing one stone."[17] Westerners in particular were blamed for "urging on the people around to attack the police." Chinese television carried extensive coverage of the rock-throwing mob and the burning of the police station. There was no mention of the beating and arrest of the monks — just that some monks had been brought to the police station for an "education session to dissuade them."[18]

About fifty foreigners witnessed the demonstration on 1 October and were present during the violent confrontation at the police station. Some of them remained in the middle of the Tibetan crowd, and a number of them took photographs. Five foreigners were arrested on 1 October for taking photographs and had their film confiscated; three of them had their passports and cameras impounded for two days. One foreigner, arrested and held for some time within the police station for taking photographs, saw monks being beaten inside with shovels. Tibetans urged foreigners to take photographs of the demonstrations, and of the dead and wounded, and to carry the news of what had happened to the outside world.

Tibetans were grateful for the presence of Western witnesses. Their presence brought international attention to the situation in Tibet. Tibetans also believed that the presence of Westerners protected them from the full force of Chinese brutality. Equally important, foreigners

[16] Lhasa Xizang Regional Service in Mandarin, 9 February 1988, in *FBIS*, 10 February 1988: 38.

[17] Beijing Xinhua Domestic Service in Chinese, 3 October 1987, in *FBIS*, 5 October 1987: 26.

[18] Beijing Television Service in Mandarin, 4 October 1987, in *FBIS*, 5 October 1987: 27.

found themselves targets, along with Tibetans, of the security apparatus, as the Chinese government attempted to control the flow of information to the outside world and restrict the movement of foreigners. Foreigners were thus in a position to function as brokers and translators to the outside world of the conditions of Chinese rule in Tibet and refute Chinese claims that the situation was "normal."

With the opening of Tibet in 1985 to "individual travellers" — tourists making their own travel arrangements and not part of organized group tours — Lhasa had assumed some of the characteristics of Kathmandu as a gathering-place for this kind of tourist in Asia. Prices in Lhasa for food and lodging in the cheaper Tibetan-run cooperative hotels and restaurants were comparable to Kathmandu. The opening of relatively inexpensive road travel from the Nepali/Tibetan border made Tibet accessible to budget travellers. One of the attractions of the Tibetan-run cooperatives in Lhasa was the extent to which individual travellers were in control of tourist services — able to have parties and hold meetings, rent or borrow bicycles, make their own travel arrangements with bus and truck operators, and come and go as they pleased at all hours. A "traveller's co-op" was established at one Tibetan-run hotel, functioning as an information centre, with about 1,000 books for loan donated by travellers, as well as a supply of donated medicine (it operated for a year and a half, run by volunteers, and was closed a few days after 1 October for containing "reactionary" literature).

In the weeks after the demonstrations, foreigners — particularly those belonging to the traveller community in Lhasa — were persistently harassed by the Chinese authorities. Westerners had their rooms searched and passports checked and were told that they had to leave Tibet by 16 October (though nothing in fact was done to those who stayed beyond that date). Visa extensions could no longer be obtained from Public Security in Lhasa, and thus travellers had no choice but to leave as their visas ran out. It became impossible to buy plane or bus tickets for travel to Lhasa from Nepal or the regular entry-points in China. Over the next several months the number of foreigners in Lhasa dwindled to a handful. An effort was also made to expel the long-staying foreigners in Lhasa — mostly English teachers who had made arrangements with individual work-units to provide language instruction to Tibetans. Some of these foreigners were interrogated by Public Security and accused of instigating Tibetan protest. Items found when foreigners' rooms were searched, such as pictures of the Dalai Lama and books about Tibet, were used to justify expulsions.

Phone and telex lines to Tibet were blocked on 1 October following the violence at the police station, and buses in and out of Lhasa were cancelled. Foreigners in Lhasa at the time expressed a good deal of fear and uncertainty about their own situation. Two had been arrested on 28 September, the day after the first demonstration, for having Tibetan flags displayed on their gear. Tibetan flags and pictures of the Dalai Lama had become common accessories and part of the regalia of travellers in Tibet. Before the demonstrations their possession was usually ignored. Four Western travellers had been observed throwing stones alongside Tibetans in front of the police station (their participation appeared to be spontaneous and unpremeditated and no action against them was taken by the authorities). But accusations in Chinese accounts of the demonstrations that foreigners had instigated them also contributed to the feeling that as a group they were under attack by the Chinese government.

Foreign correspondents began to arrive in Lhasa following reports reaching Beijing of the 27 September demonstration. The cutting of communication lines with the outside world hindered the filing of stories after 1 October, which had to be carried out to Chengdu by travellers leaving Tibet by plane. The fifteen foreign correspondents in Lhasa were ordered to leave by 9 October on the pretext that they had violated a largely ignored rule that journalists must request permission to visit so-called "open areas" ten days in advance.

The Chinese authorities continued to maintain that the situation in Tibet was "normal" and that Tibet remained "open". In fact only pre-arranged supervised group tours were allowed in. Tourists were required to stay in the modern hotel (managed by Holiday Inn) next to the Norbulingka in the Chinese part of Lhasa and opportunities for contact with Tibetans were limited. The Tibetan-run cooperative hotels emptied out. The policy discouraged unsupervised individual travellers from visiting Tibet. These were the kind of travellers most likely to establish relationships with Tibetans and witness unrest when it occurred.

The policy relaxed somewhat in the spring of 1988 — largely because Chinese tourist companies, starved for business, were prepared to arrange bogus "group tours" for individual travellers. Some hundreds of individual travellers did manage to make it to Tibet and travel around with relative freedom until the declaration of martial law in March 1989, but Tibet remained officially closed to individual travellers throughout this period. Access to Tibet for journalists was also severely restricted, particularly when protest was expected, and required advance permission from Beijing.

The principal fear of the Chinese government was that foreigners would witness and report on demonstrations when they occurred. From the autumn of 1987 onward, with journalists largely barred from Tibet, travellers became the major source of information about the situation there. They were warned to stay away from demonstrations and threatened with punishment for watching or taking photographs — with the implication that to do so constituted a form of support or participation. But the warnings were ignored by many of the travellers in Tibet during this period.

Violation of the regulations contained in the "No. 3 Announcement by the People's Government of the City of Lhasa", which was conspicuously posted in the Tibetan-run hotels after 3 October, was cited by Public Security officers when foreigners were arrested in the vicinity of demonstrations and questioned:

1. We extend welcome to friends from the different countries in the World who come to our region for sightseeing, tour, visit, work, trade discussion and economic cooperation.

2. Whoever comes to our region must respect our State sovereignty, abide by the laws of our country. They are not allowed to interfere in internal affairs of our country and engage in activities that are incompatible with their status.

3. Foreigners are not allowed to crowd around watching and photographing the disturbances manipulated by a few splittists, and they should not do any distorted propaganda concerning disturbances, which is not in agreement with the facts.

4. In accordance with our laws we shall mete out punishment to the trouble-makers who stir up, support and participate in the disturbance manipulated by a few splittists. [Spelling corrected]

The No. 3 Announcement reflects the shift in attitude of the Chinese government following the demonstrations in the autumn of 1987. It marks the end in Tibet of a period of relative openness to the outside world during the 1980s. Foreigners now fall under growing suspicion as the Chinese government becomes preoccupied with suppressing protest. It also marks the end of a period of ideological relaxation during which Tibetans enjoyed a measure of respite from the political campaigns that are a recurring feature of the Chinese political system. The mobilization of the whole apparatus of social control used to suppress dissent is also something that the Chinese government has tried to conceal from foreign eyes by closing Tibet. Continuing Tibetan protest since 1987 has thus evolved in part as a response to these intensified efforts at social and political control.

3

THE ANTI-SPLITTIST CAMPAIGN

The front page of the *Tibet Daily* on 2 October 1987, the day following the violence at the police station, contained an announcement from the People's Government of the city of Lhasa to the city's residents. The announcement repeated the government's version of the events on the preceding day: Tibetan "troublemakers" had seized guns from the police and shot at Tibetans. It did not matter that no one in Lhasa believed the official account. It was meant partly to influence Tibetans outside Lhasa, and partly to provide a palatable version of events for Chinese consumption; but primarily it set the stage for the ensuing political campaign. The discrepancy between people's own experiences and the official line is a familiar feature of the Chinese political system. In the public meetings and police interrogation sessions that followed, those who objected to the official version of events were identified as potential dissidents.

The announcement goes on to lay out a series of "directives" that mark the beginning of the campaign against "splittism":

1. The broad cadres, workers, city residents, and monks and nuns of the entire city, forcefully standing up for the promotion of the unity of nationalities and the unification of the motherland, fully comprehending the serious significance of the incident at this time, must clearly distinguish whether it is right or wrong and adhere to a correct ideological view and a correct standpoint. In particular, the broad Party members, members of the Communist Youth League, and the nation's cadres, must have a firm standpoint on what is right and wrong in this important issue, clearly show the flag, and be politically clear-minded. Doing this without wavering in the slightest is a serious test for each and every Communist Party member and member of the Communist Youth League.
2. Departments and units must do good ideological work with the cadres and workers under their jurisdiction, and the broad cadres and workers must do good ideological work with their family members, children, and relatives. The neighbourhood committees must do good ideological work with the broad residents of the city. Moreover, they must explain exactly the circumstances of this event at this time to the broad cadres and workers, and in a broad and deep manner publicize the Party's policy and carry the

43

work through to completion in the ranks. Then not only will the broad masses of the people reject the actions of a few people, but those few will be quite without friends and isolated. They must clearly understand this and be confident that it is impossible for the disturbance caused by a few people to change the Party's policy. Continuing to raise firmly the flag of patriotism, unity, and progress, by generating great enthusiasm, a united effort must be made for the purpose of creating a new Tibet of unity, wealth, and education.

3. It is necessary to take even greater precautions than before. The departments and neighbourhood committees, doing even more than before to protect security, must immediately report any special information that they come to know. Through a united effort, the broad cadres, workers, residents of the city, and monks and nuns must report in time to the concerned units if they see a disturbance. Likewise, they must not support the activities that incite disturbances, should not remain within them, and should not watch or join them. If they are at a place where a disturbance is occurring, they must immediately leave. If they are in the middle of a crowd and not able to leave, then they must diligently support the concerned units in trying to quell the disturbance.[1]

The tone of the announcement is reminiscent of earlier political campaigns, with its emphasis on a "correct view and standpoint" (*yang dag pa'i lta tshul dang lang phyogs*) and the necessity for "good ideological work" (*bsam blo'i las ka yag po*). In this, party members and cadres working for the Chinese administration are expected to set an example, and their readiness to do so "without wavering in the slightest" is a test of their loyalty. As in other political campaigns, political study sessions are to be initiated by the pervasive apparatus of Party control that extends through government departments, work units, and the neighbourhood committees that incorporate city residents. The object of the campaign is to isolate the "few" — the splittists, reactionaries, troublemakers — from the broad masses, who are loyal to the motherland and support the Party's policies. Tibetans are warned not to participate in demonstrations and encouraged to inform on each other.

The anti-splittist campaign occupied the government and the security apparatus in Tibet from 1987 onward. As the demonstrations continued and the scope of unrest broadened throughout 1988 and into 1989, the

---

[1] "Announcement [*brda khyab*] of the People's Government of Lhasa City", 1 October 1987, *Tibet Daily* (*bod ljongs nyin re'i tshags par*), 2 October 1987.

campaign went through several phases. The first phase spans the period from the first demonstrations in the autumn of 1987 to the riot on 5 March 1988 following the close of the Mönlam festival. During this phase the authorities believed that local administrative structures were adequate to deal with the problem. The emphasis was on reminding Tibetans of the benefits they had experienced as a result of the reforms during the 1980s.

After 5 March, in the wake of widespread arrests and imprisonment, the burden of dealing with the unrest shifted to the security and prison apparatus. The brutal treatment of prisoners was designed to frighten potential dissidents and organizers. Tibetans were warned that any demonstrations would be violently suppressed. The third and final phase is marked by the declaration of martial law on 8 March 1989. Martial law was in a real sense an admission of the failure of the anti-splittist campaign. Demonstrations could be suppressed, but only through a continuing display of military force in the streets of Lhasa. Given an opportunity, Tibetans would demonstrate. This has required that administrative measures implemented to search out splittists, originally a temporary expedient, have become permanent and institutionalized. Each phase of the campaign has thus added an additional layer of organized repression.

To follow the evolution of the anti-splittist campaign that began in 1987 it is necessary to understand how the reforms of the 1980s were instruments of Party control. It has become something of a cliché that China has pursued economic reforms without corresponding political reforms. The point that needs to be made, however, is that the economic reforms — along with other recent policies in Tibet, like the relaxation of restrictions on religious practice — are themselves part of a political strategy. The hope of the reformers was that economic development would guarantee social stability and the harsh apparatus of collectivization could be lifted without popular unrest. Tibetans would thus come to accept Chinese rule and see the Chinese as modernizers rather than oppressors.

Defending the reforms

Immediately after the demonstrations in the autumn of 1987 a whole series of forums was organized within the different government departments identified with the policy of relaxation and responsible for implementing the reforms in Tibet. These include the regional Chinese People's Political Consultative Conference (CPPCC), the local Bureau of Nationalities and Religious Affairs, the Buddhist Association, and the United Front Work Department of the Communist Party. One after another, Tibetan participants came forward to condemn the "crimes of a handful of splittists", praise the Party's policy on religion, and testify to the unity of the nationalities and the unification of the motherland. On 3 October the Tibet branch of the Buddhist Association sent a letter to monks and "religious believers" saying:

> The patriotic religious circles and the vast numbers of religious believers in our region must treasure the unification of the motherland, national unity, and the excellent situation characterized by stability and unity, just as we treasure our own eyes. In the past few years in particular, the CPC's policy for freedom of religious beliefs has been resolutely implemented, temples have been renovated and reopened, and religious activities have been protected. We are gratified with this situation from the bottom of our hearts and sincerely support the Party's policy.[2]

These attestations of loyalty served two purposes. First, by saying that the situation in Tibet had never been so good — monasteries rebuilt, the economy improving, religious freedom reinstated — Tibetans holding positions within the Chinese administration lent legitimacy to the Chinese regime and provided a counterweight to the exile leadership around the Dalai Lama. But secondly, they were themselves targets of the campaign against splittism. Whatever tacit support they had given to separatist thinking had to be stopped. Their own positions of influence were at risk along with whatever progress had been made in religion and education during the 1980s.

For many of these Tibetans, denunciation of the Dalai Lama and the young monks who had demonstrated did not come easily. This was the first real test of loyalty for the group of rehabilitated non-Party leaders in Tibet (referred to by the Chinese as the "patriotic upper strata"). The reforms in Tibet have required the participation of some of the pre-1959 leadership or members of leading families from that era, many of whom are highly talented people — scholars, skilled administrators, religious leaders. Often they were branded as reactionaries after the 1959 uprising or persecuted for their "bad class origins"

---

[2] Lhasa Xizang Regional Service in Mandarin, 7 October 1987, in *FBIS*, 8 October 1987: 27.

in the 1960s and 1970s. Many of them also suffered terribly during the Cultural Revolution and have spent time in prisons and labour-camps. But they have been essential in creating the cultural institutions that the Chinese point to as evidence of modernization and reform during the 1980s — the new university in Lhasa, the Academy of Social Sciences, the Buddhist Association. In practice, their cooperation has been essential for rebuilding Tibet. Politically, their compliance was expected to legitimate Chinese rule in Tibet and defuse nationalist discontent.

The United Front Work Department has been the branch of the Party responsible for overseeing the rehabilitation of the non-Party Tibetan leadership. It controls the organizations associated with religious and cultural activities, ensuring that they implement Party policies, and has played an increasing role in the administration of Tibet in the 1980s. The regional branch of the Chinese People's Political Consultative Conference (CPPCC) has reemerged as the centrepiece of the policy of rehabilitation for the Tibetan leadership during the 1980s. This non-Party organization is (like the Buddhist Association) an advisory body overseen by the United Front Work Department. Revived on the national level in the 1980s by Deng Xiaoping, the CPPCC in Tibet has a predominantly Tibetan composition. It has no real power within the Chinese political apparatus but plays a visible role in providing Tibetan assent to Chinese policies. Its members are effectively told what to say by representatives of the Party.

The chairman of the CPPCC in Tibet is Raidi (*rag sdis*), who is deputy secretary of the regional Party central committee and the highest-ranking Tibetan in the regional Party structure. He belongs to the old guard of Tibetan cadres whose careers in the Party go back to the 1950s. This group, which was Maoist during the Cultural Revolution, continues to occupy its positions within the regional Party structure. In fact, its members have moved up in rank to head Party committees as some of the old guard of Chinese cadres were retired in the 1980s. They pay lip-service to the new policies of relaxation and reform, but their concept of Party rule remains the rigid and uncompromising approach of twenty years ago, emphasizing ideological orthodoxy as the surest guarantee of loyalty. During recent disturbances they have been the first to call for political campaigns to weed out troublemakers and correct the thinking of the masses.

In a televised speech on 6 October, Raidi defines the campaign against splittism in the harshest terms, calling on Tibetans to "thoroughly expose and criticize the criminal activities of the Dalai and his clique," to "inform against a small number of splittists," and to "thoroughly smash their criminal conspiracy." He has this warning for the protestors:

You must rein in at the brink of the precipice, stop all splittist and sabotage activities, and take the initiative and surrender yourselves to the public security organs and confess your crimes so as to seek lenient treatment. If you refuse to come to your senses and dare to engage in any further sabotage activities we will severely punish you according to the law, without any leniency. You must not miss this opportunity and destroy yourselves.[3]

The Panchen Lama arrived in Lhasa on 11 January 1988 to attend the forthcoming Regional People's Congress and make his own assessment of the political situation in Tibet. More than any other figure in the Chinese government, the Panchen Lama has been identified with the policy of reform in Tibet. Since his rehabilitation during the 1980s and appointment to the position of vice-chairman of the National People's Congress, he persistently reminded Tibetans of the contrast between their situation following the reforms and their experiences during the Cultural Revolution. Though rejecting claims for Tibetan independence, he also attacked "ultra-leftists" in the Party as the principal obstacle to further progress and development in Tibet.

In a speech to the Sixth Session of the Fourth TAR Regional People's Congress on 19 January, the Panchen Lama discussed the background to the demonstrations in Lhasa. He goes to some length to justify the policy of reform and the relaxation of control in Tibet, and attributes the demonstrations to persisting problems remaining after "twenty years under the guidance of erroneous leftist ideology":

. . . the influence of leftism in Xizang [Tibet] was particularly deep, the situation in Xizang was more complicated than in other areas, and there were greater obstacles to setting aright the guideline. So Xizang advanced more slowly than, or lagged behind other localities in the country, in setting aright the guideline. Some negative things have even occurred in the process of doing this. Because we encountered a complicated situation and major difficulties, we became somewhat hesitant in the handling of some affairs. We even delayed handling some important matters for a long time. This weakened people's confidence. This state of affairs provided an opportunity which the splittists could

---

[3] Lhasa Xizang Regional Service in Mandarin, 6 October 1987, in *FBIS*, 7 October 1987: 24–5.

take advantage of to create trouble. Various errors and loopholes in our work provided the conditions, like dry firewood, for the splittists to feed the flames and stir up trouble and disturbance.[4]

The Panchen Lama insisted that the current policies should not be reversed. But it is clear that Party leaders identified with the reforms were already under some pressure from the Party conservatives who would roll back the reforms, particularly on nationality and religious questions:

Today, I want to make one point clear. After the riots occurred in Lhasa some people thought it was because we had gone too far in setting aright the work guideline, redressing wrongs, implementing policies, and correcting errors in our previous work. Because we went too far in implementing the religious policy, the lamas became too arrogant; and because we went too far in implementing the nationality policy, narrow-minded nationality sentiments were abetted. So they held that after the riots occurred we should backtrack to the old practices, stop pursuing the current relaxed policies that we adopted after setting right the guideline, and adopt some high-handed measures; otherwise there would be no way to deal with the problems. Although not many people held such a viewpoint, they did account for a very small proportion of our cadres. We should adopt a prudent attitude toward such a viewpoint and idea and approach them seriously. Such a viewpoint and idea may cause great trouble if they continue to spread.[5]

The anti-splittist campaign thus put Tibetans cooperating with the policy of reform in Tibet on the defensive. While this group continued to stress the positive benefits of liberalization during the 1980s, the old guard within the Party pushed for a return to ideological orthodoxy and the familiar methods of repression.

The apparatus of social control

On 13 October the Propaganda Department of the regional Party issued a notice defining the "focal point" for the ongoing ideological studies initiated by units throughout the region. The points to be stressed were: (1) that the disturbances were "plotted and instigated by the Dalai clique"; (2) that national unity is vital to the "policies of reform,

[4] Lhasa Xizang Regional Service in Mandarin, 9 February 1988, in *FBIS*, 10 February 1988: 36.

[5] Lhasa Xizang Regional Service in Mandarin, 9 February 1988, in *FBIS*, 10 February 1988: 36–7.

opening up to the outside world, and invigorating the domestic economy"; and (3) the "two inseparables" — that Han and Tibetan peoples cannot live without each other.[6] These ideological studies were to be carried out within the existing administrative structure of work units, government departments, and neighbourhood committees, which has been in place in one form or another since the inception of communist rule in Tibet. An important feature of these is the provision for incorporating every individual into supervised study and discussion sessions.[7] The very same structure also provides monitoring and surveillance of the behaviour of individuals and has direct links to the Public Security Bureau (PSB).

During the reforms of the 1980s the structure had fallen into disuse. After 1984 the number of required political meetings was reduced from three to one a week. The subjects discussed at meetings could be both practical and political — health, cleanliness, and education were all regular subjects. Before the demonstrations began the political content of the meetings was largely laudatory, announcing improvements made under the "new Tibet policy" in economics and education. Questions of political loyalty and Tibetan independence never came up.

Political education went on in both work units and residential compounds, and individuals would have to participate at one or the other depending on where they were registered with the government. Within the Tibetan part of the city each residential compound (*sgo ra*) is placed under the administration of a neighbourhood committee (*sa gnas u yon lhan khang*). The neighbourhood committee has a headquarters and a permanent administrative staff. Normally its meetings consist of the staff plus the leaders (*go 'khrid*) of each of the compounds. Leaders go back to their compounds with topics for meetings. Sometimes there are combined meetings of all the residential compounds and the neighbourhood committee, and every family will be required to send a member to the large meeting, which takes place in a hall able to hold hundreds of people.

During the early period of the campaign, workers in government departments were told that they would be safer if they shifted to live in

---

[6] Lhasa Xizang Regional Service in Mandarin, 13 October 1987, in *FBIS*, 14 October 1987: 30.

[7] See Whyte (1974) for a discussion of comparable forms of political education throughout China.

their work units from their homes in Tibetan neighbourhoods. For the workers this was a way of avoiding the atmosphere of intimidation and fear in the Tibetan areas. It was probably safer for Tibetans in their work units than in the neighbourhoods, since the presence of Chinese peers insulated them from the campaign. Also, displaying "wrong ideas" in the work unit sessions might result in a warning and reprimand from the unit leader, but would normally not lead to an investigation by the PSB and possible arrest. However, as one worker in a government enterprise explained, "The government made this request because they were frightened. They were trying to separate people from the movement. Many Tibetans are very angry, but they are afraid to speak for fear of losing their jobs."

The neighbourhood committee falls under the jurisdiction of the Lhasa city government. But associated with each neighbourhood committee is a neighbourhood security department (*phe bro zo*; Chinese: *pai chu suo*), which maintains files on every individual and family, and directly oversees the political life of residents within its jurisdiction (the police station destroyed on 1 October was one such, and the files scattered and looted were those of the residents of the area). Representatives of the neighbourhood security department sometimes attend meetings of the neighbourhood committees and the residential compounds.

The Public Security Bureau (*spyi bde cus*; Chinese: *gong an ju*) has a separate administration above the neighbourhood security departments and comes under the jurisdiction of the TAR regional government. It is responsible for the arrest and interrogation of political suspects. It also maintains a network of paid informers, Tibetans with ordinary livelihoods who receive extra cash for providing information about their neighbours. Particularly in Tibetan neighbourhoods, where many people are merchants or small traders and do not belong to work units, the system of informers has many of the characteristics of a "protection racket." Licences can be revoked and trade halted if individuals do not cooperate with the PSB, while special privileges such as freedom to travel are the reward for cooperation. These informers are present at meetings and report directly to the PSB on what is said.

Following the first demonstrations in the autumn of 1987, a special unit for political education and investigation at the monasteries and nunneries was organized by the TAR regional administration of Public Security (*spyi bde thing*; Chinese: *gong an ting*). Notices were sent out to government departments, work units, and enterprises to send selected cadres for training and assignment to political education squads referred to collectively as the "Work Team" (*las don ru khag*).[8] During the course of the campaign, salaries for these cadres would continue to be paid by their units while they were on temporary leave. In addition, they received a bonus for their political work. A similar Work Team was formed from the staff of the neighbourhood committees, given political training, and then sent around to conduct political education with city residents. The units assigned to monasteries and nunneries stayed for varying lengths of time, from several weeks to several months, carrying on their investigations, identifying potential dissidents, and holding meetings.

Initially the Work Team was not responsible for political education in government departments and enterprises. Managers assumed this responsibility for themselves. For instance, in one government tourism enterprise, according to a Tibetan worker in the organization, meetings were held from mid-October 1987 onwards. Throughout 1988 they were held once a week on Saturday afternoons. All Tibetan workers (but not Chinese workers in the same enterprise) were required to attend, otherwise their salaries would be cut. The general manager, a Tibetan, would address the meeting. At one meeting, when Chinese officials from the TAR government were present, he spoke for over an hour, banging his fists on the table. He said: "I was once a serf, now I have a high position. Tsering Dorje [head of TAR People's Government] was a serf, now his children are studying in China and will get high posts when they graduate. Tibet has been a part of China since the time of Songtsen Gampo. Tibet is one kingdom of China. Mao has liberated all of China, made it one."

Nobody argued with him. The Tibetan worker who described this meeting pointed out that the general manager's mother had been very active during the Cultural Revolution. Among themselves the workers referred to what the manager had been saying as "lies." One worker had commented at the time: "My mother didn't die in the old society, she died of starvation during the Cultural Revolution."

That meeting later broke up into section meetings, where every individual was supposed to give his opinions. Nobody spoke, except one person who made the observation: "Yes, the riots have affected our business, tour groups have been cancelled because of it." The mandatory meetings continued throughout 1988, sometimes in a large group with the general manager leading, sometimes in section meetings. As this

---

[8] The term in Chinese is *gong zuo dui*, which also translates as "work team."

informant explained: "The subject was always the same — how China had made big improvements in Tibet. People got bored. If there were separate section meetings, the section leaders would have to report what was discussed during the meetings. They would simply fabricate reports to save everyone a lot of trouble."

As the campaign progressed and unrest continued, the effectiveness of control in government departments and enterprises also came into question. The role of the Work Team expanded and it became a permanent fixture of life in Tibet. By November 1989, 300 cadres were reported to be assigned to the Work Team in Lhasa, and 1,000 for Tibet as a whole. They remained stationed at the monasteries, but extended their work to include institutions previously exempt. Meetings of four and five hours' duration were held in offices two or more times a week, where workers were forced to discuss their views on the demonstrations. Neighbourhood committees were instructed to separate those who had been involved with the splittists from others who were suitable for re-education, and participants in earlier demonstrations were reinvestigated to determine if their views were the same.

One function of the neighbourhood committee meetings was to aid the authorities in identifying demonstrators and potential dissidents. According to one Lhasa resident, leaders of residential compounds were instructed to tell residents: "Whoever indulges in these anti-government demonstrations will be dealt with seriously. Persons who inform the *sgo ra* who indulges in these demonstrations and inform us about people putting up wall posters will be rewarded. If you cannot inform in person, then write it on a slip of paper and push it under the door of the *u yon lhan khang*. We will check on the people you name." Reports by informers were responsible for a number of arrests in the autumn of 1987. In addition, paid informers reported directly to the PSB on what was said in residential compound meetings.

Leaders of residential compounds were also asked to investigate links between families there and the Tibetan refugee community in India. Tibetans who had travelled to India in the 1980s to visit relatives were singled out. One question asked was whether families had sent children to India for schooling. This was seen as evidence of disloyalty and marked the family as politically suspect. In addition, the family would have its ration for subsidized goods cut and the children would be removed from the registration list, effectively barring them from employment and education on their return.

The political meetings in the residential compounds and work units had the form of group discussions, where participants were encouraged to give their own ideas, others were encouraged to discuss these ideas, and finally the political leader offered criticism. Residents were regularly provided with subjects to think about or questions to discuss — e.g. whether monks should be thrown out of the monasteries for demonstrating and what should be done with them afterwards. The names of those who refused to cooperate were noted. Though they were not arrested immediately, following subsequent demonstrations they were among the first to be arrested and interrogated. People would often make excuses for not participating in the discussions, claiming that they had not seen the demonstrations or that they were not well enough informed to speak. They might be coerced into declaring their support for the Chinese, but unwillingly and without enthusiasm.

The real test of loyalty was whether Tibetans were prepared to criticize the Dalai Lama. Attempts at organizing pro-Chinese/anti-Dalai Lama counter-demonstrations foundered on this point as well. Tibetans might be coerced into making perfunctory declarations of loyalty in political meetings, but they could not be coerced into attacking the Dalai Lama. The original demand that Tibetans attack the Dalai Lama was dropped around 20 October, reportedly because of an order from Beijing that it was no longer necessary.

Chinese strategy generally has been not to attack the Dalai Lama directly, referring instead to the "Dalai clique". The policy on religious freedom has required that the Chinese acknowledge the Dalai Lama as a religious figure revered by virtually all Tibetans. At the same time, his role in the cause of Tibetan independence must somehow be distinguished from his religious role if it is to be attacked. Tibetans recognized the ambiguity in this Chinese ideological fabrication and were quick to seize the opportunity. Thus, in a meeting in a government department, a young Tibetan responded: "Whatever was done may have been very bad, but we should not curse the Dalai Lama and blame what has happened on the 'Dalai clique' [*ru tshogs*] because he is our religious leader." The worker was later called into the manager's office and told that his "thinking" had to change, but nothing else was done to him.

Tibetans became adept at managing the ambiguity of the Dalai Lama's combined political and religious roles. In the face of Chinese repression it became a principal resource for resistance. In political meetings Tibetans would insist on their right to "religious freedom" as defined by the Chinese and refuse to criticize the Dalai Lama, while in the streets the Dalai Lama would resurface as the symbol of Tibetan independence.

Individuals who spoke up at meetings in support of the Chinese found their statements used in the Chinese media for propaganda. The government made an effort to win confessions from those who had been arrested. In late October, thirteen Tibetans (including nine monks from Drepung) were released from prison after they had agreed to make public statements in support of the Chinese in Tibet. These confessions were widely publicized. Those few Tibetans who did cooperate or who provided public statements that could be used for propaganda purposes were ostracized by their neighbours. What individuals said in public, they were held accountable for in private. Tibetans who challenged the political workers in meetings were spoken of as heroes.

Like the demonstrations themselves, the political meetings highlighted the separation and opposition between the Tibetan community and the alien Chinese administration. Ironically, by pitting Tibetans as a group against the Chinese, the political meetings have functioned as solidarity-building exercises for Tibetans. Without the total subordination of social life to the state achieved during the period of collectivization, political indoctrination through public meetings has been largely ineffective.[9]

The campaign against splittism attempted to revive an apparatus of social control that employs group pressures to force compliance and change thinking. During the period of collectivization in Tibet that began in the 1960s — and especially during the Cultural Revolution — this apparatus was mobilized with brutal efficiency in "struggle sessions" (*'thab 'dzings*), where neighbours and families were forced to attack and denounce targeted members of the community in public meetings. Under the guidance of political cadres the victims were singled out as "class enemies", then humiliated, beaten, and frequently executed.

There has been no return to the practice of "class labelling", singling out economic groups for persecution. The issue in the anti-splittist

---

[9] Whyte also found that political meetings generally were not an effective means of changing attitudes. But, he adds, other properties of group organization in China nevertheless contributed to social control. He found "few instances of individual deviance or open opposition within organizations, and even fewer instances of overt group resistance" — Whyte (1974): 233.

campaign remains loyalty, not economic status, and political workers have pointed out how compliance with Chinese demands and acceptance of Chinese rule is the route to further economic opportunities. Meetings during the anti-splittist campaign consisted largely of lectures by political workers. Discussion in the meetings has been used to identify potential dissidents as candidates for arrest by the PSB, who are responsible for subsequent interrogation and imprisonment. Here, more and more, the progress of the anti-splittist campaign gives the appearance of the bureaucratic consolidation of the security apparatus rather than an orchestrated popular movement.

Control over the monasteries

On 13 October, Raidi visited Ganden monastery. He was accompanied by Mao Rubai (also a deputy secretary of the regional Party committee and a Chinese functionary in Tibet for twenty-five years) and a number of Party officials, including officials from Dagze county where Ganden is located. The Party officials met the Democratic Management Committee (the monastery's *u yon lhan khang*), an administrative body which oversees the operation of the monastery and reports to relevant government departments. The purpose of the visit was to ensure that the monks of Ganden did not follow the lead of the Drepung and Sera monks and stage demonstrations in Lhasa. Raidi explained to the officials of the monastery that "it is necessary to teach the monks to abide by the law and behave themselves."[10] The chairman of the monastery's Democratic Management Committee agreed: "Although no member of our temple was involved in the two incidents aimed at disrupting the motherland, we still must strengthen education among the resident monks of our temple, dispel rumours, and restrain ourselves from being involved in activities to disrupt the motherland and undermine national solidarity."[11]

A contingent of about fifty police and representatives from the Work Team had arrived at Ganden on 5 October to prevent Ganden monks from travelling into Lhasa to take part in further protest, and about twenty members of the Work Team stayed on to lead daily political meetings. During these sessions, some monks spoke out openly,

[10] Lhasa Xizang Regional Service in Mandarin, 14 October 1987, in *FBIS*, 15 October 1987: 20.
[11] *Ibid.*: 19.

challenging the arguments of the political workers. Though not arrested at the time, these monks were among the first to be arrested following the protest in March 1988. In late November, political workers at Ganden were attacked by a group of monks and a vehicle was set on fire. Ten monks were arrested.

The Work Team was also sent to Sera and Drepung monasteries, as well as the Jokhang temple, to conduct political meetings. Initially fifty political workers were stationed at Drepung and Sera. The monasteries were closed to outsiders for weeks at a time for political education. A sign posted from the beginning of November onwards in front of Tashilunpo monastery in Shigatse, Tibet's second largest city after Lhasa, announced that the monastery was closed to visitors for "examinations." Monks there were undergoing political instruction, though they had not taken part in any protest and the monastery is the seat of the Panchen Lama. It remained possible for organized tour groups to visit these monasteries if they received special passes issued by the PSB. Monks said that they believed the authorities were trying to prevent them from speaking to foreigners about politics.

A young Drepung monk who fled to India following the March 1988 demonstrations gives this account of the arrival of the Work Team at Drepung:

Those fifty workers who formed a committee after the October riots were the Party workers sent to the monasteries. Then there was the addition of sixteen more workers, making it sixty-six. One thing they said was: "The Tibetans don't have the means to rebel against the Chinese. Demonstrating is a mistake." The classes were going on when I left Tibet too. When I left there were eight workers doing reeducation at Drepung. These workers were Tibetans, high-ranking people from different offices, Lhasa city offices. When I left about a month ago it was still going on. It started in October. The classes were sometimes in the morning, sometimes in the evening. People didn't believe in them, so people were not going for these sessions. The workers called themselves protectors of the monasteries, but they used to drink in the monastery, shit on the roof of the monastery, and gamble in the monastery. The sessions used to take place in Tiu Khamtsen. The monks would sit around and then there would be lectures. If the workers said something was right, the monks were supposed to answer the same. The monks would argue with them but nothing would happen. The workers were a little afraid, since in the monasteries they would be defenceless for a while. Nothing happens to monks who laugh or make jokes at the time, but maybe your name is taken.

The monks were not afraid to challenge the political workers:

When the Chinese were announcing on the radio that the demonstrations were caused by the Dalai clique, the monks spoke against this, saying: "It's not the Dalai clique, but Chinese beating corpses [the joke in Tibetan plays on *ru tshogs* = clique, but *ro rdzog* = beating a corpse]. We said: "When you talk about things like the Dalai clique, it's like a stab in the heart, we will definitely challenge you." The workers would say different things, starting every day with a new line, but it would always mean that today we are happy and the demonstrations were not right. By the time the session came to an end, all the monks would have left. The workers would usually start with the discipline problem in the monasteries — that the monks do not listen to their elders, that they do not study, that they are just doing nothing. Once they said they had given 80,000 yuan to the monastery. They wanted the monks to be thankful. But the monks said that before 1959 there were special carpets in the assembly hall used only when the Dalai Lama came there. So the monks did an accounting of how much compensation was paid for these carpets that had been taken from the monastery. They said: "These carpets would cost 10,000 yuan each, but you have paid only 20 yuan each for them. You have certainly not paid us enough for what you have taken from us."

For the monks the presence of the Work Team at the monasteries vividly illustrated the continuing interference by the Chinese administration in monastic life. The rebuilding of the monasteries in the 1980s has been for Tibetans a collective project, an attempt to restore the traditional relationship between the community and Buddhism as a social institution. Throughout Tibet there has been an enormous amount of spontaneous rebuilding and repopulating of monasteries and nunneries. In remote areas this has often gone on without government interference. The breakup of the communes in the 1980s and the exemption of farmers from taxation has meant that Tibetan families have been able to take their agricultural surplus and use it to support the monasteries. They have also contributed their own labour and materials to the rebuilding of local monasteries.

State support for the rebuilding of the monasteries has largely been limited to those perceived by the government to have high value as tourist attractions. This applies to historically important locations such as Samye and Sakya monasteries, Tashilunpo, and Drepung and Sera near Lhasa. Some other smaller monasteries have received limited funds, the extent of support varying considerably according to the attitude of local officials. Generally the rebuilding has been initiated by Tibetans themselves. Ganden, for instance, had undergone some of the worst destruction of any monastery in Tibet, having been shelled and dynamited in 1966 and then completely gutted by Red Guards and abandoned. The idea to rebuilding it originated with several old monks who had been turned out of the monastery during the Cultural Revolution and were living in nearby villages. They grazed cattle up near the monastery, and in the late 1970s began constructing a small shrine in the ruins. The project caught on with people throughout Tibet — nuns, monks, and lay people. Ganden, founded in 1409 by Tsongkhapa, who initiated the reformed Gelugpa sect that assumed political power under the Dalai Lamas, was the first of the "three seats" (Ganden, Drepung, and Sera) to be established. Though the Chinese government eventually authorized some funds for reconstruction, the project quickly became an expression of national purpose. By 1983 two hundred monks from all over Tibet had taken up residence at Ganden without government permission.

The continuing uneasiness of the Chinese authorities with the spontaneous reconstruction of the monasteries is illustrated by an incident that occurred at Ganden in the spring of 1983. The police from nearby Dagze Dzong arrived at the monastery and assembled the monks, informing them that they were engaging in unlawful religious activities for which they could be executed. They were told that religious freedom did not mean that they could congregate in monasteries — they could practise religion in their homes. They were also accused of reciting prayers in praise of the Dalai Lama and for Tibetan independence. The army from Lhasa arrived and two truckloads of monks were taken off to Dagze Dzong and held in the compound there for a number of days. They were finally released, but it was soon after this incident that the policy of the Religious Affairs Bureau to restrict access to Ganden to monks from the Tibetan Autonomous Region was enforced. Monks from Kham and Amdo were told to return to their homes.

In Tibet before 1959 the large monasteries received income from extensive estate holdings, as well as endowment funds, government grants, and donations.[12] Lay support for the monasteries after the reconstruction in the 1980s has been entirely voluntary, consisting of donations to temples, money and food to sponsor ceremonies, or contributions to individual monks. Monks at the large monasteries

[12] Goldstein (1989): 34–5.

report that their finances are controlled by the resident Democratic Management Committee (the monastery's *u yon lhan khang*). Donations to the monasteries — including offerings in the temples — are deposited in a bank account and need authorization from the Religious Affairs Bureau in order to be spent. While this may be an appropriate method of managing funds provided by the government, monks complain that neither they nor lay contributors have any control over donations earmarked for religious purposes. It is also generally believed that far more money is taken from the monastery than is returned to the monks for operating expenses and reconstruction.

The traditional organization of the monasteries has not been restored. The large monasteries had an elaborate system of administration and self-government. Sera, Drepung, and Ganden, for example, comprised independent colleges (*grwa tshang*), each headed by an abbot (*mKhan po*). Abbots were appointed for a fixed term of six years by the Dalai Lama from a list drawn up by the college of nominees, all of whom had completed the highest monastic degree (*dge bshes lha ram pa*). Other officials selected by the college were responsible for maintaining discipline within it, administering its finances, and overseeing the curriculum. The administration of the monasteries thus reflected the scholastic functions they fulfilled.

The colleges in turn consisted of a number of *khamtsen* (*khang mtshan*) residential units in which monks enrolled, generally on the basis of their region of origin. These too had their own economic resources and internal administration. A monk's primary loyalties were thus to his college and khamtsen, where he lived and studied. Rivalries were common, and monks from different colleges studied different texts and debated with one another. This self-governing monastic organization — with roots not merely in Tibet but in the long history of Buddhist monasticism as an institution in Asia — has been largely preserved in the monasteries established by Tibetan refugees in India. Its administrative functions, however, have been supplanted in the rebuilt monasteries in Tibet by the Democratic Management Committees established by the Religious Affairs Bureau. The structure of colleges has been abolished. The young monks are aware of the former system, and the colleges and residences retain their former names, but the monks at the large monasteries are amalgamated into one unit. An abbot is selected for the entire monastery, but he has no administrative power. Instead, important decisions are made by the Democratic Management Committee.

The members of these committees are supposed to be elected by the monks, but the monks report that they have only a small degree of control over the selection process. Some of the members, who reside at the monasteries, are lay people, or former monks who have repudiated their vows. The older members have been selected because of proven loyalty to the Chinese administration. The position carries a salary from the Religious Affairs Bureau, besides offering considerable opportunity for corruption — especially bribes to arrange the admission of novices. Members of the committee carry the title of Turin, "manager" (*kru'u rin*, borrowed from the Chinese term *zhu ren*).

Monks at Drepung, for instance, complained about the head of the Drepung Democratic Management Committee, a monk aged about sixty who spoke fluent Chinese and had remained in the monastery during the 1960s and 1970s. He was believed to cooperate with the Chinese government mainly because of the salary he received as a Turin, and the young monks at Drepung claimed he was given a raise for his work in informing on the organizers of the demonstrations in September and October 1987, which resulted in a number of arrests. In fact one Drepung monk, Ngawang Tenkyong, had been arrested a month after these demonstrations for putting up posters around the monastery criticizing Turin Tenzin for collaborating with the Chinese — describing him as a "wolf wearing a sheep's skin".

Some of the younger elected members of the Democratic Management Committee, who must still be approved by the Religious Affairs Bureau and the older long-standing members, have themselves been arrested and punished following protests. One of the Turins at Ganden, Chungdag, stood up at meetings in the autumn of 1987 and spoke openly of Tibetan history and Tibetan independence. Though he had not participated in the Mönlam demonstration, he was accused of being a "reactionary" and was arrested on 6 March 1988, the day after the demonstration. He was never released, and eventually was reported to have received a seven-year sentence for unnamed offences relating to the demonstrations. He is presently held in Drapchi prison. Ngawang Namgyal, a Turin at Drepung, was arrested along with Ngawang Gendun, the monastery treasurer, on 10 March 1988 for writing letters to the monks of Ganden monastery. The Democratic Management Committee announced in January 1989 that these two monks were to be expelled from the monastery and sent home to their villages, but they remained in Sangyip prison without trial until March 1990.

Admission to the monasteries is controlled by various departments in the Chinese administration. In some smaller rural monasteries the process of admission has been fairly informal and villagers have been able to place their children in them without government interference. A number of remote retreats have been reestablished, with resident monks and nuns living off of donations from pilgrims.[13] Even if local villagers rebuild a monastery with their own labour and materials, there is no guarantee that they will be allowed to place monks in it.[14] Policy appears to vary considerably depending on the attitude of local officials.

The formal process of admission to monasteries involves a number of steps. In addition to the approval of the candidate's parents and acceptance by an older monk who will act as teacher and supervisor, these include: (1) acceptance of the candidate by the monastery Democratic Management Committee, (2) registration with the Lhasa Religious Affairs Bureau, (3) written permission from several levels of the local administration in the candidate's home area, and (4) clearance from Public Security. The system is particularly vulnerable to bribery. Monks report that to receive official status they have had to bribe local officials

[13] Two that I visited in 1987 were Chimpu and Yerpa. At Chimpu, an important Nyingma retreat from the time of Padmasambhava, about a day's walk from Samye, there were some fifty nuns and monks receiving teachings from a Nyingma lama. They live mostly on offerings from a steady stream of pilgrims from every part of Tibet. The chorten and main temple have been rebuilt, and the place has the appearance of a small but thriving religious community. Yerpa, about a day's walk east of Lhasa, has been partly rebuilt. The whole complex, which included Drag Yerpa monastery and the summer residence of the Upper Tantric College, was completely demolished during the Cultural Revolution. Some of the Nyingma cave temples have been partly restored and are again occupied by monks and nuns. There is also a Gelugpa lama resident in a cave associated with Atisha. Here again, the restoration work has been voluntary. People from Lhasa frequently make a pilgrimage to Yerpa and leave offerings. In the Barkhor in Lhasa collections were being taken for the restoration of Drag Yerpa. After the events of October 1987, Yerpa was visited by the police and posters were pasted on the doors to the temples warning people against participating in "counter-revolutionary activities."

[14] The Drolma Lhakhang at Netang, where Atisha died in 1054, is one of the most famous sites in Tibet. Many of the relics and statues escaped the ravages of the Cultural Revolution, but the building and outside walls were extensively damaged. In 1987 it was being rebuilt by villagers without outside help. The villagers involved in the reconstruction said that they were being allowed to restore the temple and grounds, but that they had been told by local officials that, except for a couple of old monks, no new monks would be allowed to reside at the monastery.

at the township (*shang*; Chinese: *xiang*) and county (*rdzong*; Chinese: *xian*) levels or make use of personal and family connections.

Officially a quota exists for the number of monks allowed to reside at the large monasteries. Monks at Ganden, Drepung, and Sera reported that in 1987 there were 300 officially registered monks at Ganden, 450 at Drepung and 400 at Sera. Since 1987, following the demonstrations, no new official monks have been approved at the three large monasteries. The quotas are not published and it is not clear which levels of government are involved in setting quotas, though the Lhasa Religious Affairs Bureau, along with the county administration, are responsible for admitting monks. No such quotas are imposed on smaller monasteries and nunneries; here, however, official status is not extended to religious practitioners and they depend on the tolerance of local officials.

One result of the restrictions on the admission of monks to the three large monasteries has been the growth of a population of monks who reside there illegally. These are monks who have not received official permission to study at the monasteries, but whose presence is tolerated by the authorities. They are referred to as "unlisted monks" (*them mtho med pa*); in 1987 there were over 200 of these at Ganden, 100 at Drepung, and about 100 at Sera.[15] Officially registered monks have a ration card which entitles them to a monthly allotment of grain and oil; they are also entitled to attend prayer sessions where they are able to share in donations of food and sometimes money distributed to the participants. Unlisted monks are not allowed to take part in these prayer sessions or in the organized debates which are the focus of the educational curriculum in the monasteries. Instead they must arrange for private instruction with the few qualified teachers. The principal source of support for both registered and unlisted monks remains their own families, who regularly send them cash, clothes, and other supplies. Some of the unlisted monks are able to find odd jobs around the monasteries for which they receive payment.

Registered monks also report that they are required to work at the monastery for several years before being allowed to enter formal

[15] The situation is similar at the other large scholastically-oriented monasteries. Monks from Kumbum monastery in Amdo reported 100 unlisted monks along with 300 officially registered. At Labrang Tashikyil, also in Amdo, now the monastery with the largest population of monks, there were in 1987 about 800 unlisted monks to 500 registered ones.

religious studies. A Drepung monk who had taken part in the first demonstration on 27 September explains:

The registered monks have to work for a period of at least two to three years. If any monks refuse to work, then the Chinese will not allow them to stay in the monasteries. Some monks have to work for five years. As the monks have to work, they study religion in the mornings and evenings. The curriculum for religious studies is set by the teachers. But monks have to abide by the rules of the monasteries in order to get time for religious studies. The Chinese tell us that monks should be apolitical, but we follow the rules of the monasteries and keep our vows. The work which the monks have to do are such things as cutting rocks and rebuilding the monasteries. The Chinese pressure us to work but we insist that we should study religion. The reason why the Chinese make us work is because they have been telling us that in the old system monks exploited the people. Now monks should work to earn their living instead of exploiting the public.

It is not easy to study religion these days because one can't say 'I want to study religion' and not go to the labour unit. The Chinese have said that they will increase the period of religious studies but they have not done so yet. The Chinese are taking more interest in political activities and politics and do not care about religious studies and monasteries. Although most of the monks have been saying there should be some changes in the administration of the monasteries, the Chinese have not done anything about it yet. Most Tibetans had great hopes for the demonstrations for independence and the rights of Tibetans. We also hoped to improve the rules of the monasteries and increase the period of religious studies. We hoped the authorities for the monasteries would make changes. But the Chinese neglected these points.

Most of the young monks in the large monasteries are from rural backgrounds. Born during and after the Cultural Revolution, they have grown up under Chinese rule. Most have received very little formal education. Many rural areas still have no schools, and in some a rudimentary primary education in Tibetan is available. But children whose families received a bad "class label" (*gral rim pa*) during the Cultural Revolution were barred from entrance to schools even where they were available.

The Drepung monk quoted above is from a village 15 km. west of Lhasa. He attended primary school for four years and explains the difficulties he had in becoming a monk:

If a boy from a village joins a monastery as a monk, he finds a lot of difficulties studying religion, because to learn it one has to know how to read and write.

As there are no schools in villages, children do not get an opportunity to learn. If the Chinese really want to preserve our culture and tradition, they should open schools in villages as well. But many villages have no such facilities for schools . . . I went to a small school called a "people's school," financed by the people. It has classes to grade four. As far as I am concerned, I am from a poor family with five children. I did not get much time to go to school as I had to work. But I learned Tibetan mostly through self-study, although I was not able to read script and newspapers. With my little knowledge of Tibetan I was able to get admission to a monastery as a monk.

The shortage of qualified teachers is acute. Most of the Buddhist scholars able to pass on the tradition have either been killed, fled into exile, or been forced to disrobe during the twenty years following 1959 when religion was actively suppressed. In 1987 at Ganden, for instance, there were just fifteen older monks; only two have received geshe (*dge bshes*) degrees and are able to provide instruction in the scholastic tradition to the younger monks. Sera monastery had seven geshes. At Drepung twelve geshes provided instruction to about 100 registered monks pursuing the curriculum full-time, and another fifty monks received instruction in the early mornings and evenings because they were required to work during the day.

For many young monks the monasteries offer the only opportunity to receive an education in Tibetan. Sometimes, entering small monasteries near their villages while still in their early teens, they discover that they are unable to pursue an education for lack of qualified teachers. This in turn drives them to the larger monasteries around Lhasa. Here they encounter further difficulties from the quota on registered monks.

Monasteries and society: the Tibetan view

Monks cite a whole series of restrictions on religious practice in the monasteries resulting from government interference. They also complain about the shortage of living space in the monasteries, forcing monks to live in cramped quarters with many sharing a single room, as well as the absence of monetary support for food, clothing, and necessities. The monks attribute these hardships to the unwillingness of the Chinese administration to allow the monasteries to take effective responsibility for their own affairs, making decisions and managing their resources according to their own priorities.

At the same time the monks regard monastic discipline as an internal matter. Tibetan Buddhism shares the Vinaya Rule (*'dul ba*) governing the conduct of monks with the other branches of Buddhist tradition throughout Asia. This Rule lays down procedures to be followed in the ordination, discipline, and expulsion of monks. Though there is a wide range of latitude in the strictness with which all the vows are enforced within different branches of Buddhism, the basic principles of monastic self-government, as well as the regulations prescribing the relationship between the monastic community and the laity, remain the same.[16] Monks frequently expressed the view that the discipline and expulsion of monks was the responsibility of the assembly and its elected leaders, not the Democratic Management Committees and the Chinese administration, who had no place interfering in the traditional procedures and rules of the Buddhist Sangha.

Taking the vows of a monk is a religious status validated by Buddhist tradition; monks may be disciplined or lose their monastic status and be disrobed only for breaking those vows. Thus the monks regard the practice of punishing and expelling monks for political activity as a violation of traditional religious norms. As a young monk from Drepung explains: "According to our religious customs monks must decide democratically whether monks should or should not be thrown out. We think this [expelling monks for political activity] contradicts our rule. We told this to our leader [of the Democratic Management Committee], but he said that it could not be put into practice."

The restrictions on religious practice and the government control

[16] Tibetan Buddhist monks follow the Sarvāstivāda school of the Vinaya, differing slightly from the Vinaya rule of Theravādin monks. For Tibetan monks there are 253 precepts for the fully ordained monk (*dge slong*) and ten precepts for the novice (*dge tshul*). To take the full set of vows a monk should be at least twenty years old, though there is much latitude in the calculation of age. To take the novice vows a monk must be at least seven years old. The first four precepts are the most important, since their violation is grounds for expulsion: (1) the rule forbidding sexual intercourse, (2) the rule forbidding theft, (3) the rule against intentionally taking life, and (4) the rule against claiming to possess supernatural power. In practice, only a prohibition on heterosexual intercourse is strictly enforced. Here, too, it is far more likely in practice for a monk to "give back his vows" and leave the monastery voluntarily than to be disciplined and expelled. Many of the other Vinaya rules specify in minute detail proper etiquette, rules for ownership of property, relations within the monastery, and relations with the laity. Though the Vinaya is part of the monastic curriculum, many of these other rules are simply ignored by Tibetan monks (or explained as unsuitable to the conditions of Tibet). See Spiro (1982): 290–304, for a discussion of the Vinaya Rule for Burmese monks.

over the monasteries are seen by almost all Tibetans as directly interfering with the traditional relationship between the monastic community and the laity. This is a cooperative and complementary relationship, where both people and resources are willingly committed by the community to the monasteries because the benefit is understood in general social terms. With the loss of the political and economic power that the monasteries commanded in pre-1959 Tibet, this relationship stands out in stark relief. The restoration of the monasteries is very much a collective project through which Tibetans aim to recover the principal traditional means of acquiring religious merit.

Universally in Buddhist societies the laity offers support to the monks who, merely by the act of receiving, confer spiritual benefits on the laity.[17] The same logic of making merit applies to families staffing monasteries with their own children. As donations move up from the lay supporters to the monastic community, they are spiritualized. Monks are not supported simply so that they may perform rituals on behalf of the laity (though this is also an important religious function of monks within Tibetan Buddhism); the act of giving — and thereby acquiring merit — is itself a central ritual act.

The relationship of lay people to monks is expressed in traditional Buddhist terms as the relationship of patrons and benefactors (*sbyin bdag*) to an institution which embodies the highest spiritual values of Tibetan society. Yet this is precisely the relationship that Chinese religious policy finds politically threatening and attacks through sanctions. For Tibetans the political aspect of this relationship cannot be separated from the ethical and spiritual aspects. A young monk in his twenties from Ganden explains what happened in the Gyama region of Medrokunga (where many of the Ganden monks come from) after the demonstrations:

The parents of the monks were told to educate [*slob so yag po byed*] their children to be patriotic [*rgyal gces*]. They were told to tell them that in future all separatist activities and protests against the Chinese are forbidden. They said that at present it is these splittists [*kha bral pa*] who are guilty. The talk of Tibet's independence and the return of the Dalai Lama are all wrong,

---

[17] For a discussion of this relationship in the context of Burmese Buddhism, see Spiro (1982): 103–12. Though Spiro is describing a Theravādin tradition, the same principles hold for Tibetan Buddhism. Monks constitute for laymen a "field of merit" by accepting offerings. Furthermore, the amount of merit accrued is proportional to the piety of the recipient monk. See Spiro (1982): 409–14.

they said. Moreover, if in the future there was a recurrence, not only would the splittists be arrested but they, the parents, would be held responsible and arrested too. Furthermore, the villagers would be forbidden to help in the reconstruction work at the monastery and also to act as benefactors [*sbyin bdag*] for it. If the villagers took a spadeful of earth or stone to help the monastery it was wrong. And in particular, if the villagers took any of their children to a monastery to become a monk or a nun they would be arrested. They said that the admission of children into monasteries to become monks and nuns was prohibited by a law passed by the central government in Beijing and the TAR government. Despite these restrictions by the Chinese the people are still contributing funds.

The Ganden monk adds his own analysis, making it clear that he understands it is Chinese policy to curtail political activity by attacking the relationship between the laity and the monks:

The cadres did not give any reason for prohibiting donations, but I see it like this: they want to put down the monks as much as they can, so they will not be able to fight for independence. Generally, we monks are not allowed to carry out any trade or business or till the soil. We just have to take whatever the people offer. So if they cut down the government allowances and stop the contributions from the people, then we'd have to keep quiet. They probably came to this analysis.

Chinese religious policy repudiates the social foundation of religion and attempts to render it as harmless private belief. The expressed goal of post-1980s "liberal" religious policy has been the gradual withering of religion as a relic of the past. In keeping with this policy, the restoration of religious sites is to be kept to the minimum necessary to satisfy the needs of religious practitioners (apart from sites with "scenic" or historic value). Particular emphasis is placed on curtailing voluntary contributions to religious institutions. The restoration and maintenance of the monasteries must be authorized by the government and financed by government appropriations.[18]

This policy strikes at the heart of the traditional relationship between the lay community and the Buddhist clergy. Party workers describe the former status of the monasteries as "feudal" and the monks as parasites

[18] See the 1982 Party directive known as "Document 19," translated and reprinted in MacInnis (1989): 8–26, which lays down the guidelines for current religious policy. While the assumption is that religion will eventually disappear naturally through the long-term development of socialism and communism, religion in the meantime must be tolerated and brought under administrative control.

exploiting the masses. Yet Tibetans, particularly in rural areas, see the rebuilding and restaffing of the monasteries as a collective project reordering social relations in accordance with the Buddhist paradigm. Here voluntary giving has the highest religious value — yet this is precisely what Chinese policy proscribes. The Ganden monk cited above adds in this connection: "The Chinese do not realize the suffering they are causing." He is referring to the way Chinese policy interferes with the practice of giving and merit-making which is fundamental to Buddhist society.

Thus Tibetans do not perceive the recent toleration of some religious practices as constituting religious freedom. For their part, they try to ignore or work around restrictions imposed by the Chinese, sometimes getting away with it, but always aware that the policy can be quickly reversed. The Ganden monk explains:

Under the Chinese there will be no freedom of religion. If Tibet is independent and has freedom, then there will be freedom of religion as well. Until then there will be no freedom of religion. It will be only in name, not in reality. They declared freedom of religion. They also declared a policy of relaxation [*srid jus gu yangs*]. So they actually left us without any restrictions for a little while. But slowly there came to be more and more restrictions on religion. So there's no way we'll get freedom of religion.

The issue for Tibetans is not individual religious freedom *per se*, but the role of the monasteries in society. Tibetans see restrictions on religion as preventing the monasteries from recovering their former institutional autonomy, and their rebuilding and restaffing are understood by Tibetans, monks and lay people alike, as the restoration of an institution outside the government's political control. That the monasteries once exercised independent political power in Tibet is certainly implicit in Tibetan demands, but that political role is now cast in the context of Tibetan opposition to Chinese rule.

I would argue that the equation Tibetans inside Tibet draw between religiously-motivated action and political action is a product of the current situation of Buddhism which, after two decades of systematic destruction, has been reduced to its starkest and simplest terms. In the absence of the specialized ritual services that monks traditionally performed in Tibetan society, Buddhism's ethical features have assumed a special prominence. The conception of Buddhist practice in Tibet has thus come to resemble in some ways Theravādin conceptions of Buddhist practice.

Southwold writes of village Buddhism in Sri Lanka that "ethical conduct was in some ways analogous to ritual in other systems."[19] What he says of the attitudes of ordinary Sri Lankan villagers also applies to Tibetans in the current situation:

When I asked them what as Buddhists they should do, my informants regularly replied by speaking of ethical conduct; and its seemed rather evident that much of this conduct, notably not killing animals, and liberality to the clergy, was plainly emblematic if not symbolic.[20]

Southwold adds that within this framework his informants also included political action as part of religious (i.e. "ethical") practice.

From their side, the monks are expected to respect and keep their vows (*sdom pa*), which qualify them to receive offerings from the lay community and endorse giving as religious merit-making. Here the vow of celibacy epitomizes the monks' spiritual qualifications; it signifies their election to serve the religious interests of the community. The young monks I interviewed had a strong sense of their essential role as bearers and preservers of a tradition, serving Tibetans by setting an example. They especially emphasized the necessity of keeping their vows, thus fulfilling the wishes of lay people — especially their parents — for a Buddhist clergy. The Drepung monk who earlier complained of the difficulties of becoming a monk explains:

The reason why I become a monk is because I have faith in Buddhism, because according to Buddhism one can achieve enlightenment by keeping the vows. We can keep our vows better by becoming monks in the monasteries. I had no plan to become a monk in my childhood. When I grew older I heard about monks, and my parents told me the good virtues of becoming a monk. All Tibetans are fervently religious. So it was my parents' wish as well as mine that I should become a monk. When I joined the monastery and began to study Buddhism, I came to know that one can achieve enlightenment by keeping vows strictly.

The present pattern of recruitment contrasts with the "mass monasticism" described by Goldstein for Tibet before the Chinese invasion, when as many as a quarter of all adult males were monks.[21] At that time monks were placed in monasteries by their families at seven or

[19] Southwold (1983): 175.
[20] *Ibid.*
[21] Goldstein (1989): 21–4.

eight years of age, sometimes against their will, for a variety of economic as well as religious reasons — to fulfil corvée tax obligations, to reduce the economic burden at home, to gain access to monastic resources. Only a small minority actively pursued a life of scholarship and meditation. To become a monk under present conditions requires strong motivation, financial support and sacrifice from one's family, and persistence in overcoming administrative obstacles. The opportunity to pursue scholastic studies is also a major incentive for young monks enrolling at Ganden, Sera, and Drepung — and it has been the best scholars among the young monks who have been the most active in politics. Young monks today are in no sense following customary careers. The choice of a monastic career is an exceptional decision, supported by the Tibetan community, but lacking the institutional security of pre-1959 Tibet.

The monks regard their vows as empowering them to act politically. Here they claim to be acting in the general interests of the community and appeal to universal values (e.g. freedom, independence, human rights). In the words of the Drepung monk:

We were not frightened. We thought that the worst the Chinese could do was either to kill us, or put us in prison. But we were already prepared to give up our lives for the 6 million Tibetans. Anyway, sacrificing your life is not against Buddhism.

This view, that sacrificing one's life for Tibetan independence is consistent with the vows of a monk, was frequently expressed by young monks. It was also said, by monks and lay people alike, that because monks had taken vows of celibacy and therefore had no families of their own, they were better able than lay people to sacrifice their lives for Tibetan independence.

In religious terms, however, perhaps the most important justification given for dying for independence was the belief that it guaranteed rebirth in the next life as a human being. According to Buddhist doctrine, one can only work effectively toward the ultimate goal of Buddhahood through a human rebirth. This is a primary incentive for taking the monastic vows, since faithfully keeping one's vows as a monk is also believed to guarantee rebirth as a human being. Keeping one's vows as a monk and dying for independence are thus linked to the same religious motivation. In both cases, under current conditions in Tibet, this religious motivation has an altruistic orientation, stressing personal self-sacrifice and collective salvation.[22]

This sense that monks are representatives of general universal values over and against the narrowly selfish, which are identified with the Chinese, is illustrated in a discussion about the meaning of terms like "freedom" (*rang dbang*) and "human rights" (*'gro ba mi'i thob thang*) with another young Drepung monk who took part in the first demonstration in the autumn of 1987. First, the monk explains what Tibetan independence means to him:

If we get independence, from a narrow point of view all Tibetan desires will be satisfied. From a bigger point of view, if Tibet is independent, then the Buddha Dharma can prevail and be spread. So if Buddha Dharma is strong enough and good, then it can bring peace and happiness in the world, not only for Tibetans. Here we are in our own country, but our own body is not owned by us. The Chinese say they have made a lot of improvements in Tibet, that they take care of poor Tibetan families, giving them everything, and so on. This is not true for me. Everyone is seeking freedom. Without freedom the human body is meaningless.

He goes on to explain the significance of freedom:

For us the Chinese are saying that you have freedom of everything, such as freedom of religious faith and so on. Human rights includes freedom. But we need real freedom. Through freedom we can make preparations not only for this life, but work more for the future lives to come. As the Chinese reject the existence of future lives, that is one difficult point. If one is only talking of freedom to eat and drink, it doesn't have much significance. That can be done by any animal such as a dog or a cat which only worries about food or drink. So human beings are not the same. To be human has a deeper meaning.

This young monk is in his early twenties. His education in Tibetan before entering the monastery did not go beyond the six years of elementary school; he was not allowed to continue his education because

---

[22] Compare this to Ortner's description of the unsocial individualistic bias of Tibetan Buddhism, which she associates with state support of the monasteries through centralized taxation, and which enabled the monasteries in Tibet to cut themselves off from society (1978: 158–9). She contrasts Tibetan Buddhism with the successful transformation of Buddhism into a "solidarity-sustaining" religion in Buddhist Southeast Asia. Under current conditions in Tibet the differences are less significant. State support is, of course, lacking today and, more important, the Chinese state is perceived by Tibetans as a power hostile to Buddhism. Under these conditions Tibetan Buddhism is also capable of realizing a collective, communal, and political orientation.

his family received a bad "class label" (*gral rim pa*) in the Cultural Revolution. He had studied another four years in the monastery. His political education has been entirely in the hands of Party cadres.

It is not simply that as a monk he is inclined to give words like "freedom" and "human rights" a religious gloss. To give these terms meaning within a wider coherent view of the Tibetan situation under Chinese rule requires an appeal to a Buddhist framework — where a human rebirth is precious, where there is a need to do good for future lives, and where Dharma has importance for the world. Thus, independence implies freedom to practise the Dharma, but freedom in turn is senseless without acknowledging the human condition. "Human rights" in Tibetan is literally the "rights of human transmigrators/ beings" (*'gro ba mi'i thob thang*), and "transmigrator" (*'gro ba*) is a basic term in the language of Tibetan Buddhism. The three terms — independence, freedom, human rights — thus lead in order of ascending generality back to the issue of making human life meaningful.

Religious freedom implies the right to prepare for future lives, which implies unselfish actions for the benefit of others. This includes political life in general, as well as working for Tibetan independence in particular. Opposed to this are actions motivated by the selfish interests of this life — which here refers to Chinese promises merely to "make life better." Human rights, as the concept is understood by Tibetans, thus divides altruism from selfishness, the sacred (religiously-motivated action, including politics) from the profane. What in a modern Western political context are essentially secular political values (political freedoms, human rights) are, for Tibetans, identified with the sacred side of the equation and symbolically opposed to the Chinese communist system in Tibet, which belongs to the profane side.

The Drepung monk concludes: "Reciting *om mani padme hum*, visiting temples, and making offerings to deities are not considered real freedom of religion."

4

MONASTIC MILITANCY AND
POPULAR RESISTANCE

Throughout the rest of 1987 the monks arrested from Sera and Drepung monasteries continued to be held, along with several monks from the Jokhang temple and many hundreds of lay Tibetans arrested in the weeks after the confrontation in front of the police station. On 27 November, nine of the original twenty-one monks from Drepung who staged the first demonstration were released and returned to the monastery after reportedly "confessing" to their crimes (though two additional monks from Drepung and one from Sera had since been arrested for speaking out in defiance of the cadres from the Work Team).

On 19 December six nuns from Garu nunnery, 7 km. northwest of Lhasa, staged a demonstration around the Barkhor. Garu nunnery, restored in the mid-1980s, is a small retreat accessible only on foot, with about thirty nuns, mostly young, from rural backgrounds. The six nuns were arrested by security forces after completing several circuits of the Barkhor while shouting independence slogans. The incident is significant as the first public indication that Tibetans were prepared to continue demonstrating after the crackdown in October.[1] This was also the first demonstration by nuns. In the months that followed, nuns would stage a number of demonstrations as well as take part in combined demonstrations organized in coordination with the monks.

---

[1] Two demonstrations took place in November 1987, at Rigong, in Qinghai Province, south of Xining. The area is one where there has been a heavy influx of Chinese settlers. Students at the Nationalities Teacher Training School began putting up posters demanding: (1) Tibetan independence, (2) an end to forced sterilization, (3) the use of the Tibetan language in the school, and (4) improved facilities. On 6 November a number of secondary school students and local monks staged a demonstration in support of these demands. Some of the students were briefly detained, but no arrests were made. On 27 November, following a meeting of 45 senior students from the Teacher Training School, another demonstration took place, with the students marching for about a kilometre up the street to the office of the "district leader" (rdzong dpon). Teachers collected letters from the students with their demands, but did not present them to the government officials. However, during the following month 15 PSB officers were stationed at the school and made an investigation of the incident.

The test of the Chinese government's control over the situation in Tibet would be the upcoming Mönlam prayer festival, when hundreds of monks from Ganden, Drepung, and Sera would congregate in the Jokhang temple for a celebration lasting ten days. The festival was instituted by Tsongkhapa, the founder of the Gelugpa sect, in the fifteenth century and overlaid on the traditional Tibetan New Year celebrations. Originally lasting three weeks, Mönlam was a monastic ritual in which monks offered prayers for the well-being of the world, sermons were delivered to crowds of lay people (including an annual sermon by the Dalai Lama), and monk candidates from the three monasteries for the highest scholastic degree, the rank of geshe lharampa (*dge bshes lha ram pa*), took part in competitive debates on points of philosophy. In addition to some 20,000 monks from the three big Gelugpa monasteries near Lhasa, tens of thousands of pilgrims from all over Tibet arrived for the celebration, the most important in the Tibetan calendar, doubling the population of Lhasa.[2]

The first year in which the Mönlam prayer festival had been held since the suppression of the 1959 uprising and the succeeding two decades of religious persecution was 1986. Once again the celebration attracted pilgrims from all over Tibet. The examination of candidates for the geshe degree had also been reinstituted. The holding of the Mönlam festival was an important symbol of the new liberal religious policy, a spectacular and colourful public event illustrating the return of religious freedom. Thus it was imperative that the 1988 celebration should proceed as before. The potential for civil disorder, with many hundreds of monks assembled in the centre of Lhasa, was certainly not lost on the authorities. On the other hand, a successful Mönlam would be proof that the situation in Lhasa was normal, that the authorities were in control, and that current policies were effective.

Meanwhile, the monks from Ganden, Drepung, and Sera had collectively decided to boycott the upcoming Mönlam prayer festival. They regarded the idea of holding Mönlam while many hundreds of Tibetans were still under arrest and while political education sessions were continuing in the monasteries as unacceptable. They understood too that the Chinese government had a considerable symbolic investment in the festival, and the presence of large numbers of Tibetan pilgrims in Lhasa for the New Year celebrations would add to the importance of the event. The monks reasoned that the tactic of a boycott would

[2] Shakabpa (1984): 6,85.

effectively make their political point, embarrass the Chinese government, and could be done without endangering themselves.

As the authorities came to know of their plans to boycott Mönlam, considerable pressure was put on the monks to participate. Appeals for the monks to cooperate came from elements within the Chinese administration in Tibet directly responsible for implementing reform policies. Raidi, chairman of the regional CPPCC, went in person to the monasteries to plead with the monks, accompanied by religious figures serving with the CPPCC and the Buddhist Association. The monks were told that the Panchen Lama had personally requested that Mönlam be held. The monks in turn made the release of fellow monks still in prison the main condition for their cooperation. They insisted at the meetings with officials that it would be impossible to perform the ceremonies without the participation of the imprisoned monks.

On 21 January 1988, Beijing reported the release of fifty-nine people arrested after the demonstrations in September and October.[3] This included most of the remaining monks from Drepung and Sera, as well as lay people. The release of the prisoners was attributed by officials to the personal intervention of the Panchen Lama, who had arrived in Tibet just two weeks earlier. The decision was announced in a special meeting attended by monks from Sera, Drepung, and the Jokhang, and representatives of Lhasa neighbourhood committees. Several former prisoners who were prepared to make public confessions of their guilt and assent to the "unity of the Chinese motherland" were paraded in front of the meeting.

The monks saw the release of the prisoners as a move by the authorities to placate dissent in the monasteries and win their agreement to hold Mönlam. They described the release as a "bribe", which only strengthened their resolve; among themselves they continued to speak of boycotting the festival. Furthermore, not all the arrested monks had been released. Monks at Drepung reported that at their meeting with the Party leader, Raidi, they had specifically made the release of Yulu

---

[3] Beijing Xinhua in English, 21 January 1988, in *FBIS*, 21 January 1988: 33. The Chinese authorities also acknowledged detaining a total of 80 people, and claimed to have released all but 10. This may accurately reflect the number whose cases were turned over to the Procurator's office for formal charges and prosecution. It does not include the large number of Tibetans whose arrests were never acknowledged, who were detained for weeks or months without charges ever being laid, and then in many cases were simply released.

Dawa Tsering a condition for participating in Mönlam. They claimed to have received assurances that this would be done.

Geshe Yulu Dawa Tsering is a fifty-three-year-old Buddhist philosopher who spent twenty years in prison for taking part in the 1959 uprising. He was released in 1979 with the change in China's Tibet policy. After his release he was appointed a member of the Buddhist Association and the CPPCC, and given a position teaching Buddhist philosophy in the Tibetan Department of Tibet University when it opened in 1984. He is typical of the prominent Tibetan religious figures and national leaders whom the Chinese administration has attempted to recruit into showcase organizations to validate its policies.

Yulu Dawa Tsering continued to speak openly in support of Tibetan independence. He was arrested on 26 December 1987, along with his cousin, Thubten Tsering, though his arrest was not made public, nor were formal charges laid until 9 March 1988 (four days after the outbreak of protest). It has never been made clear why Yulu Dawa Tsering was arrested in December. The charges against him — "spreading counter-revolutionary propaganda" in contravention of article 102 of the PRC Criminal Law — refer to an event which took place on 29 July 1987, two months before the first demonstrations. That evening he had supper at his cousin's house with an Italian dentist on holiday who videotaped a political discussion with him about Tibetan independence in which he asked for the support of the world to achieve Tibetan independence "peacefully." According to the announcement of his arrest, he and his cousin were guilty of having "discussed Tibetan independence" and having "criticized the Chinese Communist Party and the policies of the People's Government in the course of their conversation with reactionary foreigners posing as tourists."[4]

Yulu Dawa Tsering was the first Tibetan to be formally charged. His crimes are entirely political and ideological. He eventually received a ten-year sentence on 19 January 1989 following the first trial of Tibetan protestors. The Chinese government has since treated him as an instigator of current unrest. However, he took no part in any of the demonstrations. Originally a Ganden monk, he had not lived there for many years, though the monks at Ganden still regard him as one of the luminaries of the monastery. But he had little if any contact with the young monks who planned the demonstrations. He became a

---

[4] Lhasa Xizang Regional Service in Mandarin, 9 March 1988, in *FBIS*, 10 March 1988: 12–13.

symbol of resistance for the monks following his arrest in December, and it is possible that the Chinese government chose to make an example of him because of his prominent position, thus warning other prominent Tibetans not to appear to support the protest.

The continuing recalcitrance of the monks, even after the release of a number of prisoners, posed a real problem for the Chinese administration. What finally proved effective in gaining their compliance was threatening to expel from the monasteries the large number of "unlisted monks" — monks without residence permits — whose presence had so far been tolerated. It was largely these unlisted monks who came down to Lhasa for the Mönlam prayer festival. Many of the monks with registered status at the monasteries refused to attend, continuing their planned boycott.

A young monk from Sera monastery describes a meeting of the monks shortly before the beginning of the festival:

When the Chinese announced that Mönlam was to go ahead, about a hundred monks voted against taking part in the celebration. Two days before the actual day, a meeting was called during which a pass for the festival was given to every monk. Everyone was given a card because the Chinese wanted as many monks as possible present for the occasion. Even the unlisted monks who were not formally admitted to the monastery were forced to take part in the meeting. The oldest monks accepted the passes without any reservation. But the younger monks refused to accept them. At this point the Umdze [*dbu mdzad*, the monk who leads the recitation of prayers] told the monks who were unwilling to accept the card to leave the meeting. So most of us left. The remaining monks were mostly the unlisted monks, who were intimidated by the Umdze. So they had no choice but to accept the pass.

When the actual day came, two vehicles arrived to transport the monks. Since the number of participants was so small, it was a big embarrassment for them. The two vehicles were loaded with bedding, provisions, and the monks. We who remained behind watched this. The monks of Drepung had also refused to take part. The monks of Ganden refused to participate in the festival because Yulu Dawa Tsering was still in prison. As the majority of the monks of all three monasteries remained behind, the number of actual participants was very low. Out of curiosity some of us went to Lhasa by bicycle to see how the celebration was going. The gathering was very poor. We met up with other monks from Ganden and Drepung.

In the end, forcing the monks to hold Mönlam against their will precipitated another round of protest, on a much larger scale than the demonstrations in the autumn, and expanded the scope of public opposition to Chinese rule.

The Mönlam riot — 5 March 1988

The official announcement that the Mönlam prayer festival would go ahead was made at a press briefing on 15 February by officials with the regional Buddhist Association. Tibetans were told that "our Party's policy on the freedom of religious belief has been consistent and correct. This policy will not change just because of the riots." Monks were further instructed that they must set a "good example" and "must on no account do evil, nor must they turn themselves into social outcasts."[5]

The festival lasted ten days, from 24 February to 5 March. Only about half of the monks invited to participate actually showed up. Officials acknowledged that a number of monks had refused to take part, preferring to remain in their monasteries. Those who attended were largely the unlisted monks who had been warned that they faced expulsion if they refused to comply. The monasteries continued to be occupied by units of the Work Team, who carried on with the political education sessions and continued to monitor the activities of the monks who had remained behind.

The authorities nevertheless believed that there was no danger of a disturbance occurring. A mobile van was set up next to the Jokhang temple, and the ceremony was broadcast live on television throughout Tibet. A platform was prepared on the south side of the temple for Party officials and dignitaries, next to the Sungchöra, the area from which the Dalai Lama traditionally delivers his New Year sermon.

The festival continued without a major incident through 4 March when eight monks who had participated in the debating sessions were presented with their geshe degrees by representatives of the Buddhist Association. The previous day, one monk from Drepung had stood up and begun shouting Tibet independence slogans, but he was immediately stopped by the other monks. As some of the monks explained later, this was not the time for the protest they had planned. The Chinese responded to this incident, and the threat of trouble, by warning Chinese residents of Lhasa to stay home and beefing up the police presence in the area around the Jokhang the next day.

The Mönlam festival ended on the morning of 5 March. In the concluding ceremony a statue of Maitreya (Tibetan: *byams pa*), the future Buddha, is taken from the Jokhang and paraded in a circuit around the Barkhor. A truck is now used to carry the statue. At about 9.45 a.m., just after the truck returned with the statue and it was replaced inside

[5] Lhasa Xizang Regional Service in Mandarin, 23 February 1988, in *FBIS*, 24 February 1988: 25.

the Jokhang, the monks from Ganden rushed forward toward the platform where the Party officials had assembled for the closing ceremonies.
They began to shout and argue with the group of officials, which
included Raidi, the deputy secretary of the Party who had put pressure
on the monks to participate in Mönlam. They once again demanded the
release of Yulu Dawa Tsering, who had been arrested in December and
had now been held without charges for over two months.

It is difficult to reconstruct what happened next. What follows
are first-hand accounts from three monks who were caught up in the
events. Their reports are consistent with similar accounts from other
Tibetans and there is no reason to believe that they are not substantially
accurate. The first is from an unlisted Drepung monk who had been
forced to participate in the Mönlam festival, and later fled to India to
escape arrest:

On 5 March, at the beginning of the demonstration, the monks shouted to
the government officials that Yulu Dawa Tsering must be released: "You promised to release him." So one of the officials told the monks to shut up and
threw a rock at them. A monk picked up a rock and threw it back at the
officials. At that point someone shot and a Khampa was killed. The gun was
a pistol, but the monks don't know exactly who fired it, whether in uniform
or not. Then Raidi and some of the officials ran away. After the police killed
the man, the monks started shouting "Bod rangzen" [Tibet is independent]
and going around the Barkhor. There were about two hundred monks at first,
making circuits around the Jokhang, carrying the dead body. When they
reached the Jokhang the police charged them with tear-gas and sticks, and
the crowd dispersed. When they came back again the body had been taken
by the Chinese. The body was lost.

They made the first circuit. There were two alleys. Monks were coming
from here [the Barkhor]. The Chinese police were coming from both sides,
carrying sticks and shields. They had nails going through these sticks. So when
the monks saw them coming with these sticks they started throwing stones
at them. The Chinese ran away. Then they started making the second circuit.
When they made the first circuit many lay people also joined them. When
they made the second circuit the Chinese tried to stop them. They had
increased the number of soldiers. But the crowd started throwing stones from
rooftops and different places. Then they made a third circuit. By that time
the crowd had again swelled, and there were so many people that when the
people were going around the Barkhor the front man could see the last one.
There were over two thousand people there.

In the meantime, Raidi and the other officials had taken refuge in
a suite of offices inside the Jokhang complex that had within the last

year been appropriated by the local Buddhist Association. The offices had in fact been used to house cadres of the Work Team sent to the Jokhang to oversee political education sessions. The officials were trapped for over two hours, and were finally rescued at 12.30 p.m. by climbing down a ladder from a second-storey window after the area around the offices was cleared by People's Armed Police (PAP) using tear-gas.

After completing three circuits of the Jokhang the monks sought refuge inside the temple, closing the huge wooden doors behind them to escape from the PAP who had now entered the Barkhor area in force. Skirmishes in the streets of the Barkhor continued, with Tibetans hurling stones at the armed soldiers, who responded with tear-gas and sporadically with gunfire. The death of the Khampa at the start of the demonstrations brought the Khampa population of Lhasa on to the streets as well. Khampas, who come from eastern Tibet, have retained a cultural identity and dialect distinct from central Tibetans. The Khampa population in Lhasa consists of merchants and itinerant traders, many of whom lack official residence permits for Lhasa. They migrate seasonally between their homes in Kham and the Tibetan capital. Their participation despite their insecure status as residents of Lhasa marked a significant expansion of the scope of protest.

The next account is by a monk from Ratö monastery, a Gelugpa monastery in a village 25 km. southwest of Lhasa. The monk was in the Jokhang when the demonstration began outside. He describes what happened inside the Jokhang when the PAP soldiers stormed the temple:

I was one of the monk attendants inside the Jokhang. There was a huge crowd surrounding the temple. I was unable to get out of the temple, so I went on to the roof of the Jokhang where I saw people throwing stones. I picked some up too and threw them at the soldiers and at the trucks. The Chinese soldiers had surrounded the temple and there was no way of getting out. Many monks were trapped inside. It was impossible to get out because they fired tear-gas. The soldiers burst into the temple and started to hit the monks indiscriminately. A number of monks were killed. The soldiers killed the monks with iron bars. They were carrying sticks with nails in them. Some carried iron bars. Others had hammers. There were between 100 and 200 monks from the three monasteries [Drepung, Ganden, Sera], and some from other monasteries. I heard that many monks were killed. I saw one monk from Nagchu who had been killed. He was beaten to death with an iron bar, his skull was crushed open. One monk from Ganden was thrown off the roof. The doors were shut so it was difficult for them to get in. They threw tear-gas which made your throat and your chest burn, then the soldiers burst in and started to hit anyone they could lay their hands on. Monks were hiding everywhere. The soldiers

came in and searched all the rooms. They dragged the monks into the courtyard and started to hit them indiscriminately. I was on top of the Sheri
building. When the soldiers came I ran and jumped off the roof. I passed out.
When I woke up I was in the hospital guarded by soldiers.

The third account is by a monk from Ganden who describes what
he saw from outside the walls of the Jokhang temple:

We do not know how many were killed inside as we were watching from
outside. But one monk was killed, he was thrown off the Jokhang, we
witnessed this. He was from Nechung [a monastery near Drepung], a novice
in the same class as my younger brother. Another monk was severely beaten
until he was almost dead, and later the soldiers threw him off the roof. His
head was smashed. We went to where he was and he was carried to a nearby
house. He struggled for life for some time, even at 12 midnight he was still
breathing. He died later that night. He was from Medrokunga, not far from
my home. We were from the same *shang* [from *xiang*, the Chinese term for
a township]. Four monks were called that night to say prayers for the dead.
That same night some police came and arrested the four monks. Next day
his body was cremated at Sera. I and a few other monks went to the funeral.
His dead body revealed that all four limbs were broken and that his head was
crushed. In total about sixteen people died.

It is impossible to determine exactly how many Tibetans died on 5
March. According to Tibetan witnesses, between eight and fifteen
monks may have been beaten to death by PAP soldiers inside the
Jokhang. After the beatings, four military trucks were loaded with
monks from inside the Jokhang; many were dragged out unconscious,
and some were believed to be dead. Some of the monks escaped by jump-
ing from the building and were injured. The injured monks who were
arrested were taken to the hospital under guard. Some of the injured
may have died in hiding, afraid to seek medical treatment for fear of
arrest. Tibetans looking for missing relatives reported being asked to
pay sums of several hundred yuan to recover bodies from the mortuary
at the People's Hospital. There were rumours in the following days of
teams of Chinese disposing of bodies. A wall poster circulated after
5 March stated that twelve monks had been gunned down inside the
Palden Lhamo shrine inside the Jokhang.

The skirmishes with soldiers continued in the streets of the Tibetan
quarter of Lhasa into the evening, with short lulls as Tibetans
regrouped, making barricades in the alleys off the Barkhor and waiting
to attack Chinese soldiers with rocks. The violation of the Jokhang
temple by Chinese soldiers became a call to battle for many of the

remaining monks outside. This is how the Drepung monk described what happened after the monks inside the Jokhang were taken away in trucks:

There was a lull for about half an hour, then it started again. Nine monks from Nechung came. They said that in the beginning there were 150 of them, at the end of the day only nine of them were left, the others were trapped in the Jokhang, beaten and arrested. The nine monks had changed into ordinary clothes and said, "Today we must fight to the death. Even if it means dying, we must drive away the Chinese." Some people were trying to stop them, telling them not to go, but they went. At about 4 o'clock it stopped again. So they went toward the Jokhang. There were a lot of Chinese soldiers. They started throwing rocks at them. Now it was about 5 o'clock. It went on until it became dark. Some people were using slingshots. There were Chinese trying to take photographs. They were hit by the slingshots. Then a group of Chinese soldiers came to arrest some monks. They were driven away. There were a lot of Khampas also. People were scattered everywhere. Before darkness it was everywhere, people throwing stones, all over Lhasa.

The Chinese were chasing Tibetan demonstrators. The old people couldn't run away. They were beating them with the intention of killing them. So the Tibetans said, now we must chase away all the Chinese. Then there were two groups of opinion. One group said we should not fight all the Chinese since they are human beings also. The other group said that as long as they are Chinese we must struggle against them. At that time they burned down a Chinese restaurant and pharmacy.

The restaurant and pharmacy burned down were on Dekyi Sharlam, the main east-west street running through Lhasa, opposite the vegetable market and the entrance to the Barkhor. Both were owned by Chinese families from Sichuan, and represented to Tibetans the growing encroachment of Chinese enterprises into the traditionally Tibetan part of Lhasa. This was the first time that Chinese civilians had been targeted by Tibetan protestors. The debate over whether Chinese are "human beings" (a question of Buddhist ethics) is very much in character for Tibetan protestors. During the riots which took place a year later, in March 1989, groups of Tibetan protestors protected individual Chinese civilians from injury, though there was extensive damage to Chinese property in the Tibetan part of Lhasa. Attacks on individual Chinese people have not on the whole been part of Tibetan protest performance.

The only death officially acknowledged by the Chinese government was that of a PAP soldier, twenty-one-year-old Yuan Shisheng from

Sichuan,[6] who was reported to have been thrown from the window of a Tibetan compound by a group of Tibetan protestors after being discovered with another soldier monitoring the demonstration with a walkie-talkie. Twenty-eight PAP soldiers were reported to be in hospital. Unlike the demonstrations in the autumn of 1987, when Tibetans challenged local police officers, the 5 March events were the first direct confrontation between Tibetans and uniformed Chinese soldiers.

The events which led to the death of the PAP soldier have never been clear. Four Tibetans were eventually arrested for murder, tried, and sentenced on 19 January 1989 (two other Tibetans were also sentenced at the trial for crimes connected with the death of the soldier). One of the four, Lobsang Tenzin, a twenty-five-year-old student from Tibet University was sentenced to death (with a two-year commutation since extended). He was subsequently voted "student of the year" by the Tibetan students at the University and has become a hero among young Tibetans. The other three are Sonam Wangdu, a thirty-six-year-old businessman from Lhasa who received a life sentence, Gyaltsen Chöpel, a twenty-two-year-old living in the Barkhor, and Tsering Dondrub, a thirty-year-old student at the Nechung Buddhist Institute; the latter two received sentences of fifteen and ten years respectively.

An attempt to hold a public trial of the four in early August 1988 was disrupted by students from the University. The trial was reconvened 9 January 1989 with just a few relatives of the defendants allowed to witness the proceedings. The defendants refused to admit their guilt. All the accused were identified as participants in a crowd of Tibetans that stormed the compound in the Barkhor where the Chinese soldiers were stationed. After their arrest, none of the four was willing to implicate other Tibetans in the death of the PAP soldier.

The following is an account of what happened at the compound from someone who accompanied one of the accused, Gyaltsen Chöpel, on the day of the riot:

The crowd heard there were soldiers inside the house. They shouted at the soldiers, "If you don't come down we will burn the house." The rioting Tibetans then discussed among themselves the consequences of burning down

[6] Beijing Renmin Ribao, 7 March 1988 p. 4, in *FBIS*, 8 March 1988: 14. In an interview on 30 March, the Panchen Lama admitted that, in addition to the PAP soldier, a monk and two civilians had died (interview with Seth Faison, *South China Morning Post*, 30 March 1988: 7).

the house, whether Tibetans would be hurt also. They continued to shout at the house. Then one little boy climbed up to the top of the compound and looked inside and saw soldiers. He shouted this information down to the crowd. Gyaltsen Chöpel was in the crowd. He climbed up to see for himself. Two monks and his friend and some other people followed him. They looked through the crack of a door and saw the movement of feet. They didn't know who they were or how many. Gyaltsen Chöpel went into the house and was beaten by a soldier with a large stick. His hand was fractured. There was a fight. The small group continued to fight until they reached the top of the compound. These four people — Gyaltsen Chöpel, his friend, and two monks — were arrested. The fighting continued. A Chinese military officer came to the place where they were.

While they were being held, one of the monks from Nechung was thrown from the roof of the house. He was badly injured, his hands and feet were broken. They also saw other people thrown from the roof, but they couldn't see what happened to them. Another school friend was thrown from the roof and died from his injuries. Then the fighting continued and the Tibetans managed to throw one soldier from the roof. When he landed below, the crowd threw stones at him. Gyaltsen Chöpel was afraid, but as the fighting continued he managed to escape and ran from the room where he was being held. All over the area there were more soldiers. Then he saw the dead body of the soldier disappear. There was a lot of confusion. Gyaltsen Chöpel managed to get back to his house and there relaxed a bit.

Gyaltsen Chöpel remained at home for three days. During that time neighbours were arrested for taking part in the riot. Finally the police came to his house:

That night the Chinese called from the outside. They called for Gyaltsen Chöpel, asking where he lived. The neighbours had to tell the Chinese where he lived. The Chinese called for him to come out and see them. The family kept the door closed and told the Chinese he was sleeping. His mother opened the door and they went into the house. The Chinese soldiers took him away. She didn't know where they took him.

He told us later that they took him to the headquarters and beat him badly, saying "This is your punishment for going to the demonstration." They asked him about all the other people in the demonstration, wanting their names. They said: "If you tell us five names, we won't keep you. If you give us ten names, there will be no more trouble for you, no more punishment." At first he didn't accept. He denied seeing anybody. Then they said, "You must tell us. We have pictures, you are in those pictures. We can see you clearly."

They told him, "Today you can go home. But tomorrow morning at 10.30 you must come to the restaurant and drink tea alone. We will come there and check on who comes to speak to you. We will see who is connected with you. You stay in the restaurant. Don't leave with anyone." The police didn't see anyone come to talk with him. They said, "Now you can go, but never tell anyone we beat and punished you."

The next day they came for him and took him to the back door of the prison. He saw many people, some with ropes, some were beaten, people ill, in bad condition. They brought him there to scare him. Later, while he was in the restaurant, he saw police dressed in street clothes, looking like workers, office employees, farmers, but he knew who they were. They looked everywhere. They stayed for an hour, then they left. They gave one poor boy some money to sit and watch him. The boy followed him home. The boy spoke to him and told him that he must tell them everything. The boy said, "They say you have today and tomorrow to think about it. You must tell them who you were with." Gyaltsen Chöpel said, "I have nothing to tell. I have no reason to tell the police anything."

During this time they arrested Lobsang Tenzin and one other boy from the Jokhang. Also one monk from Nechung monastery. They asked all of them to tell who was with them. Gyaltsen Chöpel told them, "Only myself. I decided to demonstrate by myself because I am Tibetan. I went to the demonstration for Tibet. We are demonstrating for the rights of Tibet, not to break the law. I demonstrated for my country. For the rest, I don't know. This country belongs to us. We are not lying, this is the truth. We have the right to demonstrate." Gyaltsen Chöpel thought he had done something good, not wrong. He said, "I didn't do anything against the laws of the country or the constitution." For two more days he was at home, then on the third day they came again at night and took him to prison.

This was the first time that the People's Armed Police had been deployed in Tibet to deal with unrest. The PAP is a separate para-military security force created in 1984, following a reorganization of the People's Liberation Army, to deal with internal disturbances.[7] The units in Tibet are largely made up of young recruits from Sichuan. In January and February 1988, large numbers of PAP troops arrived in Lhasa — presumably brought in to deal with any further demonstrations. They could be seen practising riot-control exercises on the grounds of their bases around Lhasa. Nevertheless, their performance on 5 March suggests that they were badly trained and commanded, as bands of soldiers were frequently cornered by angry Tibetan crowds. There appeared to be no coherent plan for controlling the demonstrators.

---

[7] Bullard (1985): 35.

The significance of Mönlam: monks and the state

The Ganden monks responsible for initially confronting the Party officials after the close of Mönlam had not planned a demonstration similar to the ones the previous autumn. Nor did they anticipate a major riot involving many hundreds of monks and lay people. Their aim was to challenge the Chinese administration for reneging on the promise to release all the monks under detention. However, by March 1988 the discontent of the monks was focused on government interference in the affairs of the monasteries. Protesting in support of Tibetan independence was secondary to contesting the authority of the state over religion and what they saw as a cynical attempt by the Chinese government to manipulate and exploit the religious observance of Mönlam.

Mönlam has a special significance among Tibetan religious festivals. It rededicates Tibetan society each year to the supremacy of Buddhism. When Tsongkhapa instituted the festival in Lhasa in the fifteenth century, he joined monastic rituals to a collection of customary rites marking the transition from the old year to the new. In Tibet, as in many other cultures, the New Year is a liminal period, fraught with dangers, when the forces of evil must once again be challenged and defeated. In the traditional Tibetan New Year, rites of exorcism are performed to drive away threatening demonic powers. This function of the New Year period has been continued under monastic auspices, but has acquired an additional Buddhist meaning. The monastic ceremony of Mönlam celebrates the magical victory of the Buddha over six non-Buddhist teachers. Thus the ceremony signifies the triumph of Buddhism over other doctrines — first in India, then once again in Tibet. Mönlam links archaic rituals for restoring and protecting society to the more recently acquired aim of preserving and defending Buddhism.[8]

Some of the New Year ritual recalls the transformation of the Tibetan state from a Buddhist kingdom ruled by a wheel-turning king to a theocratic administration under the Dalai Lamas. In one traditional performance, a symbolic scapegoat, the King of Ransom (*glud 'gong rgyal po*), engages in a religious debate with a mock Dalai Lama; then he is defeated in a staged duel at dice and driven out of Lhasa, taking with him the accumulated misfortunes of the community. The King of Ransom is a representation of the evil king Lang Darma (*glang dar ma*), the last in the line of ancient Tibetan kings. Lang Darma turned against

[8] Tucci (1980): 149–53.

Buddhism, and during his six-year reign attempted to eliminate it from Tibet. His assassination in AD 842 by a Buddhist monk marked the end of the classic paradigm of Buddhist kingship in Tibet and led eventually to the assumption of political power by the monasteries.[9]

Mönlam has taken these ancient New Year rites and given them a special meaning in the context of the Buddhist doctrine of collective salvation. Its final ceremony, which centres on Maitreya, the Buddha of the next age, looks forward to the return of harmony to the world with the reemergence of the pure doctrine in the mythological future. The demonic powers threatening society, and bringing strife and suffering, are identified with the moral degeneration of the present age. The recommitment of Tibet as a nation to the cause of Buddhism is thus a step toward the collective salvation of the world.

The Tibetan New Year pageant involves carnival-like events (singing, dancing, clowning, athletic competition) in which the normal routines of society are temporarily suspended. The reversal of social roles, which is a general feature of this period in many cultures, has a special political significance as an expression of the structure of the Tibetan state. The political roles of the secular authorities and the monasteries were reversed during the three weeks of Mönlam in pre-1959 Tibet. The administration of Lhasa was turned over to the monastic officials of Drepung (*zhal ngo*), who are traditionally in charge of Mönlam. They were authorized to maintain order and exact fines and punishments, and they could overturn legislation passed by the government (this temporary transfer of power to the monks was not regarded without some trepidation by the population of Lhasa).

During the Mönlam festival the locus of power shifts from the Potala to the Jokhang. The Tibetan state, by publicly submitting to monastic authority, reaffirmed its raison d'être in the form that it has taken under the Dalai Lamas — a state whose secular authority is ultimately a dispensation from the monastic hierarchy. The ceremonial attendance of state officials during the events of Mönlam in pre-1959 Tibet likewise signified their submission to the authority of religion and their acceptance of the role of custodians of Buddhism. In return, the state was once again extended spiritual legitimacy. During the festival the state is ritually purified, renewed, and realigned, and its enemies are symbolically driven off. Mönlam thus acknowledged that the relationship between state and religion was always potentially strained and could never be taken for granted, but had to be corrected and reaffirmed periodically.

[9] Stein (1972): 217.

Whether the Chinese authorities were conscious of the special political significance of Mönlam is impossible to determine. Certainly, by claiming sponsorship for the festival, they were attempting to shift the ceremonial locus of Chinese power from the Norbulingka, to which they have already laid claim with secular celebrations of Tibetan "minority" culture, to the Jokhang, the symbolic centre of the Tibetan nation. It may be that the Party officials assembled on the platform on 5 March imagined that they could take the place of the former Tibetan government as legitimate patrons of religion. By sponsoring Mönlam during the previous two years, the Party may have been confident that it had successfully established itself in this role, usurping the position of the Dalai Lama's government in the eyes of the Tibetan people.

However, the symbolism of Mönlam is not so easily manipulated, since it requires the compliance of the monastic establishment. The monks responded by refusing compliance, openly challenging the representatives of the Chinese government in Tibet, and thereby denying the Chinese state legitimacy in its claim to be a patron of Buddhism (in symbolic terms a move exactly paralleling their planned boycott). Within the terms of the Tibetan construction of the state, withdrawing legitimacy remains a traditional prerogative of the monastic establishment. By coercing the monks into participating in the Mönlam festival the Chinese authorities had offered the monks the opportunity to do just that. Trapped in their office in the Jokhang for two hours, the government representatives were publicly humiliated; in the end, they had to be rescued through military intervention. Again the symbolic victory belonged to the monks.

The legitimacy of the Tibetan government in the past rested on a duality of functions. The traditional formula for the Tibetan state was "religion and political affairs combined" (*chos srid gnyis ldan*), a formula epitomized by the Dalai Lama who combined both functions in his person. The government of the Dalai Lama was both the most powerful patron (*sbyin bdag*) of religion, protecting the interests of the monasteries (and transferring revenues to them), and at the same time was itself headed by the highest religious figure, the Dalai Lama himself. The Tibetan state continued the original Buddhist paradigm of statehood — the righteous king who serves as a protector and defender of religion — but collapsed the two functions of patron of religion and head of religion into one.

This construction of the Tibetan state, which assumed its final form with the ascendancy of the Gelugpa sect under the Fifth Dalai Lama in the seventeenth century, was established under exceptional historical circumstances. It arose in response to the collapse of royal power from the ninth century onwards. The final consolidation of the Tibetan state under the Fifth Dalai Lama, which gave the Gelugpa sect and the Gelugpa monasteries a direct role in the government, required the military intervention of Gushri Khan, leader of the Qoshot Mongols, an independent branch of the Mongols whose territory bordered on Tibet.[10] Since then, the continuing autonomy of the Tibetan state has depended on maintaining a precarious balance between external power and competing internal interests.

The Tibetan state under the Dalai Lamas was a "non-coercive regime".[11] The rule of the government never depended on the mobilization of its own military forces; the means of force at its disposal were limited. The monasteries around Lhasa constituted a powerful army in their own right, and were not above challenging the Tibetan government if they felt that their interests were threatened. But, fundamentally, the question of political legitimacy in Tibet was not resolved through the monopolization of force by the state. Instead, it was achieved through an organizational balance established between the secular interests of the state and the religious interests of the monasteries. The monasteries retained the capability of withdrawing legitimacy and refusing to comply with the demands of the state.

The key to understanding the significance of the Mönlam festival is the special nature of the Tibetan state. Mönlam is the ritual expression of the formula "religion and political affairs combined". The Chinese government, by assuming the role of patron of religion, attempted to insert itself into this ritual equation, but under the conditions of Chinese rule in Tibet — and in the absence of the Dalai Lama — the ritual of Mönlam can only evoke the counter-image of an independent Tibet. The monks did exactly what they might have been expected to do, seizing the occasion to deny legitimacy to the Chinese state. Seen in terms of the traditional conception of the Tibetan polity, the revolt of the monks was the fatal and, in a sense, predictable outcome.

The threat of boycotting Mönlam in defence of monastic prerogatives is not without precedent in Tibetan history. Following an incident in 1944, when a group of monks from Sera Che (one of the colleges

[10] Shakabpa (1984): 100–24.
[11] Norbu (1985).

of Sera monastery) were accused of murdering a district commissioner in Phembo, the monks of Sera Che college began a boycott of the Mönlam festival.[12] The incident promised to be an embarrassment to the government, since this was to be the current Dalai Lama's first attendance at Mönlam. Only after receiving assurances of the safety of the monks did they agree to attend. The incident was part of an internecine political struggle between rival monastic segments; at issue was the position of Regent, the monastic leader selected to rule during the period of the Dalai Lama's minority. This struggle culminated in 1947 in the open armed rebellion of the Sera Che monks against the Tibetan government. The uprising was put down by the Tibetan army, resulting in the death of several hundred monks.[13]

On the face of it, the motivation underlying the Sera Che rebellion bears little similarity to the current situation in Tibet under Chinese rule. In defying the Tibetan government, the Sera Che monks were taking sides in a factional struggle for power. They were also defending the special economic interests enjoyed by monastic institutions under the estate system in traditional Tibet. A large segment of the monastic leadership of Tibetan society was at the time favourably disposed toward the Nationalist Chinese government, which appeared prepared to protect their privileges against encroachments by an increasingly powerful central Tibetan government. Nevertheless, the incident both indicates the willingness of monks to challenge political authority when their principles or interests are threatened, and suggests the form that such challenges can take. In defense of monastic autonomy, Tibetan monks are prepared to take forceful and sometimes even violent action.

---

[12] Goldstein (1989): 437–40.

[13] *Ibid.*: 496–506. Goldstein gives an account of another confrontation between the monks and the central government that took place in 1921, during the reign of the Thirteenth Dalai Lama. The incident, which almost precipitated a full-scale civil war between the monasteries and the Tibetan government, began with the arrest of three managers of Drepung Loseling college in a dispute over ownership of a monastic estate. Several thousand monks of Loseling marched to the Norbulingka, vandalized the Dalai Lama's gardens, and demanded to see the Dalai Lama. Government troops eventually surrounded Drepung and demanded the surrender of the protest ringleaders. The Loseling monks appealed for support from the other monasteries, but were refused, and in the end were forced to turn over the leaders of the protest. Relations between Loseling and the government had been strained since 1912, when Drepung had supported the Chinese at a time when, following the collapse of Manchu rule, the Dalai Lama and the government were attempting to drive the Chinese from Lhasa. See Goldstein (1985): 104–8.

Young monks in Tibet have certainly heard accounts of the actions of monks in the past, and have a conception of the behaviour appropriate to monks in confronting authority. Since 1959, however, acts of insurrection by monks have been directed against the Chinese and in defence of the Dalai Lama and the Tibetan government. The period of liberalization during the 1980s marks the first time since 1959 that the monasteries have been in a sufficiently strong position to mount collective action against Chinese authority. Chinese policy, in turn, has required the restoration of the monasteries in order to placate Tibetan discontent and counter criticism for the persecution of religion.

There is a crucial difference between monastic protest in pre-1959 Tibet and current protest. Protest under Chinese rule is directed against political institutions that are perceived by Tibetans as alien and imposed by force. Furthermore, current monastic protest has an explicitly nationalist content. Tibetan nationalism is very much a modern phenomenon; the thinking of the young monks today has been politicized in a way that would not have been possible in pre-1959 Tibet. The articulation of Tibetan independence as a political ideology is a response to the conditions of Chinese communist rule in Tibet, which has attempted to validate the reorganization of Tibetan society along Chinese lines through communist ideology. In this regard, the monks see themselves as acting for the general interests of society in a specifically political sense, allied with ordinary Tibetans against foreign invaders. They do not see themselves as acting to protect special rights or privileges.

Nor are the monks defending religious orthodoxy. In pre-1959 Tibet the monasteries were generally hostile toward Western ideas and influences, perceiving a threat to the centrality of religion in Tibetan society. Chinese rule, however, has threatened Tibetan religion through forcible suppression and persecution, not by enticing Tibetans to abandon traditional culture for an attractive modern alternative. Tibetans have not been persuaded by the Chinese communist claim to represent modernity — a claim always accompanied by the use of force. Today, in fact, Western political ideas — democracy, human rights — are perceived as compatible with Tibetan nationalism. Western cultural influences, which are condemned by the Chinese government, are valued positively by Tibetans, and Westerners are generally regarded as allies in the struggle for Tibetan independence.

Arrests, torture, interrogation

Monks who had been hospitalized following the beatings inside the Jokhang were taken to prison after several days of treatment. Others were taken directly to prison. During the next several weeks, hundreds of Tibetans were arrested in their homes, many having been identified from police photographs taken during the demonstration. Rewards were offered for turning in demonstrators: 300 yuan for a stone-thrower, 1,000 yuan for people who started fires. As the interrogation of prisoners got under way, new arrests were made on the basis of information extracted from those already arrested. Public Security broke into rooms at the monasteries, searching for "counter-revolutionary" documents. Over the next couple of months a number of monks were arrested as "ringleaders" who had not participated in the demonstrations at all, but had decided to boycott the Mönlam festival. This included monks who had spoken out in the political meetings organized by the Work Team in the monasteries. Also included in the arrests were many lay people who had been identified as political dissidents during political meetings in neighbourhood committees.

The overwhelming impression gained from the reports of prisoners held following Mönlam in 1988 is that brutality in prison was intended to intimidate and create an atmosphere of fear. It was systematic and widespread, and only incidentally related to the need to obtain information and extract confessions. Those arrested after 5 March were subjected from the outset to beatings by police, soldiers, and prison guards. The harsh treatment of prisoners — which included repeated beatings, shocks from electrified batons, suspension from ropes, shackling, and attacks by dogs — continued throughout the period of imprisonment up to the time of their release. Most of the approximately 800 people arrested after 5 March were released in July, several months later, with no charges laid. The arrests were never officially acknowledged by the Chinese government.

Most of the prisoners were taken to two prisons near Lhasa. Gurtsa, about 10 km. east of Lhasa, contains both political prisoners and ordinary criminals, and is used primarily to hold prisoners while they are interrogated and detained without trial. Sangyib, a complex of prisons about 5 km. north of Lhasa, appears to have been used after 5 March for holding prisoners singled out for their political views. A third prison, Drapchi, about 3 km. north of Lhasa, holds both ordinary criminals and political prisoners after they have been tried and sentenced, and is where many of the prisoners who were never released were eventually transferred to serve their sentences.[14]

In the following two accounts, released prisoners give details of their treatment after arrest. The first is from a Tibetan man in his twenties, arrested on 6 March and released on 10 July:

I was arrested and kept at a police station where I was constantly beaten by the police. I was then taken along with other prisoners to Sangyib prison. Altogether 147 prisoners were there. Five were from Lhasa, sixty from Kham, and the rest were monks from various monasteries. I was kept at Sangyib for 12 days and transferred to Gurtsa, where I was kept for 4 months and 4 days. At Gurtsa there were 138 prisoners. The prisoners were released in groups. There was one of twenty-five, and another of twenty-seven. There was a mixture of prisoners, monks, nuns, women, and men. When I was there, eighty-six prisoners were in the group. At present there are twenty prisoners. The fourteen men are monks. Of the six women, four are nuns.

At Sangyib we were kept in a small cell. My hands and feet were shackled for three days. There were no lights in the cell. The cell was totally bare. We were not provided with a mattress or a blanket. We were sleeping on a cement floor. I was kept like this because I refused to give names of other people who took part in the demonstration. In Gurtsa, I shared my cell with nine other prisoners. We were provided with a blanket and had to share a mattress. The prisoners were beaten by different guards daily. However there were a few guards who were very cruel. There was no set time when they beat us. They usually used an electric baton or an iron rod. The police place an electric baton inside a prisoner's mouth, which causes the tongue to swell. They beat us until they were exhausted. They also used a rifle butt. Another method was a guard holding our hands stretched out and one guard hitting the elbow with a stick. Some prisoners had their hands tied behind their backs and were hung from the ceiling. A prisoner named Nyima Tsering was kept like this for 11 days and nights. Another person named Tsering Dorje was also kept hanging from a ceiling for 7 days. Some prisoners were stripped and tied with a rope.

The second account is from an older Tibetan, married with a family, who had been a monk before the uprising in 1959, and had then been imprisoned for two decades. He had been photographed passing letters

---

[14] The names of these three prisons as they are used by Tibetans refer to Lhasa-area neighbourhoods. Drapchi is the only institution officially designated as a prison: TAR Prison no. 1. Prisoners judicially sentenced for political offences are mostly held in the 5th Division of Drapchi. Gurtsa is an "interrogation centre" run by the Lhasa Municipal Public Security Bureau. Sangyib contains a "labour reform camp" (*lao gai*) and a "reeducation through labour" (*lao jiao*) centre, as well as detention and interrogation centres.

to foreign tourists after the demonstrations in October 1987, but had not participated in the 5 March disturbance. He claimed that a local policeman had been given a photograph of him and told to find him because of his association with foreigners:

On 8 March at 12.30 midnight they arrested me. I was asleep and was woken by a knock on the door. The military had surrounded the house — they had machine-guns, and were accompanied by police with guns and electric batons. Some police had guns and walkie-talkies too. Some carried very big torches. There were five jeeps altogether, and very near to the house was a truck. One soldier took my left arm and another my right, and they twisted them behind my back. They started to take me outside the house, but a policeman stepped forward and said to take me inside the house. So they took me inside and a policeman read a charge against me. "You have to sign this document," he said. So I said I didn't know how to sign. "Don't you know how to write?" So I wrote my name down. On it was written, "On 8 March 1988 — 's house will be searched." And I had to sign that paper also. My family were very worried. They got up and the children started to cry, and they said to the police, "What has he done?" The police told them to shut up and then said, "You will not know about his activities. He has been plotting against the people and the country." I was taken out and as soon as we got outside, I was handcuffed. In the car, they talked on the walkie-talkie in Chinese and said, "We have arrested the man and we're on our way."

When I reached Gurtsa, there was a line of people who had been arrested from all over Lhasa. We had to take off all our clothes except our under-garments. I had a rosary and a watch, and they were confiscated. The guards question you and ask what crime you've committed, and then they kick you. I said, "I have not done anything." They said, "Do you think the Communist Party is lying? They would not arrest you if you have not done anything." That night I was kicked and punched and severely beaten. I asked, "What did they say I have done?" Then a guard slapped me and said I was being a loudmouth. We were taken inside the cell. There were six prisoners already in there. The cell number was 29. Except for one, all of them had bandages on their heads and had wounds. Some had broken arms. These injuries happened at the Jokhang. Some had broken ribs, some badly damaged eyes. There was a monk from Ganden who had his hands shackled all day long, and he was made to stand occasionally. Frequently, they beat him with elec-tric batons. Sometimes he was made to lie face downwards in a ditch and when the water came in the Chinese would force him down again with their feet.

The pattern that emerges from the accounts of released prisoners is that the interrogation sessions inside the prisons were an extension of the political campaign outside, with the same goals and stressing the same themes, but with the responsibility now shifted to the administrative structure of the prisons. The aim of incarceration was to root out and suppress the idea of Tibetan independence. There were no group struggle sessions in which prisoners were forced to criticize and attack each other, the principal device for social control and indoctrination during the Cultural Revolution. No attempt was made to win the loyalty of Tibetans through an appeal to the rhetoric of "class enemies." Interrogation sessions in the prisons, like the political meetings in the monasteries and neighbourhood committees, combined lectures against Tibetan independence with warnings and threats, and did not rely on group dynamics.

Systematic torture was always a feature of interrogation, which was carried out in a separate interrogation room in the presence of one or more guards, an interrogator, and sometimes a translator. Prisoners were frequently stripped naked. The beatings were administered by the guards. The accounts of prison experiences from a large number of prisoners are consistent. The ones presented here offer a picture of the experiences of Tibetan demonstrators following their arrest:

I was beaten whenever I was called for questioning and the guards continued to beat me until the questioning was finished. For me they had one Chinese and one Tibetan. I was beaten by the Chinese. On the first day we were beaten in our cells by those accompanying us. After that we were taken separately into another room whenever we were questioned. We were questioned one at a time. We were always beaten before and during questioning. They beat us with whatever was at hand, including wash-basins and mugs. They kicked us and used machine-gun and rifle butts. They used wooden sticks on us after the first day. They hit us anywhere, all over the body, including the head, face, eyes, groin, legs. The electric baton is one of the main instruments used for torturing. They used them every day after the first stage of beating — whenever we were questioned.

Another account of interrogation at Gurtsa prison comes from a shop assistant who was arrested for throwing stones on 5 March and released around 25 July:

I was interrogated eight times during the first half of the month. They asked me, "Why did you take part in the demonstration? What are your views? What does your family do?" They punched my stomach quite frequently during the interrogation. One night they made me stand outside without sleep. It was very cold. The interrogator would say that Tibet could never be independent and asked what I thought we could achieve. Some of the interrogators were Tibetans. There were two or three police in the cell and one interrogator. At first it was a different interrogator each time. Later on, the same one would come. Sometimes the questions were similar, "How many times did you throw a stone?" Afterwards, they ask you about other people. This was really very difficult. I know how much I have suffered. I don't want to be the cause of this kind of suffering for anyone. If I had named someone, how could I face him or his relatives? When you don't give names of other people they really start to beat you. If you don't say anything they beat you. Later on they ask you, "Who was the leader? Who incited you to revolt?"

Protest by nuns

The worst treatment in prison was reserved for nuns. On the morning of 17 April, at about 11.00 a.m., a group of thirteen from Garu nunnery staged a small demonstration in the Barkhor. Some of them had already participated in the demonstration on 19 December, had been arrested, and had been released shortly before Mönlam. The group left the monastery the night of 16 April, slept out in the open in the valley below the nunnery, then proceeded to circle the Barkhor three times, distributing hand-printed leaflets and shouting independence slogans. They were arrested near Sera monastery as they were returning to the nunnery.

The treatment of the nuns, both at the time of their arrest and during subsequent interrogations sessions, was especially brutal. They were all in their teens and early twenties, from rural backgrounds. One of them describes what happened after she was taken to Gurtsa prison:

When we arrived we were taken to a room. There we were handcuffed and poked and beaten with electric batons many times. We were also slapped and kicked and hit everywhere, without mercy. There were four soldiers standing at the door. We were taken there one by one and beaten and kicked indiscriminately and then thrown out of the door. Then we were made to kneel down on the ground with our hands handcuffed behind us. Soldiers and prison officers again hit our heads and backs with electric batons and spat on us. Then my name was called out. Four or five soldiers came and tied me with a rope so my hands were at the back of my neck. I still had the handcuffs on. Then they stamped on my back and on my chest. They tied and untied me three times in this way. After me they did the same to the nun ———. I was hit many times with a rifle butt by a prison guard who was Tibetan. He looked about twenty-five. There were many Chinese with him. They hit us mercilessly with wooden sticks and the electric batons and all of us had blood flowing from our heads.

Labels in black writing were hung around our necks and we were photographed. Then we were called one by one for further interrogation. The person who interrogated me was a Tibetan from Lhasa, aged around twenty-five. He asked my birthplace, nunnery, home, and level of education. Then he asked me why I had been brought there. I replied that we had demonstrated and done nothing else. He then asked me what was the purpose of our demonstration. I replied that the purpose of the demonstration was to risk our lives by demanding independence for Tibet. Then he asked: "Who told you to demonstrate? Who was the first among you to suggest the idea? Wwho was the first to write the posters? Who is behind you? Did your teachers tell you to go?" I replied that nobody told us to go, nobody led us, and we wrote the posters together. Then he asked how long we had discussed holding the demonstration. I replied that we had discussed it four or five times. Then he again asked who the leader was. I replied that nobody was the leader, that we did it together. Then he asked if I had relatives in India.

After a while another prison officer came to me and said that I had been arrested before and was not speaking the truth. He kicked me and I passed out. He then picked me up by my chest and slapped me and punched me with his fist. I was bleeding from the mouth. I could hardly stand. I felt half-dead. Then seven or eight people came with ropes and electric batons and a dog. They beat us again and set the dog on us. Our clothes and flesh were torn. Then we were put in our cells. We were given a bowl containing a spoonful of rice mixed with half-cooked vegetables. There were bits of grass and earth in the food. That night we had to stay on the floor without any mattress or bedding.

Unlike the monks held in Gurtsa, who were put in a cell with a number of other prisoners, the nuns were separated and kept alone. Many more guards appear to have been present during their interrogation, and the beatings and torture appear to be especially intended to humiliate their victims. Here another Garu nun describes her interrogation:

They would strip us naked, bend over us, and then start beating us. They took off all our clothes. One would hold your arm and twist and drop you to the ground, while another would hold your arm and twist, and another would step on your head and keep it down. Then the fourth person would take your clothes off and beat you with a stick. They didn't tie us and hang us up, but they tied me against a wall and gave me shocks. They would prod us all over our backs. They would expose our breasts and prod us. They would make us sit on a chair and then slap our faces and push us off the chair so that we fell to the ground.

A number of nuns reported forms of sexual abuse during interrogation, including the insertion of electric batons into their vaginas and rectums, as well as their mouths. Male prison guards — and especially the Chinese interrogators — were provoked by the defiance of the women prisoners and incapable of comprehending the motivation for choosing a celibate, unmarried vocation. One nun reported, for instance, that during her interrogation a Chinese official repeatedly insisted that "the nuns were demanding the release of the monks who had been arrested only because they wanted them for husbands once they were free."

The nuns always insisted during interrogation that they had acted on their own and had not been instigated to demonstrate. Despite the brutality of their treatment, the nuns refused to capitulate, frustrating the efforts of their interrogators to get useful information and confessions. They had no names to provide, because they had acted alone and all had been arrested. They refused to confess to crimes, reiterating their commitment to Tibetan independence, which they made no effort to hide. In choosing to demonstrate, they had consciously decided to sacrifice themselves regardless of the consequences.

Demonstrations by nuns during the 1987-9 period had a special significance. They were small, unannounced, and unexpected (i.e. not timed to correspond with or commemorate important dates). Following major incidents that involved a violent confrontation with the security forces and a crackdown on protest, small demonstrations by nuns signalled the first signs of a renewed cycle of protest. This was the case for the demonstration by the Garu nuns on 17 April, which was the first act of protest after the wave of arrests in the wake of Mönlam. Nuns from Chupsang nunnery, near Sera monastery, followed with a demonstration on 25 April. Nuns from Shungseb nunnery, about 45 km. southeast of Lhasa, held a demonstration in the Barkhor on 17 May. In all these cases the nuns were arrested and taken to prison. Most of them were released in July along with protestors arrested for the demonstration at Mönlam.

There is little or no precedent for organized political activity by nuns within Tibetan society before 1959.[15] Nunneries did not command the

---

[15] Individual nuns have played a prominent role in resistance to the Chinese occupation of Tibet. Two nuns were among the organizers of the famous "women's revolt" on 12 March 1959, following the outbreak of the uprising of 10 March, when the women of Lhasa gathered in front of the Potala to challenge the Chinese army, see Havnevik (1990): 83-4, and Avedon (1986): 53. During the Cultural Revolution, a nun of Nyemoru Nunnery, Tinley Chödön, led a revolt against the Chinese at the nunnery. Until she was caught and executed, she is said to have commanded a large guerrilla army that fought the Chinese across a wide area of rural Tibet. See Havnevik (1990): 84.

same economic and political power as the monasteries, nor were they supported by subsidies from the government or grants of estates. They depended on gifts from local people and from pilgrims, and on the support of individual nuns by their families. The proportion of Tibetan women who became nuns was much smaller than that of men who became monks — probably 1–2 per cent only.[16] Nunneries never numbered more than a few hundred nuns, comparable in size to the smaller monasteries. Some were affiliated to monasteries, in which case they were formally administered by the male abbot or his monk delegates.

The rebuilding of nunneries in Tibet during the 1980s attracted little attention from the government and generally proceeded without interference, possibly because the Chinese government attaches less importance to nuns as a group. The restoration of the nunneries has been initiated by older nuns with the approval of male religious leaders. Chupsang nunnery, for instance, was only rebuilt in 1985 or 1986, after complete destruction in the Cultural Revolution. In 1988 there were some eighty nuns resident there, including two or three older nuns who had been associated with the nunnery before 1959. Chupsang is affiliated to nearby Sera monastery, and religious authority is in the hands of a senior monk there. Eight Sera monks regularly visit the nunnery to perform religious rituals and offer teachings to the nuns. Almost all the nuns are young women in their teens and twenties from rural farming backgrounds — that is, the same background as the current generation of monks (some of the nuns who had been arrested described themselves, using the Chinese communist system of classification, as coming from "middle-peasant" backgrounds). The prohibition on monks from Kham and Amdo residing at monasteries around Lhasa does not seem to have extended to the nunneries, which have admitted a number of young nuns from eastern Tibet.

The nuns at Chupsang nunnery are not officially registered as residents there; they retain the identity and ration cards of their home villages. Up to the time of the demonstrations there were no quotas or restrictions on admission; nuns were admitted as long as there was space to house them and required only the religious sanction of the Sera monk with authority over the nunnery. Chupsang received no grants from the government, and the nuns were supported by their families

---

[16] Figures compiled by the Council for Religious and Cultural Affairs of H.H the Dalai Lama indicate 27,080 nuns in 717 nunneries for all regions of Tibet compared to 565,478 monks in 5,542 monasteries — *Forbidden Freedoms* (1990): 85–6.

and by donations. There were no restrictions on attending the prayer sessions where food was distributed. The nunnery does not have a Democratic Management Committee or a government-appointed political leader. Instead, its political affairs come under the authority of the local *xiang* political leader, who visited no more frequently than once or twice a year (the same leader is responsible for Garu nunnery).

Garu nunnery, which had 130 nuns in 1988, was also restored only after 1985, receiving a grant of 10,000 yuan for this purpose from the government. It has just ten older nuns. Most of the younger ones come from Phembo, an area 60 km. east of Lhasa. As with Chupsang, the nuns are supported by their families. After the first demonstration by nuns in December 1987, Garu was subjected to increased scrutiny by local political authorities, who appear also to have regularized the status of the resident nuns and issued official registration permits for the nunnery. However, no new admissions were allowed.

The requirements for a monastic career and a career as a nun under current conditions in Tibet are similar. For both, the choice calls for strong motivation and family support. The lack of support from the government puts monks and nuns in a roughly comparable position, whereas in pre-1959 Tibet monks had a considerable political and economic advantage. The nuns stressed the same themes as the monks in describing the strength of their commitment to a religious career: the importance of keeping their vows, their sense of responsibility for rebuilding Buddhism, and a willingness to sacrifice their lives for Tibetan independence (which is synonymous with defending Buddhism). Young nuns were also keenly interested in studying Tibetan language and religion, though they experienced the same shortage of qualified teachers (especially since their only access to education was through visiting monks). Both young monks and young nuns come predominantly from rural backgrounds. For both, the choice of a religious career appears to be part of a general cultural and religious revival felt especially by the young.

Traditionally nuns have occupied a lower status than monks in Tibetan society. The most common term used to denote a nun is "ani", the term used for a paternal aunt.[17] A tradition of full religious ordination for nuns does not exist, and thus nuns are only able to receive the

---

[17] The term for a nunnery is "ani gompa" (*a ni dgon pa*). "Gompa" is a general term used to refer to any monastery or monastic retreat, no matter how small.

ordination of novices (*dge tshul*).[18] In general, Buddhist norms demand that nuns defer to monks. Monks are regarded as more learned than nuns, and rituals performed by them as more efficacious.[19] A whole collection of traditional Tibetan stereotypes diminishes the status of nuns, who are regarded as less able to discipline themselves and keep their vows. The motives for women choosing the life of a nun are doubted. Instead of a "pure" religious motivation, they are often spoken of as failures at life, ugly or handicapped and thus unable to make satisfactory marriages, running away from maltreatment by families or husbands, or widows (in this regard, a higher status attaches to women who become nuns early in life).[20]

These prejudices both reflect and justify the relative powerlessness of nuns in traditional Tibetan society. However, under current conditions in Tibet the economic situation, background, and motivation of nuns and monks is very similar. Through political protest nuns are thus in a position to change Tibetans' perceptions of their status and gain respect. Tibetans see nuns assuming the same burden of political responsibility as a concomitant of their clerical status as the monks. The young nuns have shown the same willingness to keep their vows and sacrifice their lives. Thus they have emerged as important players in the current phase of protest inside Tibet, winning the admiration of ordinary Tibetans as well as their monk counterparts. From 1988 onwards, monks and nuns coordinated their protest activity and maintained

[18] The full ordination for nuns requires, according to the Vinaya tradition accepted by Tibetans, 364 precepts (compared to 253 for monks); novice ordination for nuns involves the same ten precepts as for monks. From the point of view of Buddhist orthodoxy, the issue is a technical one: ordination must be received from an unbroken line of fully ordained predecessors. It is not enough simply to take the vows; the vows of a nun must be "received" through nuns who have themselves received them through fully ordained nuns. For this reason, once the line of transmission is broken, it cannot be restored. Full ordination for nuns in the Mahāyāna tradition continues in some Chinese communities, including Hong Kong, where it is claimed that one such lineage of fully ordained nuns has survived. Whatever the historical reasons for this predicament, it puts Tibetan women seeking clerical status at a distinct disadvantage.

[19] See Havnevik (1990): 178, who describes the situation of refugee nuns in India: "The nuns are caught in a vicious circle; as they are considered inferior to the monks as concerns religions expertise and practice, they are given fewer donations and less support from the laity. Because the nuns are poor, they cannot invite lamas to give them religious teachings that could help them accumulate learning and in this way increase their prestige."

[20] See Havnevik (1990): 141–78.

clandestine lines of communication. By the end of 1988 they were appearing together, marching side by side in demonstrations. Despite the harsh treatment following arrest, protest by nuns has continued through the period of martial law up to the present.

Aims of interrogation

The interrogation sessions in prison had several aims: to intimidate the prisoners, extract confessions, gain information about other participants in the demonstrations, and accomplish "thought reform" by convincing prisoners of the futility of the goal of Tibetan independence. Prisoners were made to witness scenes of brutality in prison in order to persuade them to confess. One prisoner in Gurtsa describes such a scene:

I saw people hanging with ropes tied to their arms behind their backs, suspended with their feet off the ground. Two of the people I saw had their shoulders dislocated by the rope. I saw twelve or thirteen, a group hanging together. This was to show the rest of us that the same thing could happen to us. They told us to tell the truth, confess our guilt. They wanted us to give the names of other participants and we were told that if we told the truth or handed over other people we would be treated leniently. If not we must suffer the heavy consequences. We were also told that Tibetan independence was a figment of our imagination.

It was never clear to the prisoners what the actual consequences of confessing would be, whether they would be dealt with leniently and released, or whether they would receive harsh sentences. Some prisoners resisted confessing because they did not believe the promises of lenient treatment:

The Chinese claim that if you confess you will be set free, but this is totally false. If you confess, you are charged with a crime and sentenced to a long term of imprisonment.

Other prisoners were afraid of being labelled as "informers" by fellow Tibetans:

The Chinese do not publicize their informers who give names of other people to them because they might be punished or beaten up later. But we know who they are, because they were suddenly released from prison. In the interrogation sessions, they have always said that those who give them names of others will be leniently treated.

This same prisoner, a construction worker from Lhasa, adds, however, that he was released in July along with a number of other prisoners from Gurtsa, though he had not provided his interrogators with any useful information:

I just told them what they already knew. I said I admired communism and also would not take part in future demonstrations. I was suddenly released. I was interrogated only eight times and most were interrogated more than ten times. They had not much to interrogate me about as I was arrested afterwards, whereas those arrested on 5 March were interrogated more in order to get names of others.

A major goal of the interrogations was to identify leaders and organizers of the demonstrations. The most significant evidence that one was a ringleader was the coherence of one's political views. The more thoughtful and intelligent one's answers to political questions, the less likely one was to be released. Prisoners were told to write down why they thought Tibet was independent. Here, it was important not to have well-thought-out political ideas or a detailed knowledge of Tibetan history. One of the lay Tibetans arrested recounts his experience:

The police said that if you say Tibet is independent, then you must explain why and recite the whole of Tibetan history. I told the police that I didn't know about Tibetan history, but that others knew. I told them that I didn't intend joining the 5 March demonstration, but others said, if you are a Tibetan then you must join.

In general, lay Tibetans were under less suspicion than monks and nuns. The assumption underlying the efforts of the interrogators was that behind the demonstrations lay "ringleaders" taking orders from Tibetans in exile — the "Dalai clique." Prisoners were sometimes presented with political ideas about which they may not have been well-informed — e.g. the Five-Point Peace Proposal of the Dalai Lama.[21] This may have been to gauge the depth of their political understanding or the extent of their contact with Tibetans in India. Prisoners were asked whether they had relatives in India or had been to India. Here,

---

[21] This proposal was presented by the Dalai Lama during his visit to Washington in September 1987. It proposed: (1) the transformation of the whole of Tibet into a zone of peace, (2) the abandonment of China's population transfer policy which threatens the very existence of the Tibetans as a people, (3) respect for the Tibetan people's fundamental human rights and democratic freedoms, (4) restoration and protection of Tibet's natural environment and the abandonment of China's use of Tibet for the production of nuclear weapons and dumping nuclear waste, and (5) the start of serious negotiations on the future status of Tibet and of relations between the Tibetan and Chinese people.

a nun accused of being an organizer of the demonstration by nuns from Garu nunnery in April 1988 describes in detail the attempts of her interrogator to discover the depth and source of her ideas about Tibetan independence:

I was taken to a room and asked whether I knew, first, how many other nuns in the prison were from my nunnery, secondly, what I thought when they had been arrested, and thirdly, if I knew they had left the nunnery to take part in the demonstration. I said I didn't know anything about that. He claimed I knew about everything and it was I who had organized it all. Since he kept on insisting that I was the leader behind the demonstration, I had no choice but to say that I did organize it. Then he asked what my aims had been. I said, to have Tibet free. He asked if I would get something to eat if Tibet becomes free. I told him we do not fight for a free Tibet in order to get something to eat, but for the same reason as you. You cry out to the outside world for your rights and fight to get them. We too strive for the rights we are entitled to. Secondly, we strive so that one day all Tibetans will get the opportunity to see the Dalai Lama in a free Tibet.

He asked if I had gone to India to attend the Kālacakra initiation last year. I replied that I did not know the way to get there. Then he asked if any monk had come to our nunnery after the Kālacakra. He said someone had incited us and asked who it was. I answered that we had received no incitement and that whatever we had done, we had done of our own accord. He then asked whether there really had been no one inciting us. I said we had done everything on our own initiative and that moreover we did not need anyone to incite us.

Then he said, "This means you are a supporter of Kusho Yulu?" [Yulu Dawa Tsering]. I said, "Yes, I am a supporter of Kusho Yulu." He said, "Then are all these people in the prison supporters of Kusho Yulu?" I replied, "Yes we are." He asked if I knew what crimes Kusho Yulu had committed and I said, "Our crimes are the same — to fight for a free Tibet. Other than this I do not know." The officer said that a free Tibet is impossible no matter how much we fight for it. Then he began telling a history about which I have no knowledge, so I kept quiet. He asked if I would be happy if Tibet became free, and I said, "Yes, when Tibet is free there will be much happiness." Then he said that the policy of the present Chinese government is good, so I asked him, "In that case, why are there so many beggars around the Barkhor?" He said this was nothing special, there were more beggars under the old government. I replied that we were not talking about the old government, but about the present one. He said I should also know that there were many beggars in India, and I told him that I had no idea since I had not been there. I said that he had started talking about the present government and therefore I had to say what I thought. He then said that would be all for now, but that I should think well for three days.

The interrogator must have decided that this nun was not after all one of the organizers. She was released in July with most of the other nuns from her nunnery. When the release of prisoners came, the fact of having confessed or not seems to have made little difference. What appears to have been decisive was whether or not a prisoner conformed to the assumption of the interrogators that they had been instigated to participate in the demonstrations by the so-called ringleaders.

In Gurtsa the prisoners were required to attend large meetings where political workers lectured the assembled prisoners on the "causes" of the demonstrations — i.e. deception by a small group of splittist agitators — and the inseparability of Tibet and China. These meetings were attended by all the prisoners, including those arrested before 5 March (the only exceptions were a few Chinese prisoners held for criminal offences). Between 5 March and 10 July, by which time the bulk of the prisoners had been released without charges being laid, there were three large political meetings in Gurtsa. In addition, groups of prisoners attended another final meeting just before their release.

The political meetings lasted about an hour. Prisoners were first reminded that if they gave names of others and confessed their crimes they would be leniently treated. The point most strongly emphasized in the meetings, however, was the futility of revolt. The shop assistant arrested for throwing stones provides this account:

They always began with saying how powerful China is and how could we ever think of overthrowing them. In 1959 the rebellion was crushed, they said, although we Tibetans were well armed and supplied from abroad. They say, "You have nothing now, what can you achieve?"

The lectures in the meetings were gauged to influence the politically unsophisticated. Besides emphasizing the military strength of China, they played on themes of foreign aggression and imperialism (against China), as well as the harm which the demonstrations had done to the development of the Tibetan economy. The cadres were careful not to attack the Dalai Lama personally, recognizing that most ordinary Tibetans retain a strong religious devotion to him:

They said His Holiness is like a faithful dog who has been deceived by foreigners and is following them. They said, "You are only doing these things under the influence of a few bad foreigners and have been deceived by their tricks. You should not do this. Tibet and China cannot be separated. In terms of past history or in terms of the future, it is impossible for you to gain Tibetan independence."

Release of prisoners

Prisoners were released in batches during the summer of 1988. The majority of the prisoners held at Gurtsa were released on 10 July — eighty-six prisoners, about fifty men and the rest women. On 11 July, thirty male prisoners were released from Sangyib. The prisoners were instructed at their final meeting inside the prison never to talk about their treatment or prison conditions. No reasons were given to the prisoners for the release of some of them and not others. On 12 July the Chinese government announced that it had released fifty-two monks and nuns, declaring:

The public security bureau has found that their cases are less serious. Most of them have confessed their crimes, some have even informed against other criminals and thus made contributions to the investigation. In this connection, the regional and Lhasa city political and legal organs, after making a careful study, decided not to prosecute these monks and nuns, have released them from custody, and have given them lenient treatment . . .[22]

A total of twenty-five monks and three nuns continued to be held. These included the fourteen monks from Ganden who initiated the 5 March demonstration by confronting the government officials at the conclusion of the Mönlam ceremony. Three of these monks, including the monastery Turin, Chungdag, had not even participated in the demonstration. Chungdag was described by another Ganden monk as

. . . our leader, the leader of all the monks. He is an honest monk and all the monks liked him. He spoke up during political meetings and the officials didn't like him. They say he is one of the main trouble-makers.

The other Ganden monks held had been singled out for speaking up in political meetings, for writing letters and posters, or for attempting to organize a boycott of Mönlam.

Of five Drepung monks who continued to be held, two had been arrested for writing letters to the monks of Ganden advocating a boycott of Mönlam and had not demonstrated on 5 March — Ngawang Namgyal, also a Turin at Drepung, and Ngawang Gendun, monastery treasurer (both were held in Sangyib until March 1990). Ngari Rinpoche, an important teacher from Sera, also continued to be held for recommending that monks boycott Mönlam (he was finally released in November 1988).

[22] Lhasa Tibet Regional Service in Mandarin, 12 July 1988, in *FBIS*, 13 July 1988: 46.

The two Garu nuns who continued to be held had been singled out for similar reasons. One of the nuns who was released explains:

From the documents issued, we have concluded that one of the nuns was held because it was her second demonstration. This was considered a major crime. As for the younger nun, before the demonstration the participants prepared small pieces of paper with "Free Tibet" on them, to be thrown in the air during the demonstration. These were written in her room and kept there the night before. At the time of the "confession" session, they did not mention finding them in her room but just detained her without giving a reason.

When we were released, the Chinese made it look as if we had confessed to the charges against us, although we hadn't made any such confession. We said we had all committed the same crime, asking for a free Tibet, and that unless everyone was freed, we would refuse to leave. We noticed that our bedding had been thrown out and was lying at the gate, then they kicked us and expelled us. They said we had been released because of our confession. We stayed outside for about two hours. Since that day we have not been allowed in the prison.

Between fifty and seventy-five lay Tibetans, both men and women, also remained in prison. They too were not necessarily held because of their participation in the demonstrations, but because of what they had said in meetings or under interrogation, or because they had been caught putting up wall posters or had been found with Tibetan independence literature in their possession. These prisoners included some who had been held since September 1987, such as Sonam Gyalpo, a thirty-eight-year-old resident of Lhasa who had been arrested and kept in solitary confinement at Gurtsa for putting up posters (he was sentenced in 1989 to three years' imprisonment).

Most of those who had been identified as stone-throwers on 5 March had been released without charges. Only Lobsang Tenzin and the other three Tibetans accused of murdering the Chinese security police-man, and two prisoners remaining from 1 October who had been arrested for destroying property, were held for crimes of violence. A number, like Yulu Dawa Tsering, had been arrested in their homes for activities not directly connected with the demonstrations. The group of political detainees included every stratum of Lhasa society — students, teachers, government workers, labourers, independent business people, and pilgrims. Some of these would eventually be released without being charged while others would receive prison sentences in the wave of trials following the declaration of martial law in 1989.

5

A BATTLE OF IDEAS

By September 1988, Tibetans in Lhasa expected further demonstrations for Tibetan independence. The outbreak of protest following the Mönlam festival may have been caused by the insensitivity of the authorities to the demands of the monks, but the invasion of the Jokhang temple by Chinese soldiers, and the subsequent mass arrests, provided a focus for Tibetan defiance and contributed to a widespread sense of solidarity. Unlike the violence on 1 October 1987, when local Public Security officers opened fire on a Tibetan crowd, the events of 5 March 1988 pitted Tibetans against units of the PAP moved in from Sichuan to suppress protest. The conflict had been reduced to its starkest elements, a direct confrontation between Tibetans and uniformed Chinese soldiers. For the people of Lhasa the choice was clear: as long as Chinese troops maintained their presence around the Barkhor, Tibetans would continue to demonstrate.

The political meetings were clearly ineffective, with more and more Tibetans speaking out against the Chinese. Wall posters regularly appeared around the Barkhor, and demonstrations to commemorate the anniversary of the first demonstrations on 27 September and 1 October 1987 were anticipated. In the neighbourhood committee meetings the principal message communicated was that Tibetans would be "gunned down in the streets" if there were any further demonstrations. To back this up, ever larger military patrols began to appear in the streets of Lhasa, especially when demonstrations were expected.

On 15 June 1988 Qiao Shi, member of the Politburo and secretary of the Party's Political and Legal Commission, began an inspection tour of Tibet. His posts in the government and the Party put Qiao Shi in charge of China's security apparatus, including the People's Armed Police. Coinciding with his visit, a special unit of the Chinese People's Armed People — the No. 2 Detachment — was "organized and established . . . in light of the antiseparatism struggle in Tibet." The unit was created to "coordinate with the public security organs" and "to focus on combat-readiness and patrol and fulfil mobile missions."[1]

---

[1] Lhasa Tibet Regional Service in Mandarin, 16 June 1988, in *FBIS*, 17 June 1988: 50.

In a widely reported speech to Party officials, Qiao Shi is said to have called for a policy of "merciless repression" in dealing with future Tibetan protest.[2] At the same time, Party officials, relaying Qiao Shi's instructions, called for greater supervision of the masses. In a meeting of city Party committee secretaries on 11 July, Dorje Tsering, head of the regional government, demanded that

. . . the leading party and government cadres at all levels frequently go deep into reality and keep close touch with the masses, so as to get to know their views and demands and help them to solve practical problems and difficulties . . . We must take a firm and clear-cut stand in informing the masses of all nationalities in Tibet: there can be no restoration of reactionary rule in Tibet. The dream of a handful of separatists to split the motherland can never be attained. Tibet cannot be separated from the leadership of the CPC or from the PLA.[3]

On 7 September, at about 6 p.m., a group of seven or eight nuns from Tsangkhung nunnery in the old part of Lhasa staged a small demonstration, circling the Barkhor and shouting independence slogans. No Tibetan flags or pictures of the Dalai lama were displayed. After circling the Barkhor, the nuns dispersed before they could be arrested. The next day PSB officers visited the nunnery. The nuns involved were identified and interrogated, but no arrests were made. The leniency of the authorities may have had something to do with the fact that the political manager of the nunnery (*srid don go 'khrid*), a former nun, was a government appointee friendly to the Chinese.

Around noon on 27 September, the anniversary of the first demonstration by Drepung monks in 1987, nine monks from Drepung staged a small demonstration on the Barkhor. They were dressed in lay clothes and carried only a small photograph of the Tibetan flag along with a picture of the Dalai Lama. Tibetans had been expecting a demonstration by monks on this day, but the massive military presence, with armed PAP patrols continuously circling the Barkhor, made it impossible for a large number of lay people to fall in behind the monks. Fearful Tibetans persuaded the monks to escape into the side-alleys off the Barkhor before confronting an approaching patrol (six of them were eventually arrested at Drepung on 10 October).

[2] See *Merciless Repression* (1990): 5–8, for a discussion of the implications of Qiao Shi's inspection tour of Tibet and his ominous remarks.

[3] Lhasa Tibet Regional Service in Mandarin, 14 July 1988, in *FBIS*, 14 July 1988: 17–18.

PAP reinforcements were brought into the square in front of the Jokhang, and squared off against a crowd of several hundred Tibetans who were beginning to assemble. At this point a riot might easily have erupted. One young Tibetan boy, a seventeen-year-old carpenter, threw a rock at the soldiers, who charged into the crowd to arrest him, firing off a tear-gas canister to cover their retreat. As the boy was hustled into a nearby police station, the crowd slowly dispersed.

During the afternoon of 27 September, about 200 lay Tibetans gathered in the Sungchöra, the teaching area along the south wall of the Jokhang, to recite *mani* for those who had died the previous year. This prayer-session had been organized by a developing network of lay Tibetans who had come to define their role as providing "support and backing" (*rgyab skyor*) to the monks. The security police did not interfere with the gathering because its purpose was ostensibly religious. To have attacked people reciting prayers would have violated the official policy of tolerating individual religious observance. The organizers, however, were able to collect money from the crowd to be used to buy food and clothing for political prisoners. On the platform where the Dalai Lama traditionally gives his teachings during the Mönlam festival (also the scene of the confrontation between monks and Party officials the previous March) monks recited a prayer for the long life of the Dalai Lama. This improvised performance, with its political content barely disguised, had to suffice in the face of the Chinese military presence.

The incident in the morning of 27 September showed the continuing readiness of Tibetans, given an opportunity, to protest. It also showed the increased tension caused by the presence of armed soldiers in the Barkhor. The elements constituting Tibetan independence protest were now clearly understood by both sides, Tibetans and Chinese. First, Tibetans felt compelled to stage demonstrations on the Barkhor and in front of the Jokhang. The possibility of demonstrations elsewhere in Lhasa was not considered. The Chinese authorities felt equally compelled to prevent demonstrations around the Barkhor, regardless of the cost. Secondly, demonstrations were initiated by monks and nuns, with lay people falling in behind to lend support and protection. The continuous patrols by the security forces thus aimed to prevent a demonstration from starting in the first place — or, if one did, to bring it to a halt quickly by arresting or dispersing the demonstrators before large numbers of lay people could be drawn into the procession.

The final element defining Tibetan protest that needs to be present consists of the symbols of Tibetan independence — most important, the Tibetan national flag bearing two facing snow lions (signifying the traditional formula of the Tibetan state: "religion and politics combined"). In place of a full-scale demonstration, at least the flag might be raised on the roof of the Jokhang or on the pole in the square in front of the Jokhang.

Thus, on the morning of 1 October 1988 a flag appeared in front of the Jokhang. The residents of Lhasa expected the monks of Sera monastery to stage a demonstration on that day, the first anniversary of the bloody confrontation in front of the police station. But on the night of 30 September a convoy of thirty-three trucks passed through Lhasa and unloaded some 800 PAP troops in the square in front of the Jokhang, where they camped for the night. Forming into units of 100 soldiers, armed with automatic weapons, rifles with bayonets, and riot shields, troops continuously circled the Barkhor all through the next morning, making a demonstration impossible. Word spread among Tibetans waiting along the Barkhor that no demonstration would take place that day. The appearance of the flag in front of the Jokhang, which was quickly removed by police, was the sole gesture by the monks of Sera that they had intended to demonstrate.

The return of the Work Team

In the first week of September 1988 units of the Work Team (*las don ru khag*) returned to the monasteries and nunneries in the Lhasa area — Ganden, Sera, Drepung, as well as Garu, Chupsang, and Shungseb nunneries, and the Jokhang. The Work Team was sent to try to prevent further demonstrations with a new round of political education. Monks at Drepung, for instance, reported that twenty-seven cadres had arrived on 2 September and announced that they planned to stay for forty days, coinciding with the period when new demonstrations were expected.

The monks were questioned one at a time by teams of three cadres about their views on Tibetan independence. They were also asked to confess their involvement in previous demonstrations. The cadres said to them: "We already have information on who was involved. If you don't acknowledge what you did, we will not spare you." The twenty-one Drepung monks from the first demonstration on 27 September the previous year were targeted for special treatment. Each monk was asked whether he believed in an independent Tibet. All were told that they could be executed for this. Then they were threatened with expulsion:

1, 2. Demonstration by monks and nuns in the Barkhor, 10 December 1988

3. The Jokhang surrounded by PAP soldiers, December 1988

4. Chinese troops marching through the Barkhor, December 1988

5. Arrested monks being taken to prison after the demonstration on 5 March 1988

6. Monks demonstrating in the Barkhor, 5 March 1988

7. Tibetan prisoners on display in Gyantse, September 1988

8. Tibetans praying for demonstrators in the Sungchöra, 27 September 1988

"It won't be easy for you in prison next time. If you confess well you can stay in the monastery, otherwise you will be sent back to your villages." Older monks were called separately to a special meeting and asked to provide the names of younger monks who had been involved in protest. Part of the purpose for investigating the older monks was to determine whether they had prompted the younger monks to demonstrate. The cadres continued to believe that the younger monks could not have organized the demonstrations on their own.

Fifteen cadres arrived at the Jokhang on 3 September, announcing that they planned to stay for forty-five days "because October is coming." Here too, monks were targeted for special treatment, sometimes being divided into four different groups and sometimes taken one at a time for meetings with the cadres. At Sera, where twenty-five cadres from the Work Team arrived on 4 September, monks reported that they were told by an Party official named Basang:

You must confess your participation in last year's demonstration. If you don't confess and if you do it again, then we will kill you. We will execute you. We will put you in prison for all of your life. The weight of the law will come down on you.

Monks at each of the monasteries were also told it was not enough to confess their own guilt for participation in demonstrations, but that they must "expose" (*ther 'don*) others. Finally, they were threatened with expulsion from the monasteries if they did not comply with the demands of the political workers.

A Tibetan working within the TAR government described a meeting on 1 September of officials from the Religious Affairs Bureau, Public Security, and the regional government. At the meeting the plan for the forthcoming Chinese National Day was laid out: (1) 150 cadres of the Work Team were to be deployed in the major monasteries and nunneries to re-educate the monks and nuns; (2) all monks and nuns not holding resident cards were to be sent home; (3) those who could not be sent home would be allowed to remain in the monastery, but would lose the right to participate in monastic life; (4) those monks and nuns who had been involved in earlier demonstrations would be compelled to confess their guilt and promise not to engage in these activities in the future, and were to be expelled if they refused to comply; and (5) all monks and nuns were to attend political meetings, regardless of age or rank.

This account from a Tibetan inside the government apparatus

corresponds with what transpired in the monasteries over the next month. The threat to expel monks and nuns without residence cards would have removed hundreds of unlisted monks from the big monasteries. Though some of those identified as politically active in the past were informed that they would be expelled, the threat of expulsion was not carried out. For their part, the monks were well aware of the government's preoccupation with preventing public displays of protest during the period covering Chinese National Day and the anniversaries of the demonstrations the previous year. At the same time, the routine functioning of the monasteries was axiomatic to government policy. They could not easily be shut down, but somehow they had to be effectively managed. The population of monks and nuns that had assembled in recent years was already too large and too representative of Tibetan aspirations simply to disperse.

The monks seized the opportunity to resist and frustrate the political workers. On the morning of 7 September a poster went up on a temple door at Sera. The next morning a flag appeared on top of a flag-pole. When ordered to take it down by the political workers, the monks refused, arguing, "Since it is not ours, why should we take it down?" On 29 September a group of cadres went to the Nechung Buddhist Institute to lecture the monks and demanded a written self-criticism from each monk. The monks refused, saying that they had nothing to confess, and then proceeded to fold the sheets of paper they had been given into paper aeroplanes and toss them around the room. A few days before 1 October, when the monks of Sera were again threatened with expulsion, they volunteered *en masse* to be thrown out of the monastery, calling the bluff of the Work Team. They were confident that the last thing the authorities wanted was hundreds of monks loose in the vicinity of Lhasa as Chinese National Day was approaching.

A young monk from Ganden who had been arrested after the demonstration on 5 March and released five months later in July provides this account of the return of the Work Team to the monastery in September 1988. The team included cadres from the county headquarters in Medrokunga, from Lhasa, and from the Gyama region where many Ganden monks have their homes. A meeting was called to discuss the expulsion of monks from the monastery and the requirements for those allowed to remain:

We were told to put forth our case and discuss. No discussion followed. Then they started questioning one after another. On that day three youths spoke from our side. They stated that the Communist Party had expelled them from the monastery and that they would have to leave, and asked to be expelled from that day. It was obvious that nothing could be done, since the Communist Party had all the power. When they said this they were accused of reacting badly. They were asked, "Why do you say you are leaving? There are two paths. If one adheres to both 'love of country' [*rgyal gces*] and 'love of religion' [*chos gces*], then one can remain in the monastery. If one rejects these, then one would have to leave." So because the monks said they were leaving they were accused of being unpatriotic.

This was on the second day of the meetings. Our youths insisted that a decision should be reached that same night. They had to begin studying the next day, they said. It was decided to reach a conclusion and a heated discussion took place. The Chinese threatened to adjourn the meeting to the next day if we wanted to get into such detailed discussion. One really could not get into a detailed discussion because there was no neutral person present. If one wanted to make a point it was useless because there was no mediator. If there were an impartial mediator, then we could state our case and the Chinese could state theirs honestly. But lacking such a mediator the situation was that the Chinese put the questions and then answered them as well. They carried on exactly as they liked, so the meeting ended this way.

In fact the monks were attempting to turn the argument with the political workers into the kind of debate they are trained for as part of their religious education — the kind of debate they practise every day in the monastery courtyard. Logical reasoning is a major component of the curriculum of the monasteries, and much of the current thinking of the young monks about Tibetan independence has been developed in this form — i.e. examining the consequences of stated premises. Clearly, the cadres were not prepared for this kind of argument. The Ganden monk explains what happened the next day:

The next morning they started by saying we had behaved disgracefully the previous night and that we were still reactionaries [*log spyod pa*] poisoned to the root. They went on, "Yesterday you demanded that the meeting should come to a decision. Do you want to go to prison again? If you want to be imprisoned we can oblige. If you want to drink the water of this land you have to observe the laws." The chairman of the sub-committee [*las don tshogs chung*] spoke a lot. He was from Lhasa — a "collaborator" [*a skul slong* — literally, someone who has been "mobilized"]. The young monks did not say anything more. Then I spoke, "This is not the right way to speak to us. You are cadres [*las byed pa*], we belong to the public. Speaking for myself, I have just been released from prison. On the whole, I was not happy there, but I had no worries. I just had to think of myself. After coming here, there has been so much talk with the Chinese about this and that. You set me free from prison, but the feeling that I have is that I have been re-imprisoned. I did not ask to be released from prison and if it does not suit you, and you want to imprison me again, then send me back." When I said this they accused me of having the wrong attitude. I added, "When you start questioning us, why don't you hear us out?" They kept telling us to speak out, then interrupted us.

This same Ganden monk, an intellectual leader among his peers, had thought extensively about Tibetan history and independence. The scope of his thinking is typical of the kinds of arguments in which the monks attempted to engage the political workers:

Although my knowledge of Tibetan history is limited, I am sure that Tibet has never been a part of China. There is no single book in which one finds that Tibet is part of China. Even the books published by the Chinese give no evidence of this.

It is very important that Tibet become free. Why is it necessary? The Chinese say that the question of Tibet is the question of the personal position of the Dalai Lama. But it is not. The question of Tibet is a question of the well-being of six million Tibetans and not the position of the Dalai Lama. He is our legitimate leader. We trust in him and his leadership. From the first to the fourteenth, the Dalai Lamas, have always worked for the well-being of the Tibetan people and there has never been a time when they thought of their own well-being and power.

When the People's Liberation Army invaded Tibet it came to liberate the country. If its assumption that Tibet is part of China is true, then from whom did it come to liberate Tibet? The fact that it felt Tibet must be liberated shows that Tibet is an independent nation. Ever since the Chinese first set foot on the soil of Tibet, they have tried to change the facts of Tibetan history.

Tibetans used their knowledge of Tibetan history to challenge the cadres in political meetings — action which frequently led to arrest and imprisonment. Here the young Ganden monk explains what happened to an older monk, Tenpa Wangdrag, who had argued against the cadres in meetings at the monastery:

He is a learned monk. He knows much about the independent status of Tibet. He even challenged the Chinese many times over this matter. When the Chinese said that Tibet has always been a part of China, Tenpa did not hesitate to say it is untrue. He said: "From the time of our great Dharma kings, Tibet has been a free nation. The Chinese must produce a valid document in which it should be stated when and how Tibet has been part of China". Because he spoke so openly about such a sensitive matter the Chinese took it as a crime and arrested him.

Tenpa Wangdrag was one of the fourteen Ganden monks arrested after Mönlam in March 1988. At the time of writing, he is in Drapchi prison serving a fifteen-year sentence.

The monks saw disputation about Tibetan history and politics as a natural extension of their intellectual training, and tried to introduce the same criteria for validity as they applied to topics in logic and philosophy. The political workers had a very different view of religion. As they explained it, religious faith must be subordinated to patriotism — "love of country" — and thus religious toleration is predicated on submission to Chinese rule. The correct role of religion in society was sometimes explained by the political workers in terms of the positive service performed by religion in maintaining order and morality. It was this essentially conservative conception of religion, stressing obedience, that was held to be compatible with the needs of a communist society. At a political meeting in the autumn of 1988, a TAR government official named Phurbu directed the monks at Drepung:

We should abide by the rules of the monasteries. We are not allowed to get involved in political activities. He told us to study Buddhism thoroughly so we would be able to serve the Communist Party. We should also be able to answer the questions asked by foreigners about religion.

Instead of convincing Tibetans of the correctness of the Chinese position, the political meetings had the opposite effect, provoking resistance. Individuals might be identified as troublemakers by the political cadres and arrested, but there were always others to take their places as spokesmen when the occasion arose. By providing a forum for Tibetan grievances through the meetings, however biased and intimidating the setting, Tibetans were able to confront Chinese authority collectively, even as they watched their "heroes" taken away for punishment. The Chinese leadership knows that in the final analysis the hegemony of the Party depends on maintaining its monopoly over political ideology. The principal challenge posed by Tibetans in recent years has been ideological, and it is here that the Chinese are now on the defensive. Tibetans are, after all, invited to listen to Chinese arguments and discuss them. The exercise is largely a sham; but despite Chinese efforts to enforce ideological conformity and restrict discussion, Tibetans are capable of finding their own answers to Chinese arguments.

Perhaps the best illustration of Tibetans taking the offensive in the debate with the Work Team is the village uprising precipitated by the visit of eight cadres of the Work Team from the local county head-quarters to Ratö monastery, 30 km. west of Lhasa. Five monks from Ratö had been arrested for taking part in the Mönlam demonstration in March 1988. They had undergone interrogation in prison and been released. A meeting on 29 September 1988 was called by the Work Team to read out their confessions. At the meeting a monk from Ratö, Tsering Dondrup, stood up and began arguing with the political workers. The cadres had been lecturing the monks on the "zombie" (*ro langs*) of feudalism. Tsering Dondrup answered, "I didn't say anything about feudalism. Tibet has been independent for thousands of years. I said that Tibet has been subjected to Chinese imperialism." Then forty or fifty monks all stood up and shouted, "Tibet is independent."

Tsering Dondrup was arrested that night. The next day officials and police from the county headquarters arrived, and on 4 October a meeting was called to announce that he would be taken away for trial. As he was led away, the monks began throwing stones at the cadres and police. That night farmers from the nearby village joined the monks in attacks on police and stoning cars. Most of the young monks at Ratö are children of local families. The police and cadres left, but on 6 October about 200 People's Armed Police arrived from Lhasa and sur-rounded the monastery and the nearby village. Skirmishes broke out again, but were quelled by the troops using tear-gas and firing guns into the air. People were beaten and four more monks were arrested. A young monk from Ratö recounts the attitude of the monks during the incident:

We monks tried to keep the situation under control that night and to fight for human rights peacefully, but the soldiers beat us with sticks and forced us back inside the monastery. Then later, as we were coming back from the meeting, they arrested some of our people and took them to prison. We pleaded for their release, but the soldiers surrounded us, threatening us, point-ing their guns at us and throwing things. Unable to take any more of their threats and aggressive behaviour, we also started throwing stones and some of our people approached the soldiers shouting anti-Chinese slogans. The Chinese had told us before in the meeting that in talking about independence we were not abiding by their political law and were not behaving like monks. So we asked them to tell us what was unlike a monk in that.

There is perhaps some significance in the fact that the confrontation with the cadres took place in the monastery courtyard — the place where the monks practise debate. The cadres had set foot on Tibetan ground reserved for argument and discussion. The political meetings were sufficiently like traditional debate for the monks to draw the comparison, yet sufficiently unlike free and fair discussion for the monks to find them intellectually deficient and absurd:

All these troubles had started in the courtyard of our monastery because we had chosen not to listen to what the Chinese were saying. The Chinese told us we were not behaving like monks, and therefore we were not monks. We asked them to give their reasons for making this statement. It was on that night also that Tsering Dondrup stood up and asked them if there was anything more they would like to tell us. They replied that if we monks thought we were so great, we should go and shout about it in Lhasa. It was after this that Tsering Dondrup, who could not take any more of this Chinese talk, shouted for an independent Tibet.

For their part, the arguments of the political workers lacked even ideological substance. They were little more than boasts of Chinese power and threats that served only to provoke the monks:

What did they say at the meeting? They said that Tibet had no army and that we were in a hopeless situation. The Tibetan government had once had army barracks all over the place, but they, the Chinese, had destroyed them in three months and we could not do anything about it. There was no one as powerful as they were left in Tibet now, and even if they were to give each monk a rifle and a machine-gun we would still be helpless against them.

They told us that in old Tibet we had all been serfs and slaves and Tibetans had not been free although it had been an independent country. They also said that during the Cultural Revolution we had not had the freedom to practise our religion, but we had now been given this freedom and could do so as we wished, but we were not allowed to become involved in anything political. Activity of this sort would be a criminal act which would destroy the monastery, they said, and force the authorities to close it.

They said "Tibet is not an independent country. You cannot lift the sky with fingertips, or put it in your mouths." They asked us if we thought that tsampa and barley would fall from the sky if we got independence. "You think if you become independent that life will be easier for you and that you won't have to work so hard? That is not the case, your present life is much better than before. You were all slaves and serfs then, and you had no food to eat although it was an independent country. There is no better policy than what you have now."

Ideology: old and new

Mönlam, its tragic outcome notwithstanding, had convinced the monks of the strength of their position. The Chinese government needed the monasteries to validate its religious policy in Tibet, and this gave the monks some leverage in their dealings with it. The monks were also confident that they had the backing of the Tibetan population, who had come to see them as the principal spokesmen for the cause of Tibetan independence. Reassertions of monastic authority, and the pivotal role of the monasteries in Tibetan life, had become the leading edge of Tibetan nationalism. But most important, the monks saw their contribution in intellectual and ideological terms. They saw their role as being to formulate a coherent answer to Chinese claims. Hostility to Chinese rule in Tibet is widespread and longstanding, but this has been the first time since the invasion in 1959 that Tibetans have been able to confront the Chinese on their own ground ideologically.

The principal line of argument taken by the cadres in political meetings was that the monks want to restore feudalism. Tibetan demands for democracy and human rights were in turn dismissed as attempts to restore the "old society" (*spyi tshogs rnying pa*). Characterizations of pre-1959 Tibet as "feudal" are used to justify Chinese rule in Tibet. Tibetans are told that only the Chinese communist system is compatible with the conditions of the modern world. A Ganden monk recounts this line of argument in a political meeting at the monastery:

The Chinese say that our past government, which was temporal as well as spiritual, is totally unsuitable for the present situation. They say the Chinese government is much more advanced and more suitable for the present-day situation of the world. They have a very high regard for their socialism and communism. They said our past government was unsuitable because religion and politics are incompatible. They blame us for wanting to revive the old government, and claim that in our minds we have the goal to become the leaders. In fact we didn't shout to become leaders, but to bring happiness to the majority of the Tibetan people. We appealed to human rights organizations of the world and to the supporters of Tibet. For that reason we went on peaceful marches.

During the 1980s, Tibetans inside Tibet have come to view the question of modernization and progress in very different terms from the Chinese government, focusing particularly on Western democratic freedoms, which the Chinese political system cannot deliver. No real attempt has been made to dismantle the economic reforms of the 1980s and reinstitute collectivization. On the other hand, modernization and economic development cannot function as effective ideological substitutes for socialism, which has come to signify little besides Party domination. The vocabulary of "class warfare" has not figured in the lectures of political workers, and Tibetans have come to take economic liberalization for granted. However, they have simply identified their own aspirations for "modernity" with the larger world outside China, a point of view that further highlights the deficiencies of Chinese rule in Tibet. The influx of foreign goods, foreign ideas, and foreign visitors in the 1980s only helped this along. Foreigners are almost always sympathetic to the Tibetan cause and critical of the Chinese political system. The Chinese have wrongly assumed that Tibetan thinking can be "modernized" along Chinese lines. Instead, Chinese claims in political meetings to represent progress and modernity have sharpened the Tibetan sense of nationhood.

Tibetans brush off Chinese assertions in political meetings that Tibetan protestors want to bring back feudalism and the "serf-system." Certainly no Tibetans want this. But the relative popularity of current economic policy — particularly in the countryside, where formerly collectivized land has been redistributed and taxation suspended — has not helped the Chinese politically. Current economic gains are perceived by Tibetans as the natural result of the lifting of an alien and oppressive system, not as the effect of a positive and constructive policy. Tibetans insist that whatever benefits they have obtained result from their own efforts rather than from Chinese intervention. Also, the willingness of the Chinese government to admit to the mistakes and mismanagement of the Cultural Revolution does not strengthen the Chinese case. Chinese domination of Tibet, and continuing political repression, originate from the same system. Tibetans would thus carry through the process of dismantling communist rule in Tibet to completion.

In any case, Tibetans perceive the benefits of economic development as being very unevenly distributed, with the larger share going to the continuing influx of Chinese settlers, who have seized many of the opportunities opened up by the economic reforms in Tibet. Talk of modernization under the Chinese only serves to heighten Tibetans' perception of their own relative disadvantage, and thus to increase rather than diminish nationalist sentiments. The Ganden monk above expresses the Tibetan response to Chinese claims to have brought progress to Tibet:

I personally think that the old society will never be reestablished, and that Tibetans do not want this to happen either. Even under the Thirteenth Dalai Lama, steps were taken toward a democratic Tibet. He tried to bring about many reforms, such as land, debt, and so on. None of these reforms was effective because of his early death. When the present Fourteenth Dalai Lama took responsibility at an early age, time was not on his side. Not long after his installation, Tibet was invaded by the Chinese. He did not have time to put the reforms begun by his previous incarnation into practice.

The Chinese say that the old society was dynastic, passing power from father to son. To me, it is the Chinese themselves who are like this. They took the fate of the entire Tibetan people into their own hands. They oppress Tibetans, subjecting us to poverty and the most inhuman conditions. Tibetans are living in the darkest period in their history. The great influx of Chinese immigrants into Tibet makes it impossible for Tibetans to earn a living. Furthermore, the Chinese are transporting all our resources and wealth to China.

The Chinese claim to have invested much in Tibet for the benefit of Tibetans. In practice, all this investment is going to the benefit of Chinese immigrants. Tibetans do not share the facilities that their Chinese counterparts enjoy. The Chinese claim to have come to help Tibetans because Tibetans are incapable of helping themselves and need help to develop. On the contrary, we Tibetans are capable in every sense. We have been taking care of ourselves for thousands of years without any external help.

The liberalization of social and economic policy in Tibet during the 1980s has in fact made Chinese colonial attitudes towards Tibetan society all the more visible. During the Maoist period the superiority of Chinese institutions and culture lay in adherence to Marxist doctrine. Now, Tibetan backwardness is a matter of unwillingness to participate in the development of an integrated commodity economy. Tibetans are told that only with Chinese expertise and planning will they be able to advance along the road of economic development. Furthermore, undesirable attributes of Tibetan culture impede this development and must be overcome through exposure to superior Chinese culture combined with Party leadership.

Negative stereotypes of the Tibetan character explicitly inform current Chinese propaganda in a way that would have been unthinkable in the heyday of Maoist orthodoxy, when the suppression of Tibetan culture invoked the rhetoric of class struggle. Socialist theory in China in the mid-1980s introduced the notion of the "primary stage of socialism". With the issue of class struggle successfully resolved through the accession of the Communist Party to power, the principal goal of the primary socialist stage is the modernization of society and the development of a commodity economy through a variety of proven methods, including markets and economic competition.[4]

This is the area where Tibet lags behind China, both economically and culturally. In a speech to a forum of the regional Party Committee's Party School system, reprinted in the *Tibet Daily* on 9 January 1989, Li Weilun explained that "Tibet has, like the rest of China, entered socialism, but it is at a relatively low layer of the initial stage." Tibet has "a self-sufficient natural economy, with no commodity economy to speak of." In this current formulation of socialist development theory, the principal obstacles to economic development are cultural and psychological:

The influence of religion in Tibet is profound and broad. Religion permeates all fields of social activity, and religious culture is integrated with ethnic culture. Although the masses have fine traditions such as hard work, bravery, wisdom, and patriotism, their level of modern culture and education is low, many know nothing about science, and the proportion of illiterates is high; they have little concept of a commodity economy and a weak idea of competition. The influence of the small producer mentality is profound, such as being happy with a little affluence, being unwilling to forge ahead, and so on. It is evident from this that the task of improving ideological and cultural qualities and building socialist spiritual civilization in Tibet is particularly heavy.[5]

Invidious comparisons with Chinese civilization are commonplace under the assumptions of current doctrine. Tibetans are presented as unable to think or act for themselves:

The old Tibet had no tradition of democracy or of a legal system. The masses' idea of democracy is weak and their ability to take part in or discuss politics and to exercise democratic supervision is poor. There exists a certain degree of simple gratitude and dependence on others.[6]

Tibetans, however, see no inherent contradiction between modernization in the global sense and their traditional culture. Instead, they

---

[4] See Ding (1988) for a discussion of the ideological problems engendered by the theory of the "primary stage of socialism". The attenuation of the official ideology, and the attempt to remove the economic sphere from the requirement of ideological orthodoxy have had serious repercussions for the Chinese leadership. Pressure toward the "re-ideologization" of political life remains as an endemic tendency within the system as long as functionaries feel threatened by economic reforms. In Tibet this tendency is largely expressed by the demands of the old guard in the Party for an intensification of ideological orthodoxy in the drive to combat "splittism".

[5] Xizang Ribao in Chinese, 9 January 1989, p. 2, in *FBIS*, 27 January 1989: 57.

[6] *Ibid.*

understand Chinese communism to be deficient by world standards precisely because it cannot deliver political freedoms. The relaxation of ideological orthodoxy during the 1980s opened the possibility for a meaningful discussion among Tibetans about the shape of a future independent democratic Tibet. The monks in particular are in a position to argue that it is the Chinese system as it has been experienced in Tibet which is incompatible with the modern world, not Buddhism.

Here the Dalai Lama is especially important as the central religious and political symbol for Tibetans. The dual nature of his role for Tibetans — as both political and religious leader — has been an important political resource for them. The Dalai Lama embodies the central formula of Tibetan politics: "religion and politics combined" (*chos srid gnyis ldan*). In the conditions of Chinese rule this formula has gained a new significance that contrasts with its meaning in traditional Tibetan society, where it legitimized the institutions of the Dalai Lama's government. As a formula for political legitimacy, it derives its force from the figure of the Dalai Lama, who remains a potent yet ambiguous symbol — thus enabling the formula to be applied creatively to the present situation in Tibet. Tibetans understand the formula as being essentially open-ended; they have no difficulty equating its political side with democracy, since the Dalai Lama is acknowledged as a world leader who symbolizes democracy and human rights.[7]

The Chinese, on the other hand, are under an obligation to attack both religion and democracy. Power as it is understood by the Chinese state is unitary and reductive, concentrated in the Party apparatus. Religious faith must be subordinated to "patriotism" — love of the "nation" — and thus religious toleration requires submission to Chinese rule. Tibetan aspirations for democracy are in turn dismissed as attempts to restore the "old society."

The Drepung manifesto: the meaning of democracy

Perhaps the most important political document to come out of Tibet since the current wave of protest began is "The Meaning of the Precious

---

[7] Margaret Nowak (1984) discusses the role this formula plays in the political thinking of young exiled Tibetans in India. As she explains, along with the symbol of the Dalai Lama, it enables young Tibetans in a refugee environment to "interpret the lessons of contemporary, alien, social experience in the familiar light of the traditionally ambiguous and therefore flexible ideology of *chos-srid zung-'brel*, 'religion and politics combined' " — Nowak (1984): 157.

Democratic Constitution of Tibet" (*Bod kyi dmangs gtso'i rtsa khrims rin po che'i dgongs don*)[8] produced by a group of Drepung monks in the summer of 1988. Printed as an eleven-page pamphlet using woodblocks, the text is a manifesto for an independent democratic Tibet. The Drepung monks who composed it had all taken part in the first demonstration in the Barkhor on 27 September 1987. They began publishing leaflets after their release from prison in January 1988. From the outset the group described its aims as political education; one of their first projects was to print and distribute a Tibetan translation of the Universal Declaration of Human Rights. From rural backgrounds themselves, the Drepung group intended their literature to be taken back to villages to counter Party propaganda and educate villagers on the meaning of democracy. The Drepung manifesto provides an illustration of what an independent Tibet might look like. Much of it specifically counters the claims made by Party workers in political meetings that the Chinese have brought progress and democracy to Tibet.

On 30 November 1989 Ngawang Phulchung, the thirty-year-old leader of the group, was sentenced at a mass sentencing rally to nineteen years in prison for "organizing and joining a counter-revolutionary clique and spreading counter-revolutionary propaganda." He was convicted along with ten other Drepung monks of producing "counter-revolutionary literature" attacking the Chinese government and "venomously slandering our socialist system characterized by the people's democratic dictatorship." An official statement broadcast by Radio Lhasa on the day of the sentencing denounced the ideas of the Drepung monks, declaring that the "crimes committed by Ngawang Phulchung and other criminals demonstrate that the so-called human rights, freedoms, and democracy played up by the separatists both at home and abroad are nothing but a pack of deceitful lies." The monks were described as the "scum of the religious circles" who had "thoroughly betrayed the religious doctrines and canons of Buddhism by their actions." The severity of the sentences, the intensely ideological denunciation of their "crimes," and the public spectacle of a mass sentencing rally indicate how seriously the Chinese government perceives the threat posed by the ideas of the Drepung monks.[9]

---

[8] See Appendix A, p. 232 below, for a complete translation of this document.

[9] Lhasa Xizang Regional Service in Mandarin, 30 November 1989, in *FBIS*, 1 December 1989: 38.

Much of the vocabulary used by the Drepung monks is borrowed from the communist lexicon. Terms like "the broad masses" (*rgya che'i mi dmangs*) and the term for "democracy" itself (*dmangs gtso*) were introduced into the Tibetan language to translate Chinese communist material. Thus, outlining the conditions necessary for a "people's government" (*mi mang gi gzhung*), the term "people" is explained as referring to the "broad masses," and democracy is defined as "a popular system which fundamentally accords with the needs, wishes, and choices of the broad masses."[10] Chinese rule in Tibet is understood throughout not merely as foreign occupation, which Tibetans do not need to be convinced of, but as undemocratic and unrepresentative. The Drepung manifesto emphasizes the limited and representative character of democratic government:

As for the means for progress in the future, it is necessary to build political and social organization on the basis of the cooperation and consent of the broad masses of Tibet. This kind of organization must be constructed by the broad masses or by their representatives whose powers are limited by the people. Apart from that, an organization built on the rule of force and coercion can never be justified. As for the representatives, both their nomination and their election must be decided according to the wishes of the masses. Such a system of government is a democratic system.

The Drepung manifesto restates the principles of the 1963 constitution drawn up by the government of the Dalai Lama (and influenced by the 1948 Universal Declaration of Human Rights).[11] It calls for "equality without discrimination" (*dbye 'byed med pa'i 'dra mnyam*) based on sex, social origin, language, religion, race, wealth, or region, and declares the equal right to free speech, freedom of thought, freedom of assembly and association, and freedom of movement. These are the obligatory political rights and freedoms of Western societies. But, in the context of Chinese rule in Tibet, freedom to speak out against the government is the focal point of democracy:

Under the broad framework provided by the democratic constitution, people with different individual views of what course of action to follow, by

[10] *rgya che'i mi mang gi dgos 'don 'dod babs gtso bor bstun dgos pa'i spyi mos kyi lugs srol.*
[11] See Avedon (1984): 106–9, for an account of early experiments with democracy and the conditions surrounding the writing of the original draft constitution for a democratic Tibet by the Dalai Lama and the government-in-exile following their arrival in India. See also the *Constitution of Tibet* (1963).

exercising their democratic prerogatives, will also be able to practise what they think without need of fear, hypocrisy, or concealment.

The Drepung manifesto does not discuss a political role for either the Dalai Lama or his traditionally-appointed cabinet, the Kashag — though it does use the Tibetan government in India as an example of representative government. Most important, the Drepung manifesto explicitly rejects the "old society" (*spyi tshogs rnying pa*), and insists that an independent democratic Tibet will mark a break, politically and socially, with the past:

Having completely eradicated the practices of the old society with all its faults, the future Tibet will not resemble our former condition and be a restoration of serfdom or be like the so-called "old system" of rule by a succession of feudal masters or monastic estates.

In taking up the question of the "old society" in detail — rejecting the restoration of "serfdom" (*shing bran gyi lam lugs*) and the "old system" of feudal succession and monastic estates (*bkas bkod brgyud 'dzin pa*) — the Drepung monks are responding to the principal line of argument taken by the cadres in political meetings, who insist that the "splittists" want to restore "feudalism". The undesirability of the old society is a point that the monks willingly concede. The terminology they use to describe the old society is the same as that used by the Party cadres themselves. But as the monks see it, the Chinese political system is now the main obstacle to social progress. Thus they focus on the political rights and freedoms which they understand to be characteristic of contemporary democratic societies, but which Chinese rule in Tibet denies.

The monks are also accused at political meetings of wanting to restore the political privileges of the monasteries ("lamaism" in the Chinese lexicon). Significantly, the Drepung manifesto excludes any special political role for the monks or the monasteries in an independent democratic Tibet. It is religiously undogmatic, and Buddhism is characterized as a set of moral principles compatible with democracy and human rights. From Buddhism also comes a commitment to non-violence and respect for the integrity of the individual. The manifesto insists that it is Buddhism that "accords with the general practice of the contemporary world" (*deng dus 'dzam gling spyi srol dang mthun pa*), not communism. At the heart of the text is the traditional legitimizing formula of Tibetan politics — "religion and politics combined" (*chos srid gnyis ldan*). But this formula is now used to establish the political legitimacy of democracy. Thus the Drepung manifesto speaks of "democracy embodying religious and secular principles" (*chos srid gnyis ldan gyi dmangs gtso*).

As the manifesto illustrates, Tibetans have the confidence to borrow words and phrases from the Chinese political lexicon and use them against the Chinese. One poster distributed in Lhasa in the autumn of 1988 asserts: "However much a few communist Chinese reactionaries try, using various lies and deceits, to incorporate Tibet into their territory, all Tibetans, both inside and outside Tibet, will never accept it." [12] Here it is the Chinese who are described as the "reactionaries" (*log spyod pa*) — reversing the standard Chinese formula. Similarly, Tibetans now apply the term "imperialism" (*btsan rgyal ring lugs*), originally used by the Chinese in propaganda campaigns to attack the West, to the Chinese themselves. "Communist Chinese imperialist" (*btsan rgyal rgya dmar*) has become a standard phrase in Tibetan political literature.

Human rights

Posters and pamphlets appearing around Lhasa from the autumn of 1988 onwards increasingly stress the theme of "human rights" (*'gro ba mi'i thob thang*). Tibetans described their protests not merely as a struggle for democracy and independence, but as a fight for human rights. The continuing flow of information from the outside world on democracy, human rights, and other national struggles has provided Tibetans with an alternative point of reference, and an alternative vocabulary, to the Chinese. Thus they have come to regard their own struggle against Chinese rule in Tibet as representative of a contemporary worldwide movement. For instance, in the days preceding the demonstration on 10 December 1988, International Human Rights Day, a political leaflet circulated informing the people of Lhasa: "Today is a day commemorating the struggle for human rights. Therefore, along with appealing to the United Nations and friendly countries in order to restore our just rights, we Tibetans would like to commemorate this day.[13]

---

[12] . . . *rgya dmar gyi log spyod pa 'ga' zhig gis g.yo sgyu dang rdzun 'gebs sna tshogs kyis kho thso'i mnga' khongs su 'jug gang thub byed dang byed bzhin pa 'di nga tsho gzhis byes bod mi kun gyis gtan nas khas len gyi ma red.*

[13] *de ring ni 'gro ba mi'i thob thang la rtsod len byed pa'i dran gso'i nyin mo zhig yin/ der rten nga tsho bod mi rnams nas rang re'i bden pa'i thob thang slar gso yong ched 'dzam gling rgyal tshogs dang de bzhin mthun phyogs yul khag rnams re 'bod dang bcas te dran gso bya rgyu yin.*

These leaflets, letters, and posters, crudely reproduced by wood-block or handprinted mimeo, were signed by groups giving themselves a variety of names — "The Victorious Three Realms" (*khams gsum dbang 'dus*), "Association of Tibetan People of the Three Provinces" (*chol gsum bod mi'i mthun tshog*), "The Independence Uprising Organi-zation" (*rang btsan sger langs tshogs pa*), and frequently just "From the Tibetan People" (*bod mi mang nas*). The names often changed, reflecting a loose-knit network of dissidents forming a cross-section of Tibetan society — from shopkeepers in the Barkhor to monks and nuns, office-workers, students, and Chinese-educated cadres. The posters were often put up by women making their rounds of the Barkhor in the early morning. The penalty for being caught producing or distributing this literature is always imprisonment.

It is not surprising that Tibetans have been able to utilize ideas of democracy and human rights to endorse demands for independence. They do not see any contradiction between their own national and cultural aspirations and political modernization. A wall poster that appeared around Lhasa on the morning of 10 December included the following slogans:

Long live the long-established country!
Long live the succession of glorious religious kings!
Long live the Dalai Lama!
Long live the great unity of the people of the whole nation!
Long live the restoration of Tibetan independence!
Long live the new constitution of democratic freedom!
Remember the courage of our brave departed heroes!
Remember the human rights of the United Nations!

Alongside invocations of Tibetan history and culture, and reminders of past struggles, are appeals for human rights and democracy. Tibetans perceive a relationship between the suppression of their history and culture and the suppression of human rights. Human rights in this sense are conceived as a condition of collective freedom rather than as abstract individual liberties. Tibetan terms for both "freedom" (*rang dbang*) and "independence" (*rang btsan*) can be glossed as "self-rule" or "self-determination" — literally, control over one's own destiny.

The Tibetan conception of human rights is *substantive* rather than *formal*. When asked to discuss the meaning of human rights, Tibetans will detail concrete instances of suffering — beatings, arrests, torture, the mistreatment of monks and nuns, restrictions on the practice of religion, economic discrimination, and political powerlessness. These are seen not so much as violations of specific individual rights, but rather as symptomatic and illustrative of a general condition in which the humanity of Tibetans goes unacknowledged.

Closely associated with human rights in Tibetan thinking is the idea of "truth" (*bden pa*) — which in Tibetan also conveys the meaning of "justice." Tibetans speak of the "truth" (or "justice") of their cause, their "true rights" (*bden pa'i thob thang*), and their "true history" (*bden pa'i lo rgyus*), to which the Chinese have denied them access. They see "truth" as a weapon in the fight against Chinese rule. The Drepung manifesto opens by calling on Tibetans to struggle against the "foreign Chinese invaders" with a determination based on the "force of established truth" (*bsgrub bya bden pa yin pa'i rang bzhin gyi nus shugs*). A younger generation of Tibetans equates its recovery of Tibetan history, despite Chinese efforts at its suppression, with the eventual success of its cause. The political leaflet circulated before 10 December proclaims: "Today, recounting even a brief history will make the communist Chinese invaders feel ashamed."

The Tibetan commitment to non-violence largely hinges on this faith in the power of truth. It is how Tibetans reply to Chinese assertions at political meetings that Tibetan independence is impossible because they have no army and cannot defeat the Chinese militarily. In the words of a young Drepung monk:

The best way and the only way is to talk using the power of truth, otherwise we can't fight them. Even if we have the power to fight them, we won't do that. Instead we will fight with the truth.

It has been no small task for a younger generation of Tibetans, educated under the Chinese, to reconstruct an alternative to the official Chinese version of Tibetan history. An important genre of clandestine political literature consists of handwritten synopses of Tibetan history, detailing historical events and examining the relationship between Tibet and China. Sources include various Tibetan-language Chinese publications (which are scrutinized for contradictions), smuggled literature from Nepal and India, and, most important, Shakabpa's political history of Tibet, which is perhaps the most treasured reference work in the country and circulates underground among Tibetan intellectuals in government offices, the university, and the monasteries.[14]

---

[14] The Tibetan text has been published in Dharamsala, India. A number of copies have been smuggled into Tibet. For the English version see Shakabpa (1967).

Ironically, the political meetings succeeded in their expressed aim, raising political consciousness among Tibetans, though not in the way the political cadres intended. The result has been to take long-simmering Tibetan hostility to Chinese rule and sharpen it by identifying Tibetan demands for independence and the return of the Dalai Lama with modern political ideas like democracy and human rights. This is perhaps all the more surprising because it has occurred in the middle of a brutal campaign to suppress dissent. The level of real understanding may vary considerably throughout the population, but the majority of Tibetans at least know the words for democracy and human rights, and associate these terms with the Dalai Lama and Tibetan independence. If nothing else, democracy and human rights mark for Tibetans the limits of Chinese ideology and propaganda.

Continuing tension

The demonstration anticipated for 1 October 1988 had not taken place. However, Tibetans in Lhasa spoke of it as being postponed, not cancelled. The Chinese authorities also anticipated further demonstrations. One Tibetan working in the regional government reported that the security forces had a list of likely dates for demonstrations, largely corresponding with days for religious observances. One date was 23 November, a day associated with the protector-goddess Palden Lhamo (*dpal ldan lha mo dus chen*), the patron deity of Lhasa and a fierce deity very much connected with the cause of Tibetan independence and the protection of Tibet from foreign invaders. Early on the morning of 23 November, posters with independence slogans had appeared around the Barkhor. From 10.30 a.m. onwards, PAP units of ten soldiers each continuously patrolled the Barkhor, one after another, armed with rifles and pistols and carrying walkie-talkies.

No demonstration took place that day — nor did the monks at the monasteries around Lhasa report that a demonstration was planned. The mere potential for demonstrations was enough to force the Chinese authorities to maintain a highly visible and ugly presence around the Barkhor. The next day, 24 November, groups of uniformed PSB officers paraded around the Barkhor with pistols drawn. This intensified activity by security forces continued through to 27 November, with armed roadblocks on all the roads leading into Lhasa.

On 3 December, the evening of the Butter Lamp festival, an important religious holiday marking the anniversary of the death of Tsongkhapa in 1419, more than 1,000 Tibetans gathered in the square

before the Jokhang to chant the "Prayer of Truth" (*bden smon*), a prayer
with an explicit political message. It was composed in exile in 1960
by the present Dalai Lama, and refers to the "ruthless evil conquest"
(*brtse med du ngan dgus 'joms pa*) of Tibet by "the forces of the Chinese
barbarians" (*nag phyogs kla klo'i dpung*), and calls for "complete freedom
for the whole of Tibet" (*yongs rdzogs bod ljongs rang dbang gtsand ma*).
Most Tibetans know the prayer by heart. The recitation was led by
monks from the Jokhang standing on the balcony of the temple
overlooking the square. Though police circulated in the crowd, no
attempt was made to break up the gathering, which appeared on the
surface to be a religious event — similar in this regard to the prayer
gathering in the Sungchöra on 27 September.

The poster campaign that continued throughout the autumn of 1988,
kept up by Lhasa residents working in support of the demonstrating
monks and nuns, was not without its costs. A thirty-two-year-old
Tibetan employee of the Bank of China, Lhakpa Tsering, was arrested
on 28 September for putting up posters around the Barkhor and
immediately taken back to his office for a political meeting where he
was denounced in front of his fellow workers as a "reactionary".

Meanwhile the political meetings in the neighbourhood committees
continued. Political workers seemed particularly concerned with the
support offered by Lhasa residents to the protesting monks and nuns.
According to one Tibetan who attended a meeting of the Banakshöl
neighbourhood committee on 8 September, residents were asked to
discuss the problem posed by monks arrested for participating in
demonstrations:

Many monks have been in demonstrations and have been arrested. Except for
a few, they have all been released. What is your proposal to deal with those
who have been released and those who are still in prison? Discuss among
yourselves and decide. We want a decision by the next meeting. We will meet
every Thursday until you are told otherwise.

Lhasa residents also believed that the Chinese administration was
attempting to isolate the residents of the city, punishing them for
the protests. They claimed that new PSB officers were being recruited
from the countryside in an effort to pit rural against urban Tibetans.
The Chinese administration also announced that the policy of financial compensation and reparations for losses suffered during the
Cultural Revolution, begun in the early 1980s, would be abolished
for Lhasa residents, though it would continue for Tibetans living in
the countryside.

The prospect of negotiations with the Dalai Lama

In November 1988 Yan Mingfu, head of the United Front Work Department of the CPC, made an inspection tour of Tibet, during which he continually emphasized the strategy of the United Front for securing the loyalty of Tibetans:

It is necessary to unite patriotic personages in the upper circles, expand the united front, and mobilize all positive factors in working for the development and progress of Tibet. Tibetans in the upper religious circles have withstood tests in their long-term cooperation with the CPC. It is necessary to give full play to the role of workers, youth, and women's mass organizations, as well as political consultative committees and Buddhist associations, in the patriotic united front.[15]

Echoing the Panchen Lama's comments following the first demonstrations in 1987, Yan Mingfu also stressed the need for continuing economic development in Tibet, blaming "mistakes" resulting from "leftist influences" for Tibetan discontent. Yan Mingfu's comments contrast sharply with the instructions given by Qiao Shi during his July inspection tour, calling for closer supervision of the masses, the strengthening of the Party, and intensified ideological work.[16]

The positions of Yan Mingfu and Qiao Shi reflect opposing strategies of rival factions within the Chinese leadership for dealing with the problem of Tibet. At the time of Yan Mingfu's inspection tour, a key element in the United Front strategy for Tibet was the announcement that Beijing was willing to negotiate with the Dalai Lama. Communication preparing for these negotiations was handled from the Chinese side by Yan Mingfu personally. A precondition for the negotiations had been that the Dalai Lama renounce any claim to independence for Tibet. In a speech to the European Parliament in Strasbourg on 15 June 1988, the Dalai Lama had offered to abandon the goal of complete independence for Tibet in return for self-government in the region. This proposal was publicly rejected by the Chinese government as nothing less than "disguised independence".

Nevertheless, in late September Beijing announced its willingness to meet a negotiating team appointed by the Dalai Lama for talks in Geneva. Further progress stalled over Chinese dissatisfaction with the

---

[15] Beijing Xinhua Domestic Service in Chinese, 9 November 1988, in *FBIS*, 14 November 1988: 22.

[16] Lhasa Tibet Regional Service in Mandarin, 14 July 1988, in *FBIS*, 14 July 1988: 17–18.

composition of the Dalai Lama's team, which included members of the cabinet of the government-in-exile, the Kashag, as well as a Western legal adviser.

Tibetans in Lhasa were familiar with the Strasbourg proposal, and there was considerable discussion over whether it was desirable to abandon the demand for independence. Tibetans were torn between trust in the Dalai Lama and willingness to acquiesce in his judgement, on the one hand, and their obvious distrust of Chinese intentions, on the other. The principal motivation for the Strasbourg proposal, according to the Dalai Lama, was halting the influx of Chinese settlers to Tibet, a problem keenly felt by Tibetans in Lhasa, where Chinese outnumber them and recent Chinese migrants have seized many of the economic opportunities that have opened up as a result of the reforms during the 1980s. However, the prospect of giving up the goal of complete independence was generally viewed with suspicion in Lhasa, where the Chinese government's announcement of its willingness to negotiate with the Dalai Lama was seen as a propaganda ploy to quell the demonstrations. Brief references to the prospect of negotiations appeared in the *Tibet Daily* during the autumn of 1988. However, the forthcoming negotiations were also used at political meetings in neighbourhood committees and work units to discourage further demonstrations. Tibetans were told that it was the Dalai Lama's wish that they should not demonstrate now that negotiations were pending.

Expecting the Chinese government to negotiate real autonomy for Tibet may have been unrealistic from the start, since the political enfranchisement of forces hostile to the Party is too great a risk. Real autonomy implies dismantling Party rule in Tibet, which Tibetans see as synonymous with Chinese rule. The experience of a year of protest, along with Chinese reprisals, had sensitized Tibetans to the issues of Party control and the denial of political rights. The renewed attempts at political education and the revival of ideology had become the focus of Tibetan discontent.

But what the Chinese government expected from the negotiations was always clear. In the short term, they demanded that the Dalai Lama and the government-in-exile intervene to halt the continuing nationalist demonstrations inside Tibet. They hoped that in the long term his return and that of other Tibetan leaders from exile could be used to defuse the political situation, while, in keeping with the strategy of the United Front, their loyalty could be secured through the promise of special privileges and economic benefits.

A survey of opinions

The Chinese administration was also developing other tactics to control the political situation in Tibet. In September 1988 an opinion survey was launched in Tibet to study the political attitudes of Tibetans. It was conducted jointly by the Institute of Sociology of Beijing University and the China Tibetology Research Centre in Lhasa. The survey instrument (dated 28 June 1988) is entitled "A Questionnaire for Investigating Socio-Economic Improvement of Tibet."[17] The official announcement of the survey was made in November 1988 during the visit to Tibet by Yan Mingfu.[18] The project was described as a survey of "nationalities issues in Tibet" which would provide "important reference for studies on Tibet's issues at the top level of the CPC."

Residents of Lhasa have described the conditions under which the research was carried out. The questionnaire was designed to be administered face-to-face inside the informant's household. No attempt was made to preserve the anonymity of the informants, whose names were recorded. The researchers from Beijing were accompanied by locally-provided translators — in fact local political workers — and the interviews were organized through the Lhasa neighbourhood committees. At first some 800 "middle-class" households were to be surveyed, but because of the size of the survey, it was impossible for all the interviews to be conducted by the researchers and many of the interviews were therefore conducted entirely by the political workers.

Tibetans in Lhasa expressed considerable fear that the purpose of the survey was to identify dissidents for future arrest and punishment. For instance, Section 8 of the questionnaire, "About Religion", asks "How do you view the demonstration in the vicinity of the Jokhang on 5 March by the monks and their violence against the government?" (no. 1), and "Do you retain the hope that the Dalai Lama will become the leader of the government of Tibet?" (no. 2). Question no. 5 asks "What kind of relationship do you hope for between Tibet and the central

---

[17] *Bod kyi spyi tshogs dpal 'byor gong phel gtong phyogs skor gyi rtag spyad zhu gyi 'dri shog.* Preparations for this research project, to be carried out by a team of recently returned doctoral recipients from American universities, were first reported by Tom Grunfeld following a visit to China and Tibet in the summer of 1987. See Grunfeld (1988). My copy of the survey instrument was provided by Lhasa Tibetans with contacts in the Chinese administration in September 1988.

[18] Hong Kong Ming Pao, 3 November 1988, p. 8, in *FBIS*, 7 November 1988: 35.

government?", and offers three possible answers: "complete independence", "greater autonomy", and "continuing the present arrangement".

Section 7 of the questionnaire asks about government cadres (*las byed
pa*). One question (no. 3) asks whether Chinese cadres should be
withdrawn from Tibet. Another (no. 4) asks about the benefits and bad
points of Chinese cadres with whom Tibetans have had contact. Section
6, on religion, investigates the extent of participation in religious practice, attitudes toward monks and monasteries, and satisfaction with
government religious policy. The bulk of the questionnaire contains
questions on schooling, housing, employment, and travel. It has the
appearance of a Western-style social science research project, providing
data suitable for statistical analysis.

The data from the survey could enable the researchers to draw conclu-
sions about the distribution of religious and political attitudes within
the Tibetan population, and their correlation with socio-economic
status. That the survey was publicly announced by Yan Mingfu, and
thus sponsored by the United Front Work Department of the Party,
suggests that its purpose was to vindicate current policies of development and reform, and demonstrate the relative satisfaction of the
Tibetan population.

However, Tibetans in Lhasa compared the socio-economic survey
with similar ones conducted in the 1950s, shortly before collectivization
of the economy under the "democratic reforms". At that time political
workers assigned Tibetans to "classes" (*gral rim*) on the basis of Marxist
criteria. "Class enemies" were subsequently singled out for expropria-
tion and punishment. Tibetans recognized the same potential for singling out individuals for persecution in the 1988 survey and were thus
suspicious of Chinese motives. Nevertheless, large numbers of Tibetans
were reported to be answering the questions truthfully — indicating
their desire for an independent Tibet, support for the Dalai Lama, and
their belief that economic development in Tibet was mainly of benefit
to the Chinese. They believed that demonstrating to the Chinese
widespread support for the Dalai Lama and Tibetan independence at
this time would be effective in changing the situation in Tibet.[19]

---

[19] An incident reported in November 1989, following the declaration of martial
law, indicates the potential for abuse in the idea of an opinion survey. At the time,
Tibetans who had had contact with the exile community in India were asked a similar
collection of questions, including questions about Tibetan independence and recent protest. The cadres from Public Security who carried out the interviews insisted: "There
is no need to worry, this is just an opinion survey."

International Human Rights Day — 10 December 1988

In the last weeks of November 1988, news circulated among Tibetans in Lhasa of the forthcoming International Human Rights Day, 10 December. This date, celebrating the fortieth anniversary of the United Nations Universal Declaration of Human Rights, was officially acknowledged by the Chinese government for the first time in 1988. The date has no traditional significance for Tibetans, and there is no indication that Tibetans inside Tibet were aware of its significance before 1988. The date had prompted no attempts to demonstrate the previous year; Tibetans learned of the significance of International Human Rights Day from the outside world — partly from the Chinese, who publicized the event throughout China, and partly from the Tibetan community in India.

The suitability of the date for a protest demonstration was thus determined by perceptions of its international importance. Demonstrating on this day served two purposes. First, it gave evidence of the continuing desire of Tibetans to protest against Chinese rule in Tibet. Secondly, the demonstration was staged with an international audience in mind and with a clear intention to embarrass the Chinese government. It was an act of defiance in the face of attempts by the Chinese administration to use the prospect of negotiations to quell protest. At a time when political negotiations with the Dalai Lama were still anticipated, the demonstration reiterated the Tibetan commitment to independence, while explicitly linking Tibetan nationalist protest with international issues of democracy and human rights.

The demonstration on 10 December required considerable coordination between the monks and nuns who led the protest and the support network of lay residents of Lhasa. It also involved coordination between the three big monasteries around Lhasa and several of the nunneries. The planning for it was on the largest scale of any of the demonstrations in Lhasa. Small meetings of supporters were held throughout the Tibetan quarter of Lhasa. Posters and leaflets were prepared several days in advance, and the posters were pasted on walls throughout the Tibetan part of Lhasa on the evening of the 9th and early on the morning of the 10th.

The Chinese authorities also expected a demonstration on 10 December. A convoy of twenty trucks carrying about 500 PAP soldiers drove through Lhasa on the night of 9 December. Earlier that night Tibetans were told in neighbourhood committee meetings that if they demonstrated they would be "gunned down in the streets". Tibetan workers in government offices were informed that they would not be allowed to go home after work on the afternoon of 10 December. Tibetan children were also to be kept in school in the afternoon. Foreigners in Tibet at the time discovered in the two weeks leading up to 10 December that they could not obtain extensions to their tourist visas. Public Security made it clear that they wanted foreigners out of Lhasa by that date.

A Sera monk who was shot and seriously injured during the demonstration described, while recovering in hiding, how he became involved in the demonstration on the 10th:

I came to know about it on 8 or 9 December. Tibetans in Lhasa are always trying to gather news from around the world. We heard that 10 December was the fortieth anniversary of International Human Rights Day. This reminded us of our country. To encourage our people and to commemorate this day, we decided to hold a peaceful demonstration. On the evening of the 9th I came from Sera, and stayed that evening in Lhasa. Three or four of us went that evening to stick posters on the walls. We did not come across much danger, but the Barkhor was already filled with Chinese soldiers, who were inspecting everywhere. We continued sticking the posters on the walls, taking no notice of the soldiers. Then the next day, early in the morning, we went to the Barkhor two or three times to see how our posters were and what the Chinese were doing. In the Barkhor, there were many Chinese milling around. The soldiers were going in the anti-clockwise direction. We had planned to hold our peaceful demonstration at 11 or 12 in the morning.

The Sera monks decided that it would be impossible to assemble near the Jokhang for a demonstration. Instead, they agreed to assemble in front of Ramoche temple, on the north side of Dekyi Sharlam, across from the vegetable market and several hundred metres from the north entrance to the Barkhor. Here, the Sera monk describes how they changed the plans for the demonstration:

On the morning of 10 December we were ready for the demonstration, but there were too many Chinese soldiers around. After a careful look around the Barkhor, we discussed where to start the demonstration. There was no possibility for the Barkhor. So we decided to go to Ramoche, where a monk called Tsering was to carry the flag and lead the demonstration. So we went to Tshepag Lhakhang [a temple within the Ramoche compound] to meet Tsering. He was all alone there. He said, "No one came, what should we do now?" We were thinking of having a meal, but we could not eat. We went to the Jokhang at once to call the others, leaving Tsering behind. In front of the Jokhang there were monks from Drepung, Sera, and Ganden, and many other Tibetans. We told them that Tsering was waiting at Tshepag Lhakhang. Then gradually all went towards Ramoche. There were nuns from Ani Tsangkhung [a nunnery east of the Barkhor] and Garu Gompa. Some of us went round the Barkhor to tell the Tibetans not to stay there. We told them that the Chinese soldiers were already in the Barkhor and that it was not possible to hold a demonstration there. The Chinese were showing the monks their guns and the monks were shouting back at the Chinese. I asked them to go to Ramoche, and they all set off there.

Most of the monks and nuns were dressed in lay clothes. They assembled in double file along the side-street running past Ramoche temple. At about 11 a.m. a procession of thirty or forty monks and nuns marched across Dekyi Sharlam and into the vegetable market. A crowd of Tibetans followed 20 or 30 metres behind the monks and nuns, as much because of their concern over what might happen next as out of support for the demonstrators. When they reached the entrance to the northwest corner of the Barkhor the monks and nuns split into two groups. One group set off the long way around the Barkhor, led by four Sera monks who had unfurled a second flag, each holding a corner in their hands, and the other turned anti-clockwise into the Barkhor and headed straight for the Jokhang, hoping to get there before being intercepted by security forces.

A 30-year-old Tibetan layman who works near the Barkhor describes what he saw from his place in the procession:

Half of the demonstrators went eastward around the Barkhor. The other group, which I was in, followed the flag to the west side, the anti-clockwise direction. It was not possible to reach the Jokhang going clockwise, since the Barkhor was full of soldiers. So we had to go in the anti-clockwise direction. When we were coming along the west side of the Barkhor, I saw a couple holding each other and crying. The husband was saying to his wife to stay home and look after the children, and that he would join the demonstration. Then the husband came with us. I saw this with my own eyes. I felt very sad to see the couple, but at the same time I felt more determined not being married. So I joined the demonstration and shouted even louder.

When we went a little further and turned the corner, the Chinese were coming toward us with their guns. We thought we would not be able to reach the Jokhang, so we ran faster. As soon as we came in front of the Jokhang, the Chinese didn't hesitate and started shooting at us with automatic weapons. They came running toward us shooting and firing tear gas, which hurt our eyes and made it difficult for us to see. They also shot at many old

Tibetans who were doing khorra around the Barkhor. We were left with no choice but to run away.

Each one of us tried to escape in every direction. Some of us carried away the seriously injured monks. The less seriously injured had to be left for the Chinese. There was a truck into which the Chinese were throwing nuns and many others like dead weights. They took them away. While I was running away, I heard a woman calling for help for a Sera monk who had been shot. I turned back and ran quickly to the monk, then dragged him away. The monk was shot through the shoulder. It was not possible to stay there, as the Chinese were shooting at us from every direction.

The Chinese killed and beat as many Tibetans as they could. Some of the monks were arrested. I saw ten or fifteen Chinese beating a monk with their guns and kicking him. Chinese were beating Tibetans with whatever they had to hand. Just near the medical centre there was a large crowd of Tibetans shouting that the Chinese are beating our people. The Chinese were threatening the Tibetans, telling them to go away or they would shoot.

The Lhasa PSB made an effort to prevent Westerners from witnessing the demonstration on 10 December. The management of the Tibetan-run hotels in Lhasa had been instructed the night before to keep them indoors, but in spite of that, expecting something to happen, a number of them managed to slip out of their hotels and witness the events in the square. One young American describes what he saw from a vantage-point directly in front of the Jokhang:

As the flag moved to the Jokhang square there were many demonstrations of support from the Tibetans lining the Barkhor. We heard cheers and saw women crying. Towards the foreigners people repeatedly gave two hand signals: "thumbs up" and "take pictures". The crowd following the flag grew as people along the Barkhor fell in behind the bearers. By the time the flag was in front of the Jokhang temple, there were at least two hundred people within fifteen meters of the flag. The demonstrators were completely non-violent — chanting, not carrying any kinds of weapons or throwing rocks.

The police moved towards the demonstrators, and first tried to confront them on the north side of the temple entrance, but they then back-tracked around the square structure in the middle and came out on the south side. A captain appeared waving a pistol, and motioned ten or fifteen troops into line beside him, talking to his troops and not to the demonstrators ahead of him. Blocked by the police line, the flag-bearers slowed and virtually came to a halt. There were about 3 meters separating the two groups. The marchers behind could only slow down and stop, which caused the first rank behind the flag to be very tightly packed. The captain levelled his pistol, aimed, and fired, and there was a volley from his troops. There were no warning shots, and no one gave any warning with gestures or by word of mouth. The time between the captain appearing and the volley being fired was no more than fifteen or possibly only ten seconds, so there was little chance for people to flee for safety anyway.

The demonstrators fled, most going back along the Barkhor, others going out into the square. Shooting continued as people fled — for about fifteen or twenty seconds. The shots came from a variety of weapons: pistols, rifles of various calibres, and possibly automatic fire as well.

The demonstrators had no doubt that morning that they would be killed if they appeared in front of the Jokhang. The security forces were concentrated around it precisely to prevent Tibetans from reclaiming as their own this territory, which in their terms was sacred. While preparing during the days before the demonstration, monks and nuns made it very clear in conversation that they were willing to die, and saw their protest as a meritorious act according to the tenets of Buddhism; also that being unmarried made it possible for them to take this step without regrets. As the above account from the thirty-year-old lay Tibetan participant shows, this was the general view. The aim of the demonstrators to reach the square in front of the Jokhang temple whatever the cost, running all the faster as they saw the troops approaching, also suggests that the protest contained a dimension of religious self-sacrifice.

It was planned from the outset that the demonstration of 10 December should be completely non-violent. To the extent that Tibetans in Lhasa understood the significance of International Human Rights Day, they recognized that any protest staged under its auspices must necessarily be peaceful. Given the likely outcome of the protest if the authorities carried out their promise to shoot Tibetans down in the streets, the participants realized that they must be prepared to sacrifice themselves. The need for strict discipline was understood by lay Tibetans as well as monks and nuns. Such discipline is ultimately based on religious motives — in the language of Tibetan Buddhism it means willingness to sacrifice oneself for the "sake of all sentient beings". The lay demonstrator quoted above makes this clear:

The accusation by the Chinese that we threw stones or bottles at them is all lies. Before we had time to pick up stones, they were already shooting at us. Furthermore, we had planned a peaceful demonstration. On the way there we told each other not to throw stones at the Chinese. We even told the monks that no matter if the Chinese beat or killed us, we would not throw stones. We were demonstrating for the sake of all sentient beings. We did not even pick up stones, let alone throw them at the Chinese.

Aftermath

The Chinese government reported that one monk had been killed on 10 December and thirteen others injured as a result of police firing "warning shots" at "troublemakers" throwing "stones and liquor bottles".[20] None of the Western or Tibetan eyewitnesses reported seeing anything thrown at the police. Nor were there any warning shots. One of those injured was a Dutch woman, hit in the shoulder by a bullet while standing among a crowd of onlookers watching as the demonstrators passed.

It is difficult to know how many Tibetans were injured or killed, since many of the former were treated in hiding, fearing arrest if they appeared at hospitals. A twenty-nine-year-old Drepung monk, Ngawang Kunga, who led the procession that went anti-clockwise through the Barkhor and out into the square, was shot in the head and died instantly. His body was carried back to Ramoche temple, where crowds of Tibetans gathered to say prayers for him. One of the flag-bearers for the group that went clockwise, Kelsang Tsering, a twenty-nine-year-old Sera monk, died on 25 January in the People's Hospital. He had been shot by a police sniper from the roof of a building across from the southwest corner of the Jokhang as his procession came around the Barkhor toward the square. The wounded also included ordinary Tibetans who happened to be in the Barkhor at the time. One woman was hit by gunfire as she went to fetch a child from school. A Chinese woman, a beggar from Yunnan, was hospitalized with bullets in both legs.

Probably as many as twenty people were wounded, the majority ordinary people watching the demonstration from the street. The People's Armed Police had opened fire on a large crowd of onlookers at the exact moment when the flag-bearer from Drepung was shot in the head by the leader of the unit. This was the first time Chinese security forces had opened fire without provocation on a crowd of Tibetans. The precision of the operation shows that orders were in place long before the demonstrators arrived in the square. The plan to hold a demonstration on 10 December was no secret in Lhasa. It must have been a policy decision to fire on the demonstrators, made in Beijing and passed down through the military command. In fact, a Tibetan working within the Chinese administration reported a meeting of the

[20] Beijing Xinhua in English, 11 December 1988, in *FBIS*, 12 December 1988: 44.

regional CPPCC on 12 December, two days after the shooting, at which it was announced that "what had happened on 10 December had happened before and might happen again. In every case it will be dealt with the same way, the demonstrators will be shot. This is the policy of the central committee in Beijing."

One week later, on 18 December, more than sixty Tibetan students from the Central Nationalities Institute in Beijing demonstrated in Tiananmen Square to protest at the shooting in Lhasa of unarmed demonstrators. These students are the decisive group in terms of Party strategy for maintaining control in Tibet; they are expected to return to Tibet after completing their education to staff the Chinese administration there. The demonstration by Tibetan students as far away as Beijing echoed the growing support by young Tibetan cadres for the protest initiated by the monks and nuns. They were in no position to speak openly of independence, but they shared the general alienation of Tibetans from the Chinese administration.

On 30 December, 300 students and teachers from Tibet University openly paraded past the Potala through the centre of Lhasa to the university. The demonstration had the tacit approval of the authorities, and the security forces lining the street did not interfere (though videotapes were made of the demonstrators). Banners carried by the marchers demanded the reinstatement of Tibetan as the official language of the region, as well as more respect for Tibetan religion and culture. Other banners called for disarming Chinese security forces in Tibet and condemned the killing of unarmed demonstrators on 10 December. However, there was no display of the symbols of Tibetan independence. The demonstrators did not carry the banned Tibetan national flag or shout independence slogans. The path that the demonstrators selected avoided the Barkhor and the Jokhang temple, site of independence protest by the monks and nuns. Instead, the demonstrators went from the Potala past the compound of the TAR regional government on their way to the university.

This demonstration conformed to the criteria for a limited protest addressed to the Chinese government, implicitly acknowledging the legitimacy of Chinese rule in Tibet. The authorities may have tolerated this demonstration in an effort to channel protest in a politically acceptable direction. The potential still remained for the demonstration to get out of control, and the security forces tried to prevent foreigners in Lhasa from witnessing it. There was an incident when two Americans and a German who were photographing the procession were seized by

PSB officers. Some of the demonstrators then attacked and beat up five of the police officers. The three foreigners were forced into a jeep and taken to PSB headquarters for questioning. Their film was confiscated and one of them reported that he was struck by the PSB officers and had a gun held to his head.

Following the demonstration on 10 December the campaign against splittism intensified. The Chinese administration announced on 16 December the methods to be employed in "conducting wider patriotic education for upholding a unified motherland":

First, wide publicity is given to regulations released by the Lhasa Public Security Bureau, explaining to the masses that provoking riots and advocating independence for Tibet are against the regulations and that serious lawbreakers will be punished by the law. Second, different methods are adopted for different types of units in a bid to carry out the education in depth. Third, in carrying out the education, stress is put on the small number of the masses who were fooled and spoke or did something wrong in the previous riots but were still unconscious of what they did and said.[21]

In practice this meant that Tibetans were required to give public testimonies of loyalty in political meetings in neighbourhood committees and work units. Those who had been at the demonstrations were required to make public confessions.

The campaign against splittism was also extended into middle and primary schools throughout Lhasa. Students in some Lhasa middle schools were asked to fill out questionnaires similar to the opinion survey of Lhasa residents asking their views on the Dalai Lama and Tibetan independence. The Lhasa City Education Department described some of the methods it had adopted:

Taking advantage of blackboard, newspaper, broadcasting and routine meetings of a class, lectures on patriotic education through historical facts are given to increase the ability of students to distinguish right from wrong by themselves and to guide students to speak their views on the riots that have occurred in Lhasa. Many students explained with their historical knowledge why Tibet is an inalienable part of the motherland, why Tibet cannot be separable from the embrace of the homeland, and why advocating independence is against historical development.[22]

---

[21] Lhasa Tibet Regional Service in Mandarin, 16 December 1988, in *FBIS*, 19 December 1988: 60.

[22] *Ibid.*

The extension of the campaign into the schools introduced an added dimension of intimidation. Not only were parents to be held accountable for the political ideas of their children, but school children were to be used as a means of maintaining surveillance and control over their families.

Tibetans in Lhasa remembered the technique of turning children against their families from earlier political campaigns. On 3 January 1989, a notice was posted in the Lhasa no. 1 Middle School[23] and sent to parents. It called for the appointment of cadres to monitor the political activity of students and their families:

1. To strengthen political and spiritual education, every unit must appoint a leading cadre to be in charge of the political education of the students and tell them the truth about the struggle so that they can recognize the characteristics of the struggle and so hold to the correct direction.

2. The school will appoint a person as Student Liaison Cadre. Whenever anything unusual takes place, the students must not watch, gather round, support or take part. These are the rules. All units must reeducate their students about the situation. If anyone is found to have done something against the rules, no matter why, they will be expelled. In serious cases they will be reported to the Public Security Department for punishment. All parents of students must cooperate with their unit and with the school to educate their children.

3. Every unit should have a meeting with the students and the parents to study Party policy, the relevant history, the relevant law, and the announcement published by the Public Security Bureau. They must often analyze what has happened in their unit and they must hold to the correct direction. If anything happens they are to inform. Students' parents must co-operate with the Student Liaison Cadre and inform him of anything that happens during the holidays. Every unit must co-operate with the Student Liaison Cadre.

The notice went on to require every student to complete a project of "social investigation" during the school holiday:

The School's Political Study Department has already organized social investigation for students and we demand that each student complete one task of social investigation. The main subject of their social investigation must be to eulogise the thirty years' achievement since the Peaceful Liberation of Tibet of the

---

[23] The notice is written in Chinese. It is signed and carries an official seal, indicating that this is a directive from the Party Branch Political Study Department of the School Administration.

Communist Party's Nationality Policy and its Policy of Enriching the Nationalities. When the students return to school all the investigations will be checked and assessed, and compared to see which is the best.

The Lhasa no. 1 Middle School is an élite school for children of government cadres, both Chinese and Tibetan. The medium of instruction is Chinese, and the Tibetan students can look forward to careers in the Chinese administration. The school has been an important site for protest, and some of its students took part in the 30 December demonstration. On 8 December 1989, nine months after the declaration of martial law in Lhasa, it was announced that six students from the school had been arrested for the crime of spreading "counter-revolutionary propaganda".[24] All of them had been detained on 4 November. Five were also accused of forming a "counter-revolutionary organization" at the beginning of March, calling itself the "Tibet Youth Association". The students had made copies of the Tibetan flag and put up pro-independence posters throughout the city, as well as in the school. One of these students, Lhakpa Tsering, is reported to have died in Drapchi prison a year later, on 15 December 1990.[25]

The spread of protest into the schools and the university indicates how widely the demonstrations led by monks and nuns were supported by the beginning of 1989. The Chinese government was losing the battle of ideas despite its appeals for "unity and stability" in the name of prosperity and economic development. Tibetans were certainly fearful of the intensification of the political campaign after each demonstration, and of the evident retreat of the political cadres into ideological orthodoxy in the face of their own intransigence; but they remained confident that continuing protest would obtain results. Tibetans inside Tibet were aware of the renewed interest in their plight outside the country. Young Tibetans, in particular, believed that, contrary to Chinese claims, it was they who had history on their side.

The feelings of Tibetans in Lhasa at this time were perhaps best

---

[24] Lhasa Tibet Regional Service in Mandarin, 8 December 1989, in *FBIS*, 11 December 1989: 45.

[25] Lhakpa Tsering's death was reported to the Tibetan government-in-exile by refugees arriving in India. The circumstances surrounding his death in prison are mysterious. It was claimed that he had refused to comply with an order not to make statements critical of the Chinese to a delegation of Western diplomats who had been allowed to visit the prison to investigate conditions several weeks prior to his death.

expressed in this letter from Lobsang Tenzin to students at the university, written on 1 January 1989, and smuggled out of prison:

To all my schoolmates:

I felt so happy and excited that I could not sleep when I heard on the evening of the 30th of your demonstration. It is indeed a great source of happiness because Tibet is our beloved country and the progress or degeneration of the nation has a direct effect on each citizen. Moreover, we, the younger generation of Tibet, have a great responsibility to keep up our tradition and culture, and improve our country. We must preserve the rich tradition passed on to us by our parents. From the point of view of our university, we appreciate and accept the swift changes taking place these days. But we cannot support or agree with the oppressive conditions persisting in society.

It is our responsibility to eliminate these oppressive conditions which affect every individual in society. For example, we do not enjoy equal rights in Tibet. The Chinese use every trick to make us abandon using our rich Tibetan language and convert to Chinese. They have deprived us of the right of self-determination. Chinese propaganda claims that Tibetans are happy and contented under their rule. But do Tibetans have equal rights? Do Tibetans have the right to self-determination? Do Tibetans have the right to use their own language? There are many other equally inhuman things happening in Tibet. As everyone is aware of these things I shall not dwell on them any further.

I have tried to contain the smoke from the fire of anger burning fiercely inside my body. But this time, though I knew the Chinese would arrest me, I needed to express the strong feelings I have had for many years. This is why I took part in the demonstration on 5 March. As a result of my participation in the demonstration, I was injured, but I have recovered quickly. So please do not worry about us. Our trial will be starting soon at Lhasa People's Middle Court, and a decision will be reached.

Your demonstration has encouraged not only us, but all Tibetans. On behalf of over 6 million Tibetans, I would like to extend my sincere thanks to you all. All the prisoners who support the Tibetan cause, and my fellow inmate Gyaltsen Chöpel, send their sincere thanks to you all. To achieve our goal of restoring Tibetan independence, we request that you all continue with your efforts.

6

MARTIAL LAW AND AFTER

The first trial of independence activists since the beginning of unrest in 1987 took place in January 1989. On 19 January the Chinese government announced that twenty-seven Tibetans, some of them held for more than a year, had been tried and sentenced. Yulu Dawa Tsering received a sentence of ten years for "counter-revolutionary propaganda and agitation". Lobsang Tenzin was given a death sentence, suspended for two years, for his role in causing the death of the PAP soldier on 5 March 1988. Sonam Wangdu was sentenced to life imprisonment for the same offence. The two other Tibetans accused of murder, Tsering Dondrup and Gyaltsen Chöpel, were sentenced to ten and fifteen years' imprisonment respectively. Of the twenty-seven, the five sentenced to less than three years were all convicted of crimes connected with destruction of property during the riots (one of the prisoners sentenced to three years, Tsering Dorje, had been held since 1 October 1987 for setting fire to government vans). Those accused of merely taking part in demonstrations or committing acts of violence during riots generally received much shorter sentences than those accused of political crimes.

On 11 December 1988 the Chinese government had announced that Wu Jinghua was to be replaced as secretary of the CPC in Tibet by Hu Jintao, a young reformer and protégé of Zhao Ziyang. Though the official reasons for the replacement were given as the failing health of Wu Jinghua, there was much speculation that he had been dismissed for failing to contain the protest in Tibet. Wu was of the Yi nationality, and generally well spoken of by Tibetans — if only because he appeared in public wearing Tibetan clothes and was thought to be sympathetic to Tibetan aspirations. The administration of Tibet had in fact been in the hands of Mao Rubai, Party deputy secretary and a career administrator in Tibet for over twenty years, since shortly after the Mönlam demonstration the previous March. Thus the decision to open fire without warning on the unarmed demonstrators was made at a time when there was a vacuum in the local Party leadership.

The appointment by Beijing of Hu Jintao nevertheless signified a continuing commitment to the reform policies for Tibet. Hu Jintao arrived in Lhasa on 12 January and immediately announced a package of development plans for Tibet that included an increase in investment and emphasis on the expansion of the commodity economy. A spokesman for the State Nationalities Affairs Commission also announced on 22 December in Beijing that preparations were continuing for talks in Geneva with representatives of the Dalai Lama.

The Panchen Lama arrived in Tibet on 9 January. His visit, coinciding with the appointment of Hu Jintao as the regional Party leader, suggests that he had again been called on to try bringing Tibetans into line by emphasizing the benefits of cooperation with the reformers in the Party. In speeches to Party and government audiences the Panchen Lama continued to stress not just the need for the development of Tibet's economy, but the importance of promoting Tibetan language and culture;[1] also the need to correct "leftist" mistakes — a reference to the growing split in the leadership in Tibet over how to deal with Tibetan nationalism. In a major speech on 23 January at a meeting in Shigatse of Tibetan Party officials, which included Hu Jintao and representatives of the United Front Work Department, he declared that "although there had been development in Tibet since its liberation, this development had cost more dearly than its achievements. This mistake must never be repeated."[2] The speech may have been a last desperate plea by the Panchen Lama for understanding and tolerance of Tibetan aspirations. He called for greater regional autonomy for Tibet and a drive to recruit new Tibetan cadres on the basis of "talent" rather than "servility".

Tibetans working inside the Chinese administration reported that one of the purposes of the Panchen Lama's January visit to Tibet was

---

[1] The *Tibet Daily* on 9 November 1988 was devoted entirely to outlining in detail the new language policy for Tibet. The article carried the headline "Notice about the Announcement of the 'Detailed Policy for Implementing (On a Trial Basis) the Regulations for the Study, Use, and Development of the Tibetan Language in the Tibet Autonomous Region' " ("*bod rang skyong ljongs su bod kyi skad yig slob sbyong dang bed spyod gong 'phel gtong rgyu'i gtan 'bebs 'ga' zhig* [*tshod ltar lag bstar bya rgyu'i*] *don 'khyol byed phyogs kyi zhib srol" grems bsgrags bya rgyu'i skor gyi brda tho*). The language policy, which has the status of a statute enacted by the TAR government, calls for Tibetan to become the primary language of official communication in the region within two years. It also calls for the expansion of instruction in Tibetan within the school system, and the preparation of textbooks in Tibetan for subjects such as science, where to date Chinese has been the only available medium of instruction. The Panchen Lama was a leading spokesman for this policy.

[2] Beijing Zhongguo Xinwen She in Chinese, 24 January 1989, in *FBIS*, 25 January 1989: 55.

to convince the monasteries to hold Mönlam in 1989. The Panchen Lama insisted that the decision to do so was the responsibility of the monasteries themselves. In a meeting with monastery officials on 28 January, the TAR government announced that the Buddhist Association and the Democratic Management Committees of the monasteries were to be given the responsibility for the decision to hold Mönlam. At the meeting Dorje Tsering, head of the TAR government, insisted that "the government's policy remains unchanged towards the ceremony."[3] Considerable pressure was once again put on the monks to hold Mön-lam. But on 5 February it was made public that the Buddhist Association and the Democratic Management Committees of Ganden, Drepung, Sera, and the Jokhang had decided not to do so. In any case, monks at the large monasteries around Lhasa insisted that they would not participate in the festival under any conditions. In the end, the death of the Panchen Lama provided a reason for cancelling the festival.

The death of the Panchen Lama

The Panchen Lama died of a heart attack in Shigatse on 28 January. He remains an enigmatic figure. In March 1964, while still the Acting Chairman of the Preparatory Committee for the Autonomous Region of Tibet, he defied the Chinese by refusing to denounce the Dalai Lama. Instead, in a public speech before a crowd of thousands of Tibetans gathered next to the Jokhang temple, he called for his return and the restoration of Tibetan independence. For this act of defiance he was denounced as a reactionary, put on trial, and tortured. He vanished from public view for fourteen years.

Tibetans have continued to revere the Panchen Lama. The sincerity of his commitment to Tibetan interests has never been doubted. On the other hand, he has been associated with a strategy for development that has generated considerable resentment. This is best illustrated by the Kangchen organization, the Panchen Lama's own development corporation, started in 1987. Kangchen is a business corporation that oversees a number of enterprises, solicits and channels international development funds, and exports Tibetan products. One of its goals has been to raise money to rebuild monasteries throughout Tibet, though

---

[3] Beijing Xinhua in English, 29 January 1989, in *FBIS*, 30 January 1989: 67.

most of the money has gone to Tashilhunpo, the Panchen Lama's own monastery, and to the Shigatse area.

Kangchen is administered by men associated with the Panchen Lama who had been powerful in pre-1959 Tibet. Some of them have returned from exile to resume their role as "big men", brokers of power and privilege under Chinese sponsorship. This rehabilitated feudal leadership remains hostile to the Dalai Lama and the government-in-exile, and rejects the goal of Tibetan independence. The Chinese administration in Tibet regards Kangchen as a model for development. It offers a way of absorbing and investing economic surpluses, as well as foreign aid. At the same time, rebuilding the traditional system of patronage guarantees that political stability will not be threatened by rising economic power.

Kangchen shops in Lhasa have been repeatedly attacked in riots — not out of hostility toward the Panchen Lama, but because Tibetans recognize the "big man" scheme for what it is. On a smaller scale, a number of important families have been similarly rehabilitated and are in the process of building business enterprises under Chinese patronage. Some of these families also have ties with the refugee community in India and hold out the promise of a prosperous future for those who return. Retaining foreign business interests while channelling investments back into Tibet conforms to the overall policy of encouraging overseas Chinese to aid their kin in business ventures and to invest in the motherland.

Following the announcement of the Panchen Lama's death, rumours circulated in Lhasa that he had been murdered. Tibetan suspicions here reflect growing apprehension about Chinese intentions in a political milieu in which suggestions of conspiracy come easily. The Panchen Lama was frequently described as a prisoner of the Chinese — and of the men who surrounded him. His comments on the tragic costs of development in Tibet in his last public speech, just five days before his death, had led to speculation that once again he was preparing to defy the Chinese.

A leaflet circulated in Lhasa after the Panchen Lama's death by a group calling itself the "Independence Uprising Organization" (*rang btsan sger langs tshogs pa*) illustrates Tibetan feelings at the time:

This is what all Tibetans should know: Now our saviour, the all-knowing Panchen Rinpoche, has died while in the process of renovating and consecrating the tombs of previous Panchen Lamas. We should question why he died in such suspicious circumstances. All Tibetans should be saddened by this news. We are left only with prayers for his speedy rebirth. However, in the past it has been a tradition that people should be admitted to pay their respects in person to the body. Today they have not allowed us to visit the body. This is clearly because they are hiding their guilt. There are differences in the news that was broadcast on the Chinese radio, and on the Tibet Autonomous Region radio. As a last resort we Tibetans are sending a delegation to request the Chinese to allow people to see the body.

Tibetans also feared that with the Panchen Lama's death the Chinese commitment to promote Tibetan language and culture, and toleration for religion, would disappear. Certainly his death had upset the balance of political forces in Tibet; it was a loss to the reformers, and removed an important obstacle to a crackdown on all dissent in Tibet.

The Chinese government made the mourning and funeral for the Panchen Lama a major state event, widely covered on Chinese radio and television. The memorial service in the Great Hall of the People in Beijing on 15 February was attended by the national Party leadership, including Premier Li Peng, Party Secretary Zhao Ziyang, and President Yang Shangkun. A full-page article praising the strategy for reform in Tibet which the Panchen Lama embodied appeared in the *People's Daily* on 15 February, written by Yan Mingfu, head of the United Front Work Department of the Party, and he was described as a great Chinese patriot.

In a decision issued by the State Council on 31 January, signed by Premier Li Peng, it was announced that the search for the reincarnation of the Panchen Lama would be overseen by the Democratic Management Committee of Tashilhunpo.[4] Final approval of the selection would be made by the State Council. This stipulation drew an indignant response from the Dalai Lama's government-in-exile, who warned that political interference in the selection of the Panchen Lama would render the choice invalid. Without confirmation by the religious hierarchy, the successor would lack legitimacy in the eyes of ordinary Tibetans.

This Panchen Lama had been the tenth in the line. The Ninth Panchen Lama had died in exile in eastern Tibet in 1937, having fled there in 1923 following a dispute with the Lhasa government. Of several possible candidates for his successor, the one selected by officials of Tashilhunpo had been discovered near Xining, then under

---

[4] Lhasa Tibet Regional Service in Mandarin, 31 January 1989, in *FBIS*, 1 February 1989: 18.

Nationalist Chinese control; his designation as the new Panchen Lama had not been sanctioned by the Tibetan government in Lhasa. The new Panchen Lama was finally escorted to Lhasa in 1952 by communist Chinese troops, following the capitulation of the Tibetan government, and his acceptance as the legitimate incarnation had been a precondition to completing the Seventeen-Point Agreement, which established Chinese jurisdiction over Tibet. Submitting to political pressure, the Dalai Lama's government nevertheless carried out the ritual procedures necessary to certify the Panchen Lama's authenticity.[5]

With the death of the Tenth Panchen Lama, the Chinese government is once again drawn into the logic of Tibetan religious politics. Its strategy in Tibet requires that it coopt the religious legitimization of authority for its own political purposes; thus, it is obliged to sacralize a political appointment through an appeal to ritual procedures. It is not, however, in a position to establish for itself the legitimacy of those procedures (insisting instead on the right of the central government to bestow the legal title to religious offices). This is not simply a question of the final choice being approved by the Dalai Lama. The procedures which certify the validity of the choice are essentially magical — dreams, divination, oracles. The outcome may be manipulated for political ends, but the freedom to do so is negotiated by the bearers of the religious tradition.

The institution of reincarnation is thus a valuable political resource in the hands of Tibetans. In traditional Tibetan society there were many hundreds of incarnate lamas, of whom the Dalai Lama and the Panchen Lama are the two most prominent. The institution is unique to Tibetan society, forming a hierarchy of religious and political leadership, with important incarnate lamas commanding considerable power and wealth. The Tibetan exile community in India has continued to discover successors to incarnate lamas (*yang srid*). In principle, a reincarnation may appear anywhere; in practice, incarnations are discovered among Tibetan children born in India. Thus, the Tibetan exile community has been able to secure its own political monopoly over the institution. Though the Chinese government may insist that the search for a new Panchen Lama be restricted to China and Tibet, the option remains for the Dalai Lama and his government-in-exile to reject the designated successor.

The question of the reincarnation of the Panchen Lama is ultimately one of political sovereignty. Tibetans jealously guard the traditional

[5] Goldstein (1989): 760–3.

formula for combined religious and political leadership embodied in the figure of the incarnate lama despite Chinese attempts to manipulate the institution. Thus Tibetans universally revered the Panchen Lama as a person — notwithstanding the resentment they expressed toward the uses to which he had been put by the Chinese. The religious dimension to the institution sustains a symbolic potential beyond Chinese control. As long as the Chinese government attempts to act as a patron of religion, backing the search for the next Panchen Lama, it affords Tibetans a range of freedom that they would otherwise be denied. As the monks demonstrated during the Mönlam festival in 1988, withdrawing religious legitimacy effectively enables Tibetans to challenge Chinese sovereignty.

Three days of riots, March 1989

Throughout the winter of 1989 posters continued to appear around Lhasa calling on Tibetans to demonstrate. These were the work of the loose-knit lay support network for the demonstrating monks and nuns that had formed during 1988. A poster from the "Association of Tibetan People of the Three Provinces" (*chol gsum bod mi'i mthun tshogs*), pasted around the Barkhor on 18 January, thanks "the preservers of the Tibetan race, the great warriors of Tibet University, the Beijing Nationalities Institute, and Lhasa Middle School" for the demonstration on 30 December, and calls on "all Tibetans to fight with a warrior's heart until freedom is regained."

On the morning of 7 February, the day marking the beginning of the Tibetan New Year (*lo gsar*), a Tibetan flag appeared in front of the Jokhang, and flew for several hours before being removed. Tibetans left khatas (*kha btags*), ceremonial scarves, at the base of the flagpole. Plainclothes security officers stood by and watched the spectacle, but did nothing to intervene. At the same time, a leaflet circulated throughout Lhasa laying out instructions for commemorating the independence struggle. Issued by the group calling itself the "Independence Uprising Organization" (*rang btsan sger langs tshogs pa*), the leaflet demands that Tibetans refrain from the traditional festivities marking the New Year:

Fellow Tibetans, our struggle for the rights of the Tibetan people and for independence is a just cause of which we need not feel ashamed. Although we have suffered terrifying losses in the series of demonstrations beginning 27

September last year [1987], we should never lose courage or give up the struggle. Our programme for Losar [Tibetan New Year] is to engage in religious activities and pray for the departed according to individual means. However, if anyone indulges in merrymaking like dressing up, drinking chang [Tibetan beer] or singing, we will take appropriate action against them. We mourn from the bottom of our hearts and pay homage to those heroes and heroines who laid down their lives for the cause of the rights of the Tibetan people, for the cause of religion and for all sentient beings. All Tibetans must unite as one. May His Holiness the Dalai Lama live for ten thousand years.

On the evening of 19 February, some 200 nuns from three large nunneries north of Lhasa made their way toward town with plans to demonstrate the next day in the Barkhor. They were stopped and turned back at police roadblocks north of the city.[6] The following day a Tibetan flag appeared in front of the Jokhang and posters and pamphlets were distributed around the Barkhor; 20 February was the fifteenth day of the first Tibetan month, and would have marked the climax of Mönlam had the festival not been cancelled.

Finally, on 22 February, another demonstration took place. At about 2.45 p.m. a group of ten nuns and four monks assembled in front of the Jokhang. With about forty lay Tibetans following behind, they completed a circuit of the Barkhor shouting independence slogans. As they began the second circuit, about eighty PAP soldiers arrived in two trucks at the western end of the Jokhang square, ready to confront them. The demonstrators managed to escape into alleys and houses around the Barkhor and no arrests were made. The PAP troops remained in the square for about an hour; Tibetans made catcalls and whooping sounds as they departed. However, checkpoints were established at entrances into the Barkhor and, for the rest of the afternoon, Tibetans coming into the area were screened by groups of ten to twelve soldiers.

PAP troops had been arriving in Lhasa throughout February. On 17 February, some 1,700 PAP soldiers were paraded past the People's Cultural Palace Memorial. In spite of the growing military presence, there were further small demonstrations in the first week of March, all led by nuns. On 1 March, eight nuns from Chupsang nunnery and three monks completed three circuits of the Barkhor, disappearing into the

---

[6] This incident was reported in some detail in the Chinese media. Hong Kong Zhongguo Tongxun She in Chinese, 22 February 1989, in *FBIS*, 22 February 1989: 42–3.

alleys before they could be arrested. On 2 March, a larger demonstration by thirty-seven nuns from Tsangkhung nunnery took place. Finally, on 4 March, thirteen nuns and several monks began a circuit of the Barkhor, shouting independence slogans. On the second circuit they were joined by about seventy-five Tibetans from the street, some following behind, others leading in front. The demonstrators dispersed on their own after the third circuit. Though plainclothes officers witnessed these demonstrations, there were no confrontations with the security forces, nor were there any arrests or violence.

Sunday, 5 March 1989. The demonstration on this day did not differ in any way from the other small demonstrations in Lhasa during the previous two weeks. Around noon six nuns, three monks, and a few Tibetan youths began to circle the Barkhor, displaying a hand-drawn Tibetan flag on a small sheet of paper. In addition to "Tibet is independent", the demonstrators shouted "This is a peaceful demonstration, please do not use violence" and in English, "Freedom! Freedom!". The demonstrators were observed and photographed from the roof of the police station overlooking the Barkhor. On the roof were several plainclothes police officers with pistols drawn, dangling their weapons over the edge, and at least one uniformed soldier with an automatic weapon.

As the demonstrators completed the second circuit of the Barkhor their numbers had increased to about thirty. By then a crowd of several hundred Tibetan onlookers had gathered. As they approached the police station, one of the policemen threw a bottle down at the demonstrators. A Tibetan youth responded by lobbing a single rock which hit the wall of the building. One policeman fired two shots into the air, then he and another policeman began firing with their pistols directly into the crowd below. No warning was given to the crowd, and there was no pause between the first two shots and the subsequent shots fired at the Tibetans below. The crowd had no opportunity to disperse. The first person hit was the youth who had thrown the rock. Two other Tibetans who tried to help him were also struck by bullets. At that point the crowd fled in panic. Shortly afterwards, tear-gas canisters were fired. No one was killed in this first confrontation.

A unit of fifty PAP soldiers arrived and took control of the square in front of the Jokhang. For the next couple of hours Tibetans huddled in the alleyways surrounding the Jokhang, making sporadic forays toward the square to confront the troops, who periodically fired off tear-gas canisters and automatic weapons in their direction. Several more Tibetans were hit by bullets. The PAP troops continued to occupy the square without advancing on the Tibetans.

Unable to enter the square in front of the Jokhang, the Tibetan crowd wandered through the back alleys off the Barkhor, regrouping at the vegetable market. About an hour later, having increased to about 900 people, the crowd made another attempt to circle the Barkhor and enter the square in front of the Jokhang. Eventually the PAP troops moved into the Barkhor and connecting alleys, forcing the demonstrators out on to Dekyi Sharlam, the main street running past the Tibetan quarter of Lhasa. The demonstration at this point was confused; it was no longer a peaceful demonstration led by monks and nuns, but it had also not degenerated completely into a riot and lost the features of organized protest. The crowd surged up and down Dekyi Sharlam shouting independence slogans, following behind protestors waving Tibetan flags.

The crowd had emerged out onto the street at about 3 p.m. A unit of 100 PAP soldiers, armed with automatic weapons, watched from the west end of Dekyi Sharlam as the Tibetan crowd ran up and down the street. Troops also blocked the east end of Dekyi Sharlam where it leaves the Tibetan quarter, boxing the demonstrators in. The crowd, numbering by then about 1,500 people, consisted largely of Tibetan youths in their teens, but also included many pilgrims visiting Lhasa from other parts of Tibet. At about 3.15 the PAP troops made their first advance, firing directly into the crowd with automatic weapons as they marched up from the west end of the street into the Tibetan quarter. Tibetans in their houses were hit by bullets from the street. PAP soldiers chased demonstrators into houses where they sought refuge, opening fire on the occupants inside. After twenty or thirty minutes the soldiers withdrew back up the street. They advanced a second time about 5.30, and again soldiers sprayed the street with bullets, hitting Tibetans inside their houses. Two members of a family were shot dead inside their house, one an eighteen-year-old girl. The soldiers' third advance was around 6.50, and between 7.00 and 7.30 there was heavy shooting on the street. Tibetans caught by groups of soldiers were savagely beaten and arrested. At one point PAP soldiers were observed getting out of a truck, and some went into a Tibetan restaurant near Ramoche temple, destroyed the furniture inside, and then began shooting from the windows with automatic weapons. Tibetans reported that fifty people were wounded during this shooting alone.

Following the shooting near Ramoche temple, Tibetans started breaking into Chinese shops and restaurants along Dekyi Sharlam, piling the contents in the streets, and burning them. Looting was prohibited; anyone caught attempting to steal goods taken from the Chinese shops was forced by the crowd to throw them on to the fire. A monk who had taken part in the demonstration in the square at noon and remained with the protestors throughout the day describes how the destruction of the Chinese shops began:

Nothing happened until after the shooting in the evening near Ramoche around six or seven o'clock. There was a lot of shooting and many were injured. This is how it started. There is a Tibetan restaurant where Chinese soldiers were hiding. Tibetans who went there thinking it was safe were shot at by these two soldiers. When the soldiers fled through backstreets, we discovered that everything in that restaurant had been deliberately broken, and bedding was flung out into the street. Then we decided to take things out of their shops and burn them. We caused no damage to buildings.

The soldiers had thrown a container of oil outside. One Tibetan youth picked it up and spread the oil in the road and started the burning. This is what started the destruction. I personally think that without this happening the crowd would have dispersed peacefully.

It all started because of the Tibetan restaurant. If they had not thrown and broken the cups and bedding it would not have started. The burning would not have happened. It was because of the Chinese soldiers who were smashing things in the Tibetan restaurant, so Tibetans wanted to destroy Chinese things. The Chinese went in there to hide and to shoot because people were passing by the restaurant. The Tibetans were going up and down Ramoche Lam and the soldiers could shoot from the restaurant.

The monk goes on to describe how the first shops along Dekyi Sharlam were burned. The first Chinese property attacked was a pharmacy:

The pharmacy happened immediately after the Chinese destroyed the Lhamo Restaurant. We moved to the pharmacy immediately. Things were taken outside. They say we burned houses but they were full only with Chinese goods. About fifteen small shops on Dekyi Sharlam were burnt. There were some Tibetans who said, this is what the Chinese have done to us and we must do it to them. Some said we must not, and that it would be a mistake.

I can swear that there was not a single Tibetan who stole anything. If we had, it would have been a disgrace upon the Tibetans. How can we think of stealing when they are killing our people? If we stole, the Chinese would have said we were doing this only for stealing.

After the pharmacy there was an electrical repair shop and the shop of a watch repairer who charged a lot of money. The Tibetans said, "we are always being cheated by these people." The things were taken out and burned, the shop was not burned. It was sort of a grudge people held. Along Dekyi Sharlam there were many Chinese restaurants.

Monday, 6 March 1989. Monday was quiet until about mid-morning, when crowds began to gather along Dekyi Sharlam. Numbering about 500, the crowd moved up and down the street with Tibetan flags, as they had done the day before, shouting independence slogans. Onlookers were considerably more fearful on this day than the previous day, and many were visibly crying. Tibetans began throwing rocks at passing Chinese cyclists on Dekyi Sharlam, forcing them to dismount. At least one was seriously injured after being hit by a rock and attacked by Tibetans. The bicycles were thrown on fires in the middle of the street; between one and two hundred were burned in this way on Monday. This was the first time that Chinese civilians were attacked during a protest in Lhasa. However, after having their bicycles taken, Chinese were frequently protected by individual Tibetans in the crowd from physical attacks and helped to safety. As with attacks on Chinese shops, the principal target of Tibetan protest was Chinese property.

Throughout most of Monday the PAP troops were withdrawn from the centre of Lhasa, leaving the Tibetan areas at the mercy of bands of Tibetans, who continued to vandalize Chinese property in the area. Eyewitnesses reported that Tibetan onlookers who refused to participate in the protest were taunted by the crowds and sometimes had rocks thrown at them. Sporadic shooting occurred throughout the afternoon of 6 March. Police snipers on rooftops shot at Tibetans in alleys around the Barkhor, killing and wounding several. Chinese reports referred to a demonstration at about 2 p.m. by "300 rioters" who marched west along the south side of the Barkhor, smashing shops and burning goods.[7] They also reported the destruction of several government offices at the east end of Dekyi Sharlam. But the first major advance by the PAP into Tibetan areas was not until about 7 p.m., when troops marched up Dekyi Sharlam firing automatic weapons and tear-gas canisters. At around 8 p.m., fifty protestors throwing stones at a building in the square before the Jokhang were shot at with automatic weapons; several Tibetans died in this shooting. Meanwhile the troops had withdrawn back up Dekyi Sharlam. A second advance

---

[7] Beijing Zhongguo Xinwen She in Chinese, 6 March 1989, in *FBIS*, 6 March 1989: 18.

took place at around 8.30, as PAP troops again attacked Tibetans who had returned to the street after their withdrawal. Sporadic firing continued through the night, as security forces entered Tibetan homes, shooting and beating the occupants, and making arrests.

Tuesday, 7 March 1989. The crowds on Tuesday were smaller and the participants mostly youths. No more than 400 people gathered on Dekyi Sharlam, moving up and down the street as they had done on previous days. More bicycles belonging to Chinese were burned, and more fires were lit. But the enthusiasm of the Tibetan crowd had waned. By early afternoon sporadic bursts of gunfire were heard around the city. A rumour circulated that the security forces were about to make a sweep, shooting Tibetans on sight. This drove many Tibetans indoors. No sweep occurred, and a couple of hours later they reemerged. The three days of Tibetan protest were effectively over.

In the early evening 2,000 People's Liberation Army troops arrived in trucks and took up positions throughout the centre of Lhasa. The decree imposing martial law was issued in Beijing on Tuesday afternoon by Premier Li Peng and the State Council, and came into effect at midnight. During the night security forces continued to enter Tibetan houses, arresting people and dragging them away. By dawn checkpoints had been set up at every major intersection and PLA soldiers were stationed at every alleyway leading off the main street into the Barkhor. Martial law in Lhasa was not to be lifted for thirteen months.

Why was martial law imposed?

The best estimates of the number of Tibetans killed on 5 March are about fifty, with many more wounded. The Chinese government claimed that ten Tibetans and one Chinese policeman had died on 5 March, and about 100 people — forty police and sixty Tibetans — had been injured. The Chinese policeman said to have been killed was never identified, nor were any Tibetans named as his murderers.[8] For the three days of protest the Chinese put the total number of deaths at

---

[8] Several unconfirmed reports from Tibetan sources suggest that a PAP soldier may have died when a gun accidentally discharged. Oddly, there is fairly good evidence that a Chinese policeman videoing the riot from a building across from the Snowlands Hotel was killed when he was struck by a rock and fell through a glass window. No Chinese reports ever referred to this.

sixteen. The best independent estimates fall somewhere between eighty and 150.[9]

Chinese reporting of the events leading up to the declaration of martial law differed significantly from the accounts of Tibetan protesters and Western observers. First, the Chinese gave considerably higher numbers for the size of the Tibetan crowd than did eyewitness observers, and reported escalating violence and crowds of more than 1,000 on both 6 and 7 March.[10] In fact, the demonstrations had tapered off over the final two days, with the crowd on Dekyi Sharlam numbering no more than 400 on the third day. Chinese reports emphasized the destruction of government property and attacks on government offices and enterprises. A number of buildings in the Tibetan quarter were sacked — including several neighbourhood committee offices, a taxation office, and branches of commercial bureaus — most along the 0.75 km. stretch of Dekyi Sharlam accessible to the demonstrators, and all adjacent to Chinese-owned shops. The protesters never attempted to move out of the Tibetan quarter toward the regional government headquarters.

Chinese reports also claimed that Tibetan rioters had "resorted to firing guns openly for the first time."[11] According to this account, they took over a building along Dekyi Sharlam on the evening of 5 March and shot at security forces, killing the PAP soldier said by the Chinese to have died in the confrontation with demonstrators. Tibetans had been accused of seizing guns from police officers during the incident at the police station on 1 October 1987, but this time the Chinese government maintained that firearms and ammunition had been smuggled into the country from overseas as part of a premeditated plan. Yan Mingfu, head of the United Front Work Department, claimed that "reliable intelligence showed that the rioters had smuggled weapons into Tibet from abroad and that some of them had received unofficial terrorist training abroad and had already entered Tibet."[12] The mayor of Lhasa announced that "a small number of firearms have

---

[9] See *Defying the Dragon* (1991: 28–9).

[10] For 6 March, see Beijing Zhongguo Xinwen She in Chinese, 6 March 1989, in *FBIS*, 6 March 1989: 18; for 7 March, see Hong Kong Zhongguo Tongxun She in Chinese, 7 March 1989, in *FBIS*, 8 March 1989: 7.

[11] Beijing Xinhua Hong Kong Service in Chinese, 7 March 1989, in *FBIS*, 8 March 1989: 20.

[12] Beijing Xinhua in English, 21 March 1989, in *FBIS*, 22 March 1989: 23.

been confiscated and we are in the process of finding their sources," adding "We are also sure who organized these riots" and "The truth will be made known in due time."[13] The riots themselves were described as "deliberately launched after long premeditation by a few separatist elements."[14] And Westerners were part of this plan: "Separatist groups outside the country have recently sent people into the country in the capacity of tourists to set up programs for riots, and also sent men to smuggle arms across the border."[15]

As with every major demonstration since 1987, foreigners were identified as taking part in the riots, and as being organizers and instigators. One Chinese report refers to "a foreigner with a big nose and blue eyes, in a red down jacket" seen among the rioters, and hints at "international links" with Nepalese, Russians, Americans, and Taiwanese.[16] Both journalists and travellers from abroad were certainly present throughout the three days of unrest, acting as witnesses and observers to the events, and relaying information to the outside world. Fifteen foreign eyewitnesses who arrived in Kathmandu on 14 March issued a statement denying that any Tibetans had used guns during the demonstrations, rejecting the claim that foreigners had been actively involved in the demonstrations or had provoked Tibetans, and dismissing as preposterous the suggestion that foreigners had provided arms.

Chinese reports refer to the three small demonstrations led by nuns in the first week of March.[17] These declare that the authorities "exercised restraint and tried to dissuade and educate the separatists, thereby safeguarding public order and averting direct clashes."[18] The demonstration at midday on 5 March, involving no more than a dozen protesters, was no different in size or intent from these earlier ones. There was no need for the police officers on the police station roof to fire on the demonstrators, provoking an angry response from the Tibetan

[13] *Ibid.*, 31 March 1989, in *FBIS*, 31 March 1989: 11.

[14] Lhasa Tibet Regional Service in Mandarin, 16 March 1989, in *FBIS*, 9 March 1989: 60.

[15] Beijing Xinhua Hong Kong Service in Chinese, 8 March 1989, in *FBIS*, 9 March 1989: 23.

[16] Hong Kong Ming Pao in Chinese, 9 March 1989, p. 36, in *FBIS*, 9 March 1989: 20.

[17] Hong Kong Ta Kung Pao in Chinese, 7 March 1989, p. 2, in *FBIS*, 7 March 1989: 12.

[18] Beijing Television Service in Mandarin, 7 March 1989, in *FBIS*, 7 March 1989: 8.

crowd. The small demonstration, like all the previous ones, would have dispersed on its own.

The Chinese government insisted that these demonstrations were in preparation for a major uprising on 10 March. This became the official justification for martial law. Yan Mingfu explains the government's decision:

[The Dalai Lama] and his government-in-exile made use of the opening up of Tibet to send people across the border to plot a large-scale riot in Lhasa on 10 March. To prevent violence and save the lives and property of the Tibetan people, the central government decided to impose martial law in Lhasa, thus disrupting their plan for a large-scale riot. We confirmed that they had shipped many weapons into Tibet, and sent in some people who had undergone special training in Japan.[19]

No evidence was ever presented for a plot to stage an armed uprising on 10 March. None of the reports of arrests and trials following the declaration of martial law referred to such a plot, nor were any weapons ever produced or Tibetans sentenced for possession of them. The anniversary of the 1959 uprising against the Chinese, 10 March, had not previously figured as a date for demonstrations by monks and nuns.

In fact, the demonstrations in February and early March were hastily organized, with no coordination among dissident groups in Lhasa (as for the 10 December demonstration). The demonstration on 5 March was a symbolic gesture in the face of hopeless odds. A monk who had helped organize the demonstration explains:

The evening before the demonstration we wrote a few letters which were passed around, but the message was mainly passed verbally. We asked people not to trade the next day and to join the demonstration. There were no plans prior to that.

It was not an anti-Chinese demonstration. We asked them not to use violence. We planned a peaceful demonstration. On the first walk around the Barkhor there was no trouble at all. On the second the Chinese police at the station in the Barkhor threw beer bottles down on our heads. They also threw stones and took photographs. One person in the crowd was hit by one of these stones and threw another stone back, whereupon the police opened fire.

The demonstrators on 5 March, as in the other small demonstrations, were prepared for the worst, expecting to be beaten, arrested, or possibly killed. As the monk quoted above explains, the protesters did

---

[19] Beijing Zhongguo Xinwen She, 21 March 1989, in *FBIS*, 22 March 1989: 23.

not anticipate that they would precipitate a riot: "We did not think this demonstration would become big because it was understood that the small group of protesters would all be killed, and therefore it would not proceed to a larger demonstration."

Did the events of these three days in March justify the imposition of martial law? The original demonstration on the 5th was small and peaceful, and it was only after the shooting that an angry crowd assembled. The shooting of demonstrators from the police-station roof served only to provoke the crowd; it was not part of an organized effort at crowd control. Tear-gas was used to disperse the crowd only after the shooting. Eyewitnesses indicate that in the moments before the shooting Chinese police officers were seen communicating on walkie-talkies. This suggests that the decision to open fire was not a spontaneous decision of officers on the spot, but carried out on orders received from superiors. The two shots fired into the air may have been intended to provide a photographic record of "warning shots".

The behaviour of the PAP troops during the three days appears to have inflamed the protest. The security forces had it in their power to take control of the Tibetan area and suppress the violence using established riot control techniques. Following previous demonstrations they had shown their ability to quell protest effectively. On this occasion, they allowed the protest to escalate, making periodic sweeps, firing automatic weapons indiscriminately into the street, and then retreating from the area. The use of snipers on rooftops firing at Tibetans in the streets also served no purpose in terms of crowd control. These tactics provoked the Tibetan crowd to further violence. No attempt was made until midnight on Tuesday to take control of the Tibetan area of Lhasa. When it was finally decided to move in and take control, the operation was completed quickly and easily.

The evidence suggests that the Chinese strategy was deliberately to provoke the escalation of Tibetan protest, providing a justification for the imposition of martial law. In any case, by the time martial law was instituted on Tuesday night, the protest had largely subsided. Thus the imposition of martial law appears to have been part of a coordinated plan to deal with continuing protest in Tibet.

It is possible that the violent attacks on Tibetans during the three days were initiated by the PAP command in an attempt to extend their own political and economic domination of Lhasa. By precipitating riots they demonstrated to the Party leadership the extent and violence of the separatist threat in Tibet, and the corresponding need for continuing repression, which only the PAP could provide. Since their arrival in large numbers in Lhasa after the first demonstrations in 1987, the PAP had become an increasingly visible presence and a power in its own right, displacing the local Public Security apparatus. PAP troops were generally regarded as disorderly and undisciplined, and were linked to corruption in the supply of goods and services to Lhasa. The shooting of unarmed demonstrators on 10 December 1988, carried out by a unit of PAP soldiers, may have been planned to embarrass and discredit the newly appointed Party secretary for Tibet, Hu Jintao, a reformer identified with the policy of continuing liberalization in Tibet. The death on 28 January, of the Panchen Lama, who advocated sensitivity to Tibetan religious aspirations, eliminated a major impediment to a general crackdown on the entire Tibetan population.[20]

However, the imposition of martial law ended the PAP monopoly over security in Lhasa. With the arrival of PLA troops, authority was transferred to the Tibet Military District of the Chengdu Military Region, which receives orders directly from the Central Military Commission in Beijing. Immediate responsibility for enforcing martial law in Lhasa lay with Major-General Zhang Shaosong, political commissar of the Tibet Military District, who assumed command in Lhasa

---

[20] In a document summarized in an article by Jonathan Mirsky in the London *Observer* (12 August 1990, p. 17), an exiled Chinese journalist, Tang Daxian, presents a detailed account of faction rivalries within the Chinese leadership and opposing strategies for handling the Tibet crisis. Tang describes the conflict between reformers in the Party, who favoured the United Front strategy of continuing liberalization and tolerance for Tibet's special problems, and Party centralists, who saw communist power being eroded and favoured an immediate crackdown. According to Tang, this rivalry was played out among different wings of the security apparatus, with the PAP under Qiao Shi preparing for a bloody showdown with Tibetan protestors. Tang goes on to detail an elaborate conspiracy in which a "Special Task Force" of 300 PAP soldiers, disguised as Tibetans, engaged in acts of sabotage and provocation, starting fires and destroying property, in order to instigate a violent confrontation. According to Tang, this culminated in a massacre of 300 Tibetans on the morning of 6 March.

The evidence of Western and Tibetan eyewitnesses does not support Tang's chronology of events for the three days in March. Tang's description of a massacre in the Barkhor on 6 March was never corroborated by any other observers. The credibility of his analysis of the faction rivalries played out in the events leading up to the declaration of martial law, for which Tang claims to have seen documentary evidence in the form of internal Party communications, rests finally on how much weight one is prepared to attach to conflict within the Party in the shaping of events, and how much the decision to impose martial law is seen as a unified action of the Party leadership.

on 8 March. The PLA troops under his command were better trained and disciplined than those of the PAP. The decision to impose martial law may signify a move by the Party leadership in Beijing to rein in the PAP and take direct control of the situation in Tibet.

The PLA were in a position to exercise much more extensive control over the Tibetan population. By declaring martial law the central government was implying that the rule of law was the norm in Tibet, and that only extraordinary circumstances excused extra-legal methods. Arbitrary search and arrest have always been the norm in Tibet, and demonstrations or other acts of political protest treated as illegal. But Martial Law Decree no. 1, signed by Dorje Tsering for the TAR Government on 7 March, banned "assemblies, demonstrations and strikes by workers, students, and other people" and gave the security forces the legal power to deal summarily with violators, and the "right to search the riot-creating suspects and places where criminals are possibly hidden."

Martial law sanctioned a cordon of the entire Tibetan quarter of Lhasa, with checkpoints every few metres. No movement within, into, or out of the area was possible without identity documents and permits. Tibetans were required to be in possession of identity cards at all times. Movement within the martial law area demanded a permit issued by the authorities. Martial Law Decree no. 3, also issued on 7 March, required monks and nuns to have "certificates issued by the democratic management committees of their monasteries" — a rule which voided the right of unlisted monks and nuns to remain in the area and subjected them to arbitrary removal. The security forces were sanctioned to "adopt mandatory measures on the spot" in dealing with violators of the pass requirements. Martial Law Decree no. 3 also demanded that people from outside Lhasa "on entering the martial law-enforced area must have certificates issued by the people's government of county level or above and go through formalities for temporary residence within 5 hours after entering the area."

This last requirement, though potentially applying to the transient Chinese population of Lhasa as well, was in fact directed exclusively at Tibetans. On 20 March, Dorje Tsering called for the registration of "all people who have come into Lhasa from elsewhere" and indicated that there were 30,000 to 40,000 such people in Lhasa. Referring to "certain people [who] have blindly flocked to Lhasa," it is clear that he had the large transient Tibetan population of Lhasa in mind. The requirement that people report for registration was described as an "extraordinary measure taken during the martial law period", necessary to "effectively strengthen security control" and "eliminate factors for instability". Clearly, what was feared was that a large segment of the population would escape the sweep to identify dissidents. The registration of all Tibetans was described as "essential to strengthen leadership and discipline and do a good job in ideological education and propaganda work and in providing guidance."[21]

Martial Law Decree no. 5, issued on 8 March, declared that Tibetans "who know the facts of separatists' activities and crimes of fighting, smashing, robbing and arson, etc." were required to "expose and report the cases" to Public Security. This created an atmosphere of intimidation and suspicion. Tibetans reported that rewards of 300 yuan were being paid to informers. The decree called for the protection of informers, stating that "those who retaliate against people who inform against them will be severely punished."

Finally, one of the provisions of Martial Law Decree no. 1, issued on 7 March, prohibited foreigners from entering the martial law area, and required that those already in Lhasa leave. Martial Law Decree no. 4, issued on 8 March, deals exclusively with foreigners in Lhasa. It bans "unorganized foreign tourists" from Lhasa and requires that tour groups organized by tourist agencies be accompanied at all times by Chinese guides with a pass issued by Public Security. This effectively prevented any unsupervised contact between Tibetans and Westerners. The first tour groups under the new regulations were not allowed into Lhasa till the beginning of May, two months later. They were required to stay in Chinese hotels and their movements were closely monitored. Except for two English teachers at the University and the foreign staff of the Lhasa Holiday Inn, all other foreigners were gone from Lhasa by 9 March.

By 9 March, the day the 100 or so remaining Westerners in Lhasa were expelled, as many as 1,000 Tibetans had been arrested. Hundreds more were arrested in the following days, many of whom took no part in the demonstrations or violence. Martial law provided the opportunity for a sweep through the entire Tibetan population in the search for dissidents.

---

[21] Lhasa Tibet Regional Service in Mandarin, 20 March 1989, in *FBIS*, 21 March 1989: 58.

Tibet under martial law

During the martial law period the residents of Lhasa were subjected to regular displays of military force such as had not been seen in Tibet for decades. On 10 March, the day after foreign tourists and journalists were expelled, forty truckloads of soldiers were positioned around the Jokhang, each truck equipped with a mounted machine-gun. Also deployed were trucks fitted with multiple rocket launchers, with the rockets pointed toward the Jokhang temple. Other such trucks were positioned along Dekyi Sharlam near the Potala, with rockets pointed at the palace. The Chinese had expected demonstrations on 10 March, the thirtieth anniversary of the 1959 uprising, but martial law was already in place. The intimidating display of military hardware bore no relation to any real threat posed by Tibetan protestors; rather, it was an assertion of Chinese power directed at the symbols of Tibetan national identity.

PLA troops continued to pour into Lhasa throughout March. On Sunday 23 April, troops and vehicles again moved into the square before the Jokhang, and rockets were trained on the Jokhang temple and the Potala palace. Around the beginning of May armoured personnel carriers made their first appearance in the streets of Lhasa. The military build-up continued through the autumn of 1989, and on 10 December 1989, International Human Rights Day, a year after the demonstration when troops opened fire on unarmed demonstrators, APCs were again deployed in front of the Jokhang and remained in place till 13 December, presumably to prevent a repeat of the previous year's demonstration.

Military displays continued throughout the martial law period. On 4 March 1990, in preparation for the anniversary of the protests which led to the declaration of martial law, tanks were deployed in Lhasa for the first time in many years. Four tanks took up positions in the square before the Jokhang. On the morning of 8 March the Chinese staged a huge military parade through the streets of Lhasa. The largest military display during two and a half years of nationalist unrest in Tibet, it took forty-five minutes to pass. It included five APCs, twelve trucks towing field-guns, and some fifty trucks with thirty armed soldiers each, as well as jeeps and motorcycles. The parade marked the anniversary of the declaration of martial law on 8 March 1989.

The first trial of protestors arrested during the riots in March 1989 was concluded on 29 July that year. Ten defendants received relatively light sentences of two to three years for a range of violent crimes, including looting, arson, and the destruction of public property, but much longer sentences were given to prisoners charged with non-violent political offences. On 12 September another six prisoners were sentenced in the Lhasa Intermediate Court. One of these, fifty-seven-year-old Tsering Ngondrup, received a twelve-year sentence for taking part in demonstrations and for inciting young people to sing "reactionary Tibet independence songs".[22] Two monks from Ratö were sentenced to three and four years for raising a Tibetan flag at their monastery. Two former monks were given five years for collecting information about the March uprising to send to the Dalai Lama. The charges mentioned the use of foreigners to send information out of Tibet, suggesting that the two monks may have been punished for documenting the human rights situation in Tibet. Another Tibetan received a much longer sentence of eleven years as "another spy sent by the Dalai clique".

Sentencing of prisoners charged with non-violent political offences continued throughout the autumn of 1989 and into the winter. In particular, a number of Tibetans were sentenced for producing and distributing political literature. These included the Drepung group, headed by Ngawang Phulchung, and the ten other Drepung monks sentenced on 30 November 1989 at a mass sentencing rally, and the six students from Lhasa no. 1 Middle School who were sentenced on 8 December.

One group arrested in the sweep consisted of three Tibetans — Tseten Norgye, Thubten Tsering, and Sonam Chödron, a woman; all three were detained in April 1989 and formally charged on 10 November 1989. They were lay people. The Tibetan named as the leader of the group, Thubten Tsering, who worked as an electrical technician at the Lhasa Power Station, was identified as a Party member. Tseten Norgye had worked as a receptionist at the Banakshöl hotel in Lhasa, where many Western travellers stayed. A document from the Lhasa Municipality Intermediate People's Procuracy, dated 19 January 1991, indicates that the charges against the three centred on the printing and distribution of literature explaining the Dalai Lama's Five-Point Peace Proposal and his speech to the European Parliament in June 1988. According to the court document, the group had attached the name of an underground organization, "The Tibet Independence Uprising

---

[22] Beijing Xinhua in English, 13 September 1989, in *FBIS*, 13 September 1989: 57.

Group" (*bod rang btsan sger langs tshogs chung*), to some of the leaflets, which were printed on a mimeograph machine hidden in Thubten Tsering's bedroom. The Chinese government never publicized the trial of the three, but Thubten Tsering is reported to have received a sentence of five years, Tseten Norgye four years, and Sonam Chödron two years.

An indication of the extent to which protest activity had begun to spread among Tibetans working within the Chinese administration was the arrest of Tashi Tsering, a member of the CPPCC, in Shigatse. He was arrested on 28 November 1989, and charged with "counter-revolutionary propaganda and inflammatory delusion".[23] His "crimes" were described in the Radio Lhasa broadcast announcing his arrest:

For a long time [Tashi Tsering] has been slack in remoulding his ideology, showing great discontent against the party and about reality. He wrote a total of seventy-three slogans and leaflets supporting independence for Tibet this year and put them into complaint letter-boxes at the central airport of the prefecture . . . , the general office of the CPPCC prefectural committee and the head office of the Xigaze city party committee. These slogans and leaflets, venomously slandering the CPC and the socialist system, reflected his very reactionary thinking. They have had an extremely bad influence on the public and seriously undermined political stability . . .

Tashi Tsering was eventually given a sentence of seven years and sent to Drapchi prison.

The imposition of martial law in Lhasa and the expulsion of foreigners did not halt the demonstrations. Organized protest began again in the autumn of 1989. The first demonstration under martial law took place on 2 September 1989 at the Norbulingka. As in previous years, the Chinese administration in Tibet sponsored the Yoghurt Festival (*zho ston*), a traditional secular holiday during which Tibetan opera and dance (*lha mo*) are performed in the grounds of the Norbulingka. The festival was extensively publicized in the official press since it was an opportunity to demonstrate that the Chinese government continued to support the non-political celebration of "minority" culture.

Nine nuns from Chubsang and Shungseb nunneries rushed on to the stage during the afternoon opera performance on 2 September and shouted independence slogans in front of the assembled government officials and a crowd of several thousand Tibetans. They were

---

[23] Lhasa Tibet Regional Service in Mandarin, 29 November 1989, in *FBIS*, 1 December 1989, p. 39.

immediately arrested by PSB officers, and on 8 September brought before the Lhasa Municipality Committee for Reeducation through Labour. This is an administrative body made up of representatives from government departments that oversees administrative detention — so-called "reeducation through labour" (Chinese: *lao jiao*) — which allows "anti-social elements" to be imprisoned for up to three years without undergoing criminal proceedings. On 11 September, the nuns who had demonstrated at the Norbulingka on 2 September were sentenced to two and three years' "reeducation through labour."

On 22 September another group of six nuns from Shungseb nunnery staged a brief demonstration on the Barkhor. They too were arrested within minutes of beginning to shout independence slogans, and on 24 September brought before the Committee for Reeducation through Labour and given three-year sentences. The same procedure was followed with a monk who attempted to demonstrate on 30 September, four nuns from Michungri nunnery who sang songs praising the Dalai Lama before the Jokhang on 14 October, and two more nuns who tried to demonstrate on 15 October. These are the first instances of administrative detention being used for political prisoners since the outbreak of protest in 1987. Its use following the imposition of martial law represented a new policy of quickly sentencing political activists without going through the formalities of a public trial.

Administrative detention seems to be aimed primarily at the participants in the small unanticipated demonstrations, often staged by nuns, that have recurred regularly. The sentencing of protesters to administrative detention has sometimes been publicized, as with those responsible for the small demonstrations in the autumn of 1989. Presumably this serves as a warning to others, but often prisoners are transferred to "reeducation through labour" centres without any formal acknowledgement by the authorities.

Another demonstration in the Barkhor took place on 25 October. This was led by five young monks from Palhalupuk, a small monastery on Chakpori Hill across from the Potala which was rebuilt during the mid-1980s by Lhasa youth as an explicit symbol of the revitalization of Tibetan national identity. As a result it was referred to by Tibetans in Lhasa as the "youth temple" (*gzhon nu'i lha khang*). Its twenty resident monks were known for their strong pro-independence views. The demonstration was easily broken up by a few soldiers, and Palhalupuk monastery was closed down by the Chinese administration, the five monks receiving sentences of three years "reeducation through labour."

In the small demonstrations described here there was no possibility of the protesters escaping arrest and little expectation of initiating a larger demonstration by lay onlookers. The demonstrations show the continuing willingness of Tibetans to carry on protest without the presence of foreign witnesses, the audience here being the Tibetan community itself. These were defiant acts of self-sacrifice in the face of overwhelming odds, with no expectation of immediate positive results. Small demonstrations of this scale and type, unanticipated by the authorities, have continued through the martial law period up to the present, adding to the growing number of political prisoners inside Tibet.

Nobel Peace Prize celebrations

On 5 October 1989, the award of the 1989 Nobel Peace Prize to the Dalai Lama was announced. The news was broadcast on the Tibetan Service of All India Radio, and spread among Tibetans over the next few days. On the morning of 11 October, Tibetans in Lhasa began publicly celebrating the award in the only way possible under the conditions of martial law. A political message was communicated through traditional religious practices. Large numbers of Lhasa residents poured into the Barkhor to perform khorra, circling the Jokhang temple, burning immense quantities of *bsangs* in the incense-burners along the Barkhor circuit, and throwing handfuls of tsampa, the roasted barley flour which is the staple food of Tibetans, into the air (*lha rgyal*, a symbolic gesture signifying literally the "victory of the gods", is associated with the Dalai Lama). Tibetans continued circling the Barkhor throughout the day, throwing tsampa in the air, as well as visiting the temples in the old part of Lhasa to make offerings of gratitude for what they understood to be international recognition of the Tibetan cause. The ground along the Barkhor was covered in "windhorses" (*rlung rta*), prayers written on small squares of paper and scattered to the wind. People's clothes and bodies were coated with the fine powder of the tsampa.

The celebration involved almost the whole Tibetan population of Lhasa: office-workers, school children, visiting pilgrims. Celebrants walked from the Barkhor to the Norbulingka, where white scarves (*kha btags*) were left as offerings. The next day, a crowd of up to 400 proceeded to the Norbulingka, only to find the gates of the palace closed. They left *kha btags* at the entrance, some blowing conch shells, another traditional element of Buddhist ritual here used to signify political as well as religious "victory".

Initially, the Chinese administration took no notice of the Tibetan celebration, since it fell within the bounds of traditional religious practice. The date itself did not commemorate previous protest or have any other political significance. Soldiers circling the Barkhor were themselves covered in tsampa, which they cheerfully accepted as another odd but apparently friendly Tibetan religious practice. Toward the evening the attitude of the security forces changed, and they began checking identity cards of Tibetans on the Barkhor. On the night of 11 October a number of truckloads of security police arrived in front of the Jokhang, but they did not interfere with the celebration or try to disperse the crowd. As the significance of the festivities became clear to the authorities, however, they faced a dilemma in developing a response to the situation. Tibetans mostly avoided any explicit reference to forbidden political themes; they did not display the Tibetan flag or chant independence slogans. Circumambulation of the Barkhor, burning incense, and throwing tsampa remained within the prescribed limits of religious tolerance. Nevertheless, they made no effort to conceal the cause of their jubilation, speaking openly of their delight in the award of the Nobel Peace Prize to the Dalai Lama.

On the morning of 13 October meetings were held in all major government offices to denounce the award of the Peace Prize to the Dalai Lama and condemning the tsampa-throwing celebration throughout the city. Security forces were instructed on 13 October to begin arresting tsampa throwers, whose activity was henceforth to be treated as "counter-revolutionary". Anticipating further celebrations on 10 December, International Human Rights Day, the day the Nobel Peace Prize is officially awarded, political meetings were called throughout Lhasa on 5 December in work units, offices, and neighbourhood committees to renew the ban on tsampa-throwing and declare that violators would be subject to administrative detention. Burning incense around the Barkhor was also banned. Parallel to this, security was tightened at the major monasteries, where it was announced that public religious observances were banned unless official permission had been given.

Tibetans had shown that potentially any form of religious observance could be used to convey a political message. The Chinese administration was thus forced to impose ever tighter restrictions on religious observances to suppress their latent meaning as political protest. In doing so, they were forced to violate their expressed policy of toleration for traditional religious practices. Tibetans were always quick to point out this contradiction, that the Chinese were in effect "lying" about religious freedom — even as Tibetans were themselves fully cognizant of their own intent to use religion to convey political messages. Carried to its logical extreme, the Chinese are forced to suppress all expressions of religion to eliminate political protest, which, for Tibetans, proves the point that there is no religious freedom in Tibet under Chinese rule. In this way, Tibetans are able to overcome their effective powerlessness by drawing the Chinese into a symbolic competition on Tibetan terms. The Chinese government is not in a position to control the meaning of the "symbols", which Tibetans here deploy in whatever way suits their purposes. The Chinese government may be able to suppress political protest by suppressing religion, but the symbolic victory belongs to the Tibetans, who have forced the Chinese into demonstrating through their actions that there can be no religious freedom in Tibet as long as it is under Chinese rule.

Screening and investigation

In the autumn of 1989 a new political campaign was launched in Tibet. Work units, government departments, and neighbourhood committees were required to undertake a drive for "screening and investigation" (*gtsang bsher dang zhib bsher*), investigating suspect individuals, including government workers and Party members, in an effort to identify dissidents. Detailed plans for the screening and investigation campaign are contained in a document issued by the Organization Department of the Regional Committee of the CPC on 27 July 1989. This document carries the title "Work Plans of the Regional Party and the Regional People's Government for Resolutely Striking Splittists and other Serious Criminals through Screening and Investigation."[24] Referred to as Document no. 13, it was prepared for

[24] Document no. 13 (27 July 1989) "Work Plans of the Regional Party and the Regional People's Government's for Resolutely Striking Splittists and Other Serious Criminals through Screening and Investigation" (*ljongs tang 'ud dang ljongs mi dmangs srid gzhung gi kha phral ring lugs pa dang de min tshabs che'i nyes gsog par gtsang bsher dang 'brel sems thag gtsang bcad kyis rdung rdeg gtong rgyu'i skor gyi las ka'i jus gzhi*), in "Selected Study Documents for Discussion by Party Members" (*dmangs gtsos tang yon la dpyad gleng byed pa'i slob sbyong yig cha 'dems bsgrigs*), Organization Department of the TAR Party Committee, March 1990, pp. 78–98 (for internal circulation). See Appendix B for a complete translation of this document.

internal circulation among Party members in Tibet and is described as
a response by the Tibetan regional Party Committee to a document
prepared by the Beijing Party Committee and Municipal People's
Government following the events in Tiananmen Square in June 1989,
and distributed by the Central Committee of the CPC to Party branches
throughout China.[25]

The significance of Document 13 lies in the explicit link it establishes
between the Party's response to unrest in Tibet and the larger threat to
Party control represented by demands for democracy and human rights
throughout China. These are portrayed as part of a worldwide conspiracy against the Party, orchestrated from abroad, in which the
Tibetan independence movement is just one component. Preparations
for the campaign were made before the announcement of the 1989
Nobel Peace Prize award. Nevertheless, the announcement of the award
while the campaign was in progress must have confirmed the view of
the Chinese government that international support for the Dalai Lama
was part of the same conspiracy to undermine the Party's dictatorship
in China.

Document 13 redefines the ideological challenge to the Party represented by Tibetan protest: "Their strategy has changed, and they are
trying to accomplish their conspiracy of 'Tibetan independence' by
means of 'democracy, freedom, and human rights'."[26] The screening
and investigation campaign in Tibet is described as an implementation of the Beijing document, with the same goal of exposing and
prosecuting the "behind-the-scenes conspirators". But the link with
the post-Tiananmen campaign throughout China justifies a much
greater scale of political investigation than the first anti-splittist campaign of 1987 and in turn anticipates uncovering a large number of
conspirators.

The "targets" of the campaign (*rdung rdeg gtong yul*) are specified in

---

[25] Document no. 3 (30 June 1989), issued by the Central Committee of the CPC,
"Report on Work Plans for Resolutely Suppressing Those Who Incite Counter-
Revolutionary Rebellion through Screening and Investigation" (*gsar brjer ngo rgol gyi
gdum spyod zing slong bar gtsang bsher dang 'brel sems thag gtsang bcad kyis drag gnon bya
rgyu'i las ka'i jus gzhi'i skor gyi dgongs skor snyan zhu*), in "Selected Study Documents
for Discussion by Party Members" (*dmangs gtsos tang yon la dpyad gleng byed pa'i slob
sbyong yig cha 'dems bsgrigs*), Organization Department of the TAR Party committee,
March 1990, pp. 68–77 (for internal circulation).
[26] *'thab jus thog la'ang 'gyur ba phyin nas "dmang gtso dang rang dbang mi dbang" bcas
kyi thab lam la bsten nas "bod rang btsan" gyi lkog gyo 'grub thabs byed pa.*

detail. These include "those who plan behind the scenes to cause disturbances", "those who command the organizations", and "the ringleaders and principal members of secret counter-revolutionary organizations", as well as "fabricators of reactionary rumours" and "instigators of evil counter-revolutionary propaganda". The Party's analysis of the reasons why the demonstrations in Tibet took place distinguishes organizers and ringleaders from the mass of Tibetan participants in nationalist protest, which includes "those who shout a few slogans harming the unity of the nationalities without having a clear understanding", "those who generally believe or spread rumours, and speak what they don't wish for", "those who participate in disturbances because they are deceived or are forced by others", and "those who distribute and put up documents of reactionary propaganda because of the lies and deceptions of others".

These distinctions are largely an artifact of the campaign itself, and have less to do with real guilt or innocence than with the circumstances surrounding apprehension, the extent to which individuals are intimidated and willing to confess or implicate others, and the diligence with which political work teams ferret out dissidents. The same political theory which authorizes ideological education as an instrument of social control also underlies the Party's analysis of the causes of unrest — i.e. if the "masses" can be mobilized and "led" by the Party, then they can also be mobilized and "misled" by counter-revolutionary conspirators. In neither case are they their own political masters. The outcome of screening and investigation is predictable: a number of principal offenders are identified and examples are made of them, while the full scope of popular discontent goes unacknowledged and remains submerged.

Document 13 lays out the organizational details for the formation of work teams to carry out screening and investigation. These work teams are intended to supplement the ongoing work of the regional Party's "Leading Work Group for Stabilizing the Situation" (*dus bab brtan lhing 'go khrid tshogs chung*), created after the imposition of martial law. Following the guidelines laid down in the document circulated by the Central Committee, two government offices for screening and investigation are to be established in Tibet, with work teams made up of cadres drawn from relevant branches of the regional Party. One office, under the Political and Legal Affairs Committee of the regional Party, which oversees the Public Security Bureau and the judicial system, is to carry out "special investigation work" (*ched*

mngags zhib bsher gyi las ka). The second office, under the Discipline
and Inspection Committee of the regional Party, is responsible for
"internal screening and investigation work" (*nang khul gtsang bsher
gyi las ka*), looking within government and Party organizations for
supporters of Tibetan independence. In addition, Party-led Work
Groups for screening and investigation are to be formed within a whole
range of organizations – including offices, associations, schools,
businesses, factories, state and private enterprises, and villages and
town administrations.

What distinguishes the 1989 screening and investigation campaign is
its range and thoroughness on the one hand, and on the other, the fact
that it acknowledges the pervasiveness of pro-independence sentiments
within the Tibetan population. The creation of two special government
offices for screening and investigation directly under departments of the
regional Party shows the extent to which the Party recognizes that it
can no longer trust government offices and enterprises, including the
PSB, to identify and punish dissidents working within their ranks. The
purge of dissident elements in the Party and government throughout
China in the wake of Tiananmen Square is used to justify a similar purge
of the government apparatus in Tibet.

The "internal" (*nang khul*) screening and investigation is the core of
the campaign, calling for a thorough investigation of the actions and
thinking of cadres and political workers, especially Party members
and leading cadres. The presumption is that widespread sympathy and
support for Tibetan protesters is to be found among Tibetans working
within the Chinese administration in Tibet. However, the aim of the
campaign is not only to uncover participants in the demonstrations and
members of underground organizations, but also "those who propagate
speech and action that opposes the Party and socialism". In explaining
that the most important aim of the internal screening and investigation
is the "screening and investigation of thought" (*bsam blo gtsang bsher*),
"bourgeois liberal ideas" (*'byor ldan gral rim rang dbang can gyi bsam
blo*) are listed alongside "splittist ideas" (*kha bral ring lugs kyi bsam
blo*). Party members and cadres are asked to examine what they have
done to halt the spread of both kinds of dangerous ideas. Anti-Party
thinking and "bourgeois liberalization" incline Party members and
cadres towards passive support and sympathy for Tibetan protest, if
not active involvement.

A front-page article in the *Tibet Daily* on 6 November 1989, entitled
"With Great Enthusiasm, Lhasa City Does Well the Work of

'Screening and Investigation' ",[27] documents the progress of the campaign within the Lhasa City Bureau of the Communist Party. The article explains how the office has implemented directives from the Regional Committee of the Party:

> The Lhasa City Bureau of the Communist Party, in order to further the work of screening and investigation, has repeatedly and diligently studied the document of the Regional Party Committee on the work of screening and investigation and, because they have achieved a deep understanding of its real meaning, they have obtained a unified view and a higher recognition of the important essential meaning of the work of screening and investigation.

The article reveals how the process of screening the organization has proceeded through the different divisions and departments of the city, "progressing from within the Party to outside the Party, and from the leading cadres to the general cadres and workers." As detailed in Document 13, people's thinking is also to be subjected to screening and investigation. The article explains that the Lhasa City Party organization has now been screened for participants in the demonstrations and is ready to move on to the next stage of ideological screening and investigation.

An article in the 24 November *Tibet Daily*, entitled "Party Committee of the Lhasa City Municipal District Administration Applies the Method of Screening and Investigation,"[28] explained the two stages of screening and investigation in greater detail. The first stage was "internal", i.e. within relevant government departments, and is subdivided into two phases — in the first, the target was the organization, to identify actual participants in counter-revolutionary activities, and in the second it was thinking, to identify those who hold potentially dissident views. Among the staff and workers within this district office, two participants in the "counter-revolutionary disturbances" were investigated in this process.

The article provided a detailed account of the "struggle between splittism and counter-splittism" within this organization. All members of the organization were required to expose and explain their thinking. Thus, while 84 per cent of the workers and staff "have a firm stand-

---

[27] *grong khyer lha sas hur brtson chen pos "gtsang bsher gnyis" kyi las ka yag po byed pa*, Tibet Daily (*bod ljongs nyin re'i tshags par*), 6 November 1989.

[28] *grong khyer lha sa khreng kon chus ud kyis bya thabs spyad de "gtsang bsher gnyis" kyi las ka byed pa*, Tibet Daily, 24 November 1989.

point, show the flag, and continuously protect the unity of the mother-land," another 15 per cent were shown through investigation to be "without a clear understanding" and "without a clear attitude". Finally, one or two workers and staff were found to have the "attitude of sympathizing with the disturbances", but after being subjected to "ideological education", were "able to achieve a standpoint of opposing splittism."

Finally, the article declared that the first, so-called "internal" stage of screening and investigation was drawing to a close for the Lhasa Municipal District Administration, and that the second stage, "related social screening and investigation," was beginning. Some sixty cadres were contributed by departments of various city offices to form a "related social screening and investigation sub-committee" of 100 cadres, who were able to apply the method of "area screening and investigation" throughout the jurisdiction of the Lhasa Municipal District Administration.

The screening and investigation campaign in Tibet, linking Tibetan protest to a China-wide movement to undermine Party power, was a by-product of the post-Tiananmen crackdown on dissent throughout China. The purge of the Party and government throughout China pro-vided the rationale for a sweep through the Chinese administration in Tibet in search of dissidents. In Tibet the campaign focused almost exclusively on pro-independence activity.[29] Nevertheless, the campaign significantly redefined the problem of splittism. Tibet was no longer to be regarded as a special problem demanding special treatment, nor were ideological campaigns to be couched solely in terms of the "Dalai clique" and the "return of feudalism." They would also focus on the common threat to Party rule throughout China posed by foreign ideologies. Thus, the Party's ideological appraisal of the situation in Tibet had converged with the demands of the organizers of demon-strations and the writers of pamphlets themselves, with the debate now centring on ideas of democracy, freedom, and human rights.

---

[29] On 21 May 1989, Radio Lhasa announced that some 400 of the 800 students at the University of Tibet were on strike in sympathy with Beijing students in Tiananmen Square. Though all assemblies and demonstrations had been banned under martial law regulations, authorities in Tibet allowed the demonstrations of support to proceed, describing the student's motives as "patriotic", but expressing fear that separatists would capitalize on the unrest. There is no indication, however, that the screening and investigation campaign was directed at pro-democracy Chinese cadres in Tibet as well as Tibetans suspected of pro-independence activities.

Expulsions from the monasteries

Following the imposition of màrtial law the major monasteries of
Ganden, Sera, and Drepung had permanent encampments of PLA
soldiers. At Ganden 200 soldiers were encamped in thirteen large
army tents, with armed guards posted at each entrance. Monks could
not leave the monasteries without special permission. Political work
teams continued to be stationed in the major monasteries and nunneries,
and in early November 1989 training sessions were held for cadres
assigned the task of screening and investigation there. The directives
issued for the monasteries and nunneries were: (1) to continue to resist
the splittists and the "Dalai clique"; (2) to condemn and campaign
against the award of the Nobel Peace Prize to the Dalai Lama; (3) to
continue to identify those involved in the successive demonstrations
since 1987 and their supporters, particularly those who did not actively
protest, and to expel unregistered monks; and (4) to go even to small
monasteries and nunneries looking for splittists. It was emphasized
during the training sessions that this time the screening had to be
complete.

As a consequence, between December 1989 and April 1990 more
than 200 monks and nuns were expelled from monasteries and nunneries
near Lhasa and returned to their homes and families.[30] This included
thirty-seven monks from Drepung, nineteen from Ganden, three from
Sera, seven from the Jokhang, and three monk-caretakers from the
Potala. The number of nuns expelled in the vicinity of Lhasa was much
higher: some eighty were reported expelled from Chupsang including
almost all the young ones, twenty-one from Garu, twenty-seven from
Shungseb, and sixteen from Ani Tsangkhung. The much larger number
of nuns expelled may be partly because very few of them had official
resident status in these nunneries. They had also been mainly responsible
for keeping up the cycle of small demonstrations following the imposition of martial law.

The procedure for the expulsions has been described as follows.[31] A
list of monks or nuns to be expelled was drawn up by the Screening and
Investigation Work Team and the monastery's Democratic Management Committee, and a general meeting was then called to announce

---

[30] See *Defying the Dragon* (1991: 18–19) for a breakdown of the number of monks
and nuns expelled from monasteries and nunneries in the Lhasa area.
[31] *Ibid.*

the expulsions. At the same time, the monastery was surrounded by security forces, with police vehicles waiting to transport those expelled back to their homes; the expelled monks and nuns were not allowed to return to their rooms to collect their belongings. After arriving in their home area, they were taken to the county headquarters, where the conditions of their expulsion were explained by local officials and police. Nuns expelled from Garu and Chupsang nunneries, for instance, were forbidden to wear robes or shave their heads, or to rejoin their former nunneries or other nunneries,[32] and allowed to worship in local monasteries only if they returned to their family homes in the evening. They were not allowed to perform religious rituals in other people's homes, or to leave their villages without government permission; they could only work as farmers. Though the monks and nuns are not forced formally to give back their vows and assume a lay status (as during the Cultural Revolution), these conditions constituted an insurmountable obstacle to the performance of the normal activities and obligations of the Buddhist clergy. The result has been that since 1989 many of the expelled monks and nuns have fled to India, where they have been able to continue their studies and maintain their clerical status.

On 16 April, the day after the expulsions at Drepung, the remaining monks agreed to stage a walkout in sympathy with the thirty-seven expelled monks. The Drepung walkout, which included all the younger monks, lasted a month. A number of the 200 resident monks at Sera monastery staged a similar walkout to protest the expulsion of three monks there, and locked the doors of all the temples as they left. In late May, forty young monks from Drepung submitted a petition requesting that the monks expelled from the monastery be readmitted. The petition, addressed to the monastery's Democratic Management Committee and to the Screening and Investigation Work Team stationed at the monastery, threatened that if the expelled monks were not readmitted, then the monks submitting the petition would leave the monastery themselves. The expelled monks were described as the top students in the scholastic curriculum of the monastery.

Boycotts of religious ceremonies and non-compliance with the demands of government religious authorities have become a recurring

---

[32] In the case of eighty nuns expelled from Chubsang in December 1989, fifty were allowed to join small nunneries in their local villages.

feature of life in the major monasteries around Lhasa since 1989. At the same time, monks and nuns who escaped expulsion, along with new recruits, have continued to stage demonstrations in the streets despite attempts by the Chinese administration to tighten political control within the monasteries and nunneries.

Symbolic competition

Tibetan protest since 1987 may be understood as a form of symbolic competition with the Chinese state. While the latter continues to command overwhelming military and political power, its capacity to compel Tibetans to submit to the symbols of that power is no longer absolute. Tibetans have seized the advantage, inventing new symbols and shifting the meaning of old ones, as they continue to communicate protest, express solidarity, and subvert celebrations of Chinese power. This is precisely the area in which the Chinese state has been accustomed to a near-monopoly, putting on vast displays of state power, with uniformed and costumed citizens waving flags and marching in parades. In the past no opposition or non-participation was possible. But the decollectivization of society during the 1980s weakened the coercive power of collective organizations to mobilize the Tibetan population. The cumbersome symbols and ceremonies of communist state power are no longer threatening, and each propaganda offensive in turn provokes a Tibetan response.

The limited capacity of the Chinese state to celebrate its power in Tibet is illustrated by the plans for the fortieth anniversary of the "Peaceful Liberation of Tibet" on 23 May 1991. On this day in 1951 the Seventeen-Point Agreement between China and representatives of the Dalai Lama's government was signed, allowing the PLA to enter Tibet. Tibetans insist that the agreement, which was repudiated by the Dalai Lama after the 1959 uprising, was reached under duress. Thus Tibetans were being asked to celebrate the day which signifies their defeat as a nation.

The focus of the fortieth anniversary celebrations was to be the legitimacy of Chinese rule in Tibet, stressing continuities during the forty years of "liberation", rather than the mistakes of the past. This was the theme stressed by the new Chinese Party Secretary, Jiang Zemin, during his inspection tour of Tibet in July 1990. His directives called for "Fostering the Spirit of Old Tibet", referring to the motivation of the PLA and the early Chinese cadres and settlers who came to Tibet during the 1950s.[33] The phrase itself indicates an attempt to return to a more orthodox style of propaganda work, emphasizing the good qualities of the Chinese in Tibet and the continuing progress under the Chinese administration since the 1950s, while ignoring the major shifts in policy during this period and the catastrophe of the Cultural Revolution. Jiang's directives also called on soldiers in the PLA to be "mentally prepared to settle in Tibet and take part in construction on a long-term basis."[34] Tibet is again described as China's "frontier", requiring Chinese manpower for its development.

Plans for commemorating the fortieth anniversary of the "Peaceful Liberation of Tibet" were presented to a mobilization rally for cadres on 4 December 1990, by Gyaltsen Norbu, head of the TAR regional government. In his speech he declared the day to be "an extremely important festive day" and stressed that "the Party Central Committee and the State Council have attached great importance to the commemoration and propaganda activities for the important festival day." Unlike the ongoing anti-splittist campaign, which relied on intimidation and targeting individuals, the fortieth anniversary celebrations demanded positive enthusiasm and active participation: "It is hoped that after this mobilization rally, various localities and departments will inherit and carry forward the revolutionary spirit of the 40th anniversary of the peaceful liberation of Tibet . . . and extensively mobilize cadres, staff members, and workers to do a good job in various activities to commemorate and publicize the 40th anniversary of the peaceful liberation of Tibet in a highly efficient and effective manner." In his speech to the rally, Gyaltsen Norbu called for "work at the grassroots level and among the masses," citing a warning by Jiang Zemin that the anniversary celebrations would be a "tit-for-tat struggle in public opinion."[35]

Originally, a week-long period of celebrations had been planned, including a procession of floats, a military parade, and various sports events. But the Chinese administration in Tibet no longer has the capacity for mass mobilization on the scale of the public spectacles of previous decades; instead it is forced to rely on a variety of individual incentives and threats to obtain cooperation. As a result, the planned

[33] Lhasa Tibet Television Network in Mandarin, 20 August 1990, in *FBIS*, 22 August 1990: 43.

[34] *Ibid.*, in *FBIS*, 20 August 1990: 47.

[35] *Ibid.*, 4 December 1990, in *FBIS*, 20 December 1990: 67.

celebrations were scaled back, the main event being a one-day holiday on 23 May, with a picnic at the Norbulingka with dance and music performances, and a rally at the sports arena, attended mainly by students and government workers.

In the third week of April work units, neighbourhood committees, enterprises, and schools were instructed to provide personnel for the anniversary celebrations. Quotas were assigned to each organization for the number of people required to participate. Government offices were asked to provide audiences for the meetings with officials from Beijing. Various threats were used to get employees to participate in the celebrations. At the Lhasa City Hospital, for instance, employees were told they would lose a month's salary for refusing to attend. Most of the approximately 200 employees are reported to have either made excuses to avoid participating or to have flatly challenged the order. In the end, some thirty employees of the hospital, mainly Chinese, agreed to go. In some neighbourhood committees "volunteers" for the picnic at the Norbulingka had to be chosen by lot. Residents who failed to show up after being selected were threatened with 15 yuan fines. Other residents were offered payments as high as 30 yuan as an incentive to attend. Villagers from outside Lhasa were also paid to attend the picnic in the Norbulingka.

During the months leading up to 23 May posters and leaflets appeared throughout Lhasa threatening to disrupt the celebrations. Posters described 23 May as a day of mourning for Tibetans and called on them to boycott the picnic at the Norbulingka. One poster, which appeared on the Barkhor on 20 May, ridiculed the way neighbourhood committees were recruiting participants: "We paid 30 fen for one stone, but you hire people for 30 yuan for the picnic in the Norbulingka" ("30 fen" — one hundred fen is one yuan — is a joking reference to Chinese accusations that Tibetans were paid 30 fen by splittists for each stone thrown on 1 October 1987). One underground organization, calling itself the Tiger-Dragon Youth Association (*stag 'brug gzhon nu tshogs pa*), prepared leaflets two months in advance to be distributed on 23 May. On the evening of 21 May some 600 leaflets were scattered in the Shöl area of Lhasa. At the rally in the sports stadium on 22 May young Tibetans threw leaflets into the stadium as they left.

Because of the threat of disruptions, plans for the anniversary celebrations kept changing. The rally, which was to be held outdoors in the Cultural Park in front of the Potala on 23 May, was moved to the sports stadium and rescheduled for 22 May. A delegation from the Party

Central Committee arrived on 19 May, led by Li Tieying, China's Education Minister, whose father had headed the Chinese negotiating team that signed the 1951 agreement. Secrecy surrounded the visit of the delegation, whose itinerary was never publicized. The date of a banquet at the Holiday Inn for the Chinese officials was also shifted to the 22nd. On 15 May the Chinese government announced that foreign journalists, including those from Hong Kong and Macau, would not be allowed into Tibet to cover the celebrations. Heightened restrictions were also placed on the few tourists in Lhasa, who were prohibited from visiting the Barkhor between 23 and 25 May, even in the company of tour guides. Schools and offices in Lhasa were closed on 23 May, but students and workers were instructed to stay away from the Barkhor and to remain at home for the day. They were specifically instructed not to perform khorra.

Around 20 May a meeting was held with secretaries of Lhasa neighbourhood committees to discuss screening the participants in the anniversary events. Admission to the picnic was limited to holders of tickets provided by neighbourhood committees and work units. The day before the picnic those attending were instructed to arrive at 9 a.m., after which no one would be allowed in. Identity cards had to be presented at the entrance, and those admitted were not allowed to move around inside the grounds. The picnic for the Chinese delegation was held indoors in an area separate from the Tibetans. The monasteries near Lhasa were sealed off and monks were not allowed to leave. Drepung monks were told in a political meeting at the monastery on 7 May that they would have to remain inside the monastery from the 15th to the 28th. They were also asked to send a group of eighty or ninety monks to meet the delegation from Beijing. The Drepung monks unanimously refused to comply, and the request was dropped.

There was no major incident on 23 May, but the anniversary celebrations were hardly a symbolic victory for the Chinese government. Tibetans described the intensified security arrangements during the period as similar to martial law. One Tibetan activist, in a letter smuggled out of Tibet in July 1991, wrote: "The celebration was behind closed doors among Chinese officials. The public was kept at a distance. They tried to make it a big show but failed badly." Demonstrations broke out immediately after security in Lhasa was relaxed. Three demonstrations took place on 26 May, and as many as ten more during June and July. One consequence of the preparations for the celebrations was a dramatic increase in the number of posters and

Tibetan flags that appeared throughout Lhasa. At least thirty-one Tibetans were arrested between December 1990 and July 1991 for putting up posters and flags; these were the work of the loosely-knit network of underground organizations, made up primarily of lay Tibetans. The escalation of the poster campaign marks the spread of organized underground activity within the Chinese administration in Tibet. In December 1990, posters and leaflets even appeared inside Public Security offices in Lhasa. Some of the leaflets were individually addressed, threatening reprisals against PSB officials.

Protest in Tibet since 1987 has produced a radicalized younger generation of Tibetans. Although demonstrations continue to be led by monks and nuns, protest activity has spread throughout the Tibetan population, increasingly involving both students and Tibetans working inside the Chinese administration. The heavy-handed response of the Chinese state to protest has bred widespread resentment. Although their efforts remain largely symbolic, with little hope of changing the Chinese political system, Tibetans persist in challenging assertions of Chinese authority. In this, activists command extensive sympathy and support among the general Tibetan population.

During the five-year period from September 1987 to August 1992, some 138 separate incidents of public assembly and protest by Tibetans have been reported.[36] Protest continued through the 1989–90 martial law period, reaching a peak of thirty-seven incidents in 1991, mostly in the months before and after the 23 May celebrations. This does not include other forms of protest activity, such as putting up posters, distributing leaflets, and raising Tibetan flags, which have become increasingly common in spite of heightened surveillance and security.

It is difficult to estimate the total number of Tibetans arrested during this period as a result of the disturbances. Many of those arrested have been held for several months, then released without charges. Others have gone immediately into administrative detention without appearing before the courts. A compilation made in the autumn of 1991 of Tibetans imprisoned for political offences since the outbreak of

---

[36] This figure represents a compilation of incidents reported from various sources by the Tibet Information Network in *Background Papers on Tibet* (September 1992): 46–9. For each year since 1987 the number of incidents are: 1987 September–December (9), 1988 (17), 1989 (32), 1990 (20), 1991 (37), 1992 January–August (23). Of these incidents, forty-one were protests led by nuns, five were student demonstrations, and twenty-six occurred outside Lhasa.

protest in 1987 identifies 360 prisoners by name, of whom 120 were released.[37] Two-thirds of those imprisoned were monks and nuns. One-third of the prisoners were women, 80 per cent being nuns. Most striking, however, is the age of the prisoners: two-thirds were under twenty-five. These young prisoners are a cross-section of contemporary Tibetan society — from both rural and urban backgrounds, lay as well as monks and nuns, students and cadres as well as labourers and businessmen. Having grown up under Chinese rule, these young protestors epitomized the antagonism of a new generation to Chinese rule in Tibet and to the communist political system sustaining it.

[37] See *Political Prisoners in Tibet*, Asia Watch and Tibet Information Network, February 1992. The compilation is based on three prisoner lists received from Tibetan sources including detailed information provided by former inmates.

7

THE DILEMMAS OF CHINESE POLICY

By the beginning of the 1990s the Chinese administration in Tibet had come to perceive the struggle against splittism as protracted and complex. It is now acknowledged to be a chronic problem, needing constant attention and the target of repeated political campaigns. Nevertheless, a *modus operandi* has been developed. More sophisticated monitoring and surveillance prevent any large demonstrations at all, while small demonstrations and other acts of defiance are quickly dealt with, and the protesters arrested, processed through the security apparatus, and imprisoned. Organizations such as neighbourhood committees, monastery democratic management committees, and work units have been called upon to exercise stricter control over Tibetans than during most of the 1980s, with repeated drives to identify dissidents. Finally, greater attention is given to the political loyalty of cadres, with education campaigns inside the Chinese administration to ensure that the power of the CPC does not weaken.

The new strategy for dealing with unrest was summed up in an important speech by Gyaltsen Norbu, Deputy Party Secretary and chairman of the TAR Regional Government, at a regional conference on "Strengthening Basic Work on Public Security in Grassroots Units" in October 1990. He described the anti-splittist struggle as "long, uncompromising, and complicated", and attributed the government's success in suppressing disturbances to the "higher level of initiative than in the past":

Nowadays we no longer respond passively to the situation, as we used to in the past few years. We take more initiatives nowadays than we did in 1987 and 1988. During those days, we only dealt with the problem once disturbances and riots had occurred. The situation now is that if someone is thinking of causing trouble, we do not allow the disturbance to happen. Recently (September to October), we took more and more initiatives to carry out preventive work. Generally, our work has begun to shift gradually from passivity to activity . . . So long as we do not relax our attention and we diligently implement the Party's penal laws, pay great attention to basic work in grassroots units, emphasize prevention, combine attack with prevention and implement total and coordinated control, our goal of long-term security will definitely be achieved.[1]

This chapter examines the scope and effectiveness of Chinese political and economic strategies for containing Tibetan nationalism. There is no doubt that security measures can be effective and that China, with large police and military forces at its disposal, can maintain its hold on Tibet. Nevertheless, Tibet remains an important test of the Party's ability to perpetuate its power by deploying the political and economic resources it commands. Chinese policies aim to placate Tibetan religious and cultural aspirations, legitimize the Chinese state in the eyes of Tibetans, and ultimately win acceptance of Chinese rule through economic development and prosperity. These policies, however, are conditioned by the system that implements them, and thus reflect its limitations and contradictions. Tibetan opposition to Chinese rule cannot be easily reduced to ethnic or regional antagonisms, which by themselves admit to a variety of possible solutions. Chinese rule in Tibet operates through the communist state apparatus, and thus Tibetan protest is conditioned by the response of the state to political dissidence. Assertions of Tibetan national identity are always perceived as challenges to the communist political system, and predictably this sets in motion the mechanisms of Party control. Continuing nationalist protest thus exposes an endemic crisis of political control in Tibet.

The persistence of ideological campaigns

The events in the spring of 1989 leading up to the Army crackdown in Tiananmen Square on 4 June gave a new cogency to the arguments of conservative forces in the Chinese Communist Party calling for greater supervision of the masses and more emphasis on ideological education. Although the pace of economic reform and marketization of the economy has not slackened in China, the apparatus of social control used in Tibet to combat splittism has been resuscitated throughout China to suppress demands to introduce democratic

---

[1] "Comrade Jiangcun Luobo's [Gyaltsen Norbu] speech at the Regional Conference on Basic Work on Public Security in Grassroots Units, 17 October 1990." Party Circular no. 20 (in Chinese), Office of the Tibetan Autonomous Region Party Committee, 20 November 1990, numbered for restricted circulation. Translated from Chinese by Tibet Information Network and reprinted in *Background Papers on Tibet* (September 1992: 54–6).

freedoms and rights and to promote the new "socialist" orthodoxy —
i.e. continuing Party rule based on the principle of the "people's
democratic dictatorship".

The return to political education has been a general feature of
political life throughout China in the post-Tiananmen period. It has
run parallel to ongoing economic reforms. Since 1989 there have been
movements of ideological education in work units and schools, and
among cadres within the Party and the government. The notion of
a "socialist market economy" developed by Deng Xiaoping and the
reformers within the Party may be an ideological contrivance devised
to placate Party conservatives while the non-state sector of the economy
continues to expand; nevertheless, it signifies the limits to political
expression.

Shifting political currents in Beijing are always mirrored by developments in Tibet. One manifestation of this was the "Propaganda Program for Socialist Ideological Education" in 1992. Preparations for this
political campaign began in January 1992. On 1 April teams of cadres
(*las don ru khag*) were dispatched throughout Tibet, notably to rural
areas as well as Lhasa. Frequent meetings were reported in villages and
towns throughout the TAR as well as in Tibetan areas in neighbouring
Qinghai and Sichuan provinces. The campaign displayed an unusual
intensity in some areas, reminding Tibetans of political campaigns of
the 1960s and 1970s. In one area near Gyantse Tibetans reportedly were
made to hold parades and sing Mao-era songs. Substantial fines were
also levied on families who failed to attend the meetings.

Villagers throughout rural Tibet were lectured on the three "patriotic
loves" (*dga' zhen*): (1) love for the communist party (*tang la dga' zhen*);
(2) love for socialism (*spyi tshogs ring lugs la dga' zhen*), and (3) love for
collectivization (*mnyam sdeb la dga' zhen*). Farmers in one village in
central Tibet, fearing a change in economic policy and a return to the
collective system of production, are reported to have responded that
they "knew all about the communal system" and would refuse to
grow any more crops. The Work Team were at pains to convince
the villagers that this "collectivization" was not the same as during
the 1960s.

There was considerable variation between different areas in the style
and intensity of the socialist education campaign, reflecting the orientation and enthusiasm of local officials. No doubt, some local officials
interpreted the campaign as a return to the collectivism of previous
decades, but its principal focus was ideological. However, its most

important feature was the lack, at least in its initial stages, of primary stress on the splittist threat in Tibet.

A directive issued to cadres listing the main points to be covered in the meetings outlines the reasons for socialist ideological education, emphasizing the development of "socialism with Chinese characteristics" and the need to "tighten the relationship between the party and the masses and the cadres and the masses" and to "mobilize as much as possible the masses' natural diligence and capacity for innovation".[2] In Gyantse and some other areas outside Lhasa, Tibetans were required to memorize the points contained in this directive, and would be subjected to public criticism if they failed to do so.

Splittism is mentioned only once in the directive: one of the reasons given for socialist ideological education is "to build a long steel-like wall in the struggle against peaceful evolution and against splittism."[3] "Peaceful evolution" has become ideological shorthand throughout China for the fear that the economic reforms will gradually erode the power of the communist party and lead to the emergence of Western-style democracy. The socialist ideological education campaign in Tibet was part of a China-wide campaign against "peaceful evolution", precipitated by the collapse of the Soviet Union. Political pluralism, multi-party democracy, and the influence of intellectuals are all held responsible for the demise of communism in Eastern Europe.[4]

The Party in Tibet has never been insulated from political currents in Beijing — perhaps even less so in the 1990s than in the 1980s. As we have seen, the struggle against splittism in Tibet is now equated with the wider struggle against both foreign ideologies and the erosion of Party control. Tao Siju, China's Minister of Public Security, in fact identified illegal religious activities carried out under "the banner of religious freedom" and "ethnic splittist activities" in Tibet as two of

[2] "Propaganda Program for Socialist Ideological Education" (*spyi tshogs ring lugs kyi bsam blo'i slob gso gtong rgyu'i dril bsgrags rtsa 'dzin*), Work Committee of the Bureau Office of the Regional Government (*ljongs srid gzhung don gcod khang gi las don ru khag*), undated (list of directives distributed to local cadres in April 1992).

[3] *zhi bas rim 'gyur la ngo rgol dang kha phral la ngo rgol byed pa'i 'thab rtsod kyi ngar lcags lta bu'i lcags ri ring po rgyag.*

[4] See "CPC Internal Antisubversion, Antipeaceful Evolution Materials" from Shishi Baogao (Current Events Report, CPC Central Propaganda Department), published in Hong Kong Chiushih Nientai in Chinese no. 264, 1 January 1992, in *FBIS*, 15 January 1992: 18–28.

six principal targets in the struggle against "peaceful evolution".[5] In a speech to a working committee of the regional Party on 30 October 1991, Gyaltsen Norbu outlined some of the "problems" (*gnad don*) in handling religion in Tibet:

> Because we do not adequately recognize either the nature of the long-term religious problem during the period of socialism, or the nature of the disturbances, we have not made adequate urgent ideological preparations for the use of religion as an important means of peaceful evolution by the powerful enemy side among foreign nations, who are relentlessly increasing their destructive conduct and infiltrating our side.[6]

Gyaltsen Norbu's remarks reiterate general guidelines issued by the Central Committee of the Chinese Communist Party on 5 February 1991 for "Improving Work on Religion", where religion is also described as a "strategy for bringing about peaceful evolution."[7] These guidelines were part of a China-wide effort to curtail the unregulated growth of religion from 1989 onwards, following recognition by the Party of the international orientation and links of religious bodies, and the support they provided, both inside and outside China, for human rights and democracy in China. Thus, Tibetan protest is no longer understood as a strictly local problem, requiring sensitivity to local conditions and history, but as part a general movement to undermine Party rule. As the argument between reformers and conservatives in the Party in China translates into recurring ideological campaigns in Tibet, Tibetan protest will in turn be perceived in terms of political currents

---

[5] Hong Kong *Chiushih Nientai* in Chinese no. 264, 1 January 1992, in *FBIS*, 15 January 1992: 20–1. The other four targets were: (1) Western hegemonism using the slogans of "democracy," "freedom," and "human rights" to "incorporate the Soviet Union, China and the Third World" into the Western order"; (2) infiltration from Hong Kong and Taiwan; (3) hostile elements who have settled abroad and call for "the overthrow of the socialist system in order to set up a so-called free, democratic, and pluralist country with respect for human rights"; and (4) "reactionary elements in the country" who plot the creation of an opposition party in the hope of building a political force to oppose the Communist Party and replace it once the opportunity comes along."

[6] Gyaltsen Norbu, "Speech to a Work Meeting of Regional Party Members" (*ljongs tang ud las don tshogs 'du'i thog gi gsung bzhad*), 30 October 1991, p. 28 (marked "secret" [*gsang ba*] and internally distributed in numbered copies).

[7] Document no. 6, "Circular Issued by the Central Committee of the Chinese Communist Party and the State Council on Some Problems Concerning Further Improving Work on Religion," 5 February 1991, in Appendix 1, *Freedom of Religion in China*, Asia Watch (January 1992: 27–32).

originating in Beijing, and demands to accommodate special Tibetan interests are likely to fall by the wayside.

In practice, socialist ideological education metamorphosed into another anti-splittist campaign. Political cadres interpreted the aims of the campaign in familiar terms — i.e. the principal threat to socialism in Tibet is splittism. This, after all, is the ongoing chronic problem facing the Chinese administration in Tibet, and political campaigns initiated from Beijing provide a rationale for an already functioning security and political apparatus to carry on with its work. Thus, in areas outside Lhasa the campaign became indistinguishable from previous ones, with lectures by cadres on the Dalai clique, the impossibility of Tibetan independence, and the harsh punishment awaiting splittists when they are apprehended.

Equally important, political campaigns often provoke Tibetan resistance. Tibetans in fact do not distinguish between the ideological objectives of Party-orchestrated political movements and the ongoing drive to suppress the independence movement. Protest may actually be precipitated by the arrival of political work teams in the area (as happened in the Ratö monastery incident in 1988), leading to an escalating confrontation. Thus, individuals may stand up and challenge the cadres in meetings. Posters calling for independence may appear around the village, or one or two people, perhaps monks from the local monastery, may stage a small demonstration. This in turn prompts an investigation by the authorities leading to arrests. Villagers are told that family members will be fined or arrested, and opportunities for schooling, jobs, or ration cards will be denied, if anyone in the family is caught demonstrating or putting up posters. The original ideological focus of the campaign is forgotten in the course of repeated threats and intimidation.

The socialist ideological education campaign had faded away by the summer of 1992.[8] Deng's speeches during his trip to southern China

---

[8] On 4 May, in an address to the Fifth Session of the Fifth TAR People's Congress, Gyaltsen Norbu announced that the education campaign had been a success: "In the light of significant changes in the international political situation and new features in the antiseparatist struggle, we strengthened our political and ideological work and launched an extensive and thorough reeducation campaign on the four cardinal principles and Marxist concepts on nationalities and religion. In so doing, we helped cadres and workers further consolidate their faith both in communism and in following the socialist road with Chinese characteristics." (Lhasa Tibet People's Radio Network in Mandarin, 10 May 1992, in *FBIS*, 18 May 1992: 56).

in January and February 1992 became the basis for a renewed emphasis on economic reform as the key issue rather than ideology. By the summer the study of Deng's speeches was in full swing, with the emphasis now on Deng's call to "emancipate the mind". In the Tibetan context, however, this was interpreted as meaning not only overcoming conservatism within the Party but also playing down the "uniqueness" of the Tibetan situation. Under attack were both leftists in the Party, who stressed ideology over economic reform, and the increasingly sidelined advocates of accommodation to Tibetan language, culture, and religion — i.e. the strategy of the United Front and its allied organizations. In a commentary on Lhasa radio in May, the relationship between emancipation of the mind and the Tibetan situation was discussed:

> . . . if we do not emancipate the mind, dare not make moves, only stress the uniqueness of Tibet, and procrastinate in taking actions, we will end up losing good opportunities . . . At present, some comrades, faced with the tides of reform and opening up, tend to cite the uniqueness of Tibet; when carrying out reform and opening up they say that the uniqueness of Tibet's being a border area and the religious faith of the Tibetan people must be taken into consideration. Hence they dare not give all-out efforts to reform and opening up; this is actually a misinterpretation of Tibet's uniqueness.[9]

Reformers in Tibet have hoped to sidestep the question of the political legitimacy of the Party by lifting state controls over production and offering rapid economic improvement. Here, they face the problem, however, of justifying Party rule without recourse to ideology, while simultaneously raising expectations of the state. It is not surprising that Tibetan protest has emerged during the 1980s, a period of relative political relaxation. Dismantling the collective system of production eliminated the principal basis for political participation, however onesided and oppressive, that lent substance to ideology. The commune was the basic unit of both productive organization and political control. Before the 1980s it would have been impossible to challenge the ideological legitimization of Chinese rule. Following decollectivization, the discrepancy between economic and social practices and the ideological claims of the Chinese communist state widened sufficiently for Tibetans to challenge the continuing reliance of the state on ideology.

One symptom of this widening gap between Party ideology and social practice has been the increasing scale of demands made on Party

---

[9] Lhasa Tibet People's Radio Network, 30 May 1992, in *FBIS*, 3 June 1992: 45.

officials at political meetings. Tibetans use the meetings as an opportunity to complain about the rising cost of commodities, the government's incompetence and corruption, and its failure to implement announced policies. Having invited a discussion of the situation in Tibet, cadres often find themselves at a loss to defend the government. The ideological campaigns thus provide an opportunity for expressing a whole collection of grievances against the state which, depending on how they are handled by local officials, may coalesce into nationalist protest.

Recurring ideological campaigns have certainly contributed to the spread of nationalist protest. Coinciding with the campaign for socialist ideological education, for instance, nine demonstrations by small groups of monks, nuns, and laypeople took place in Lhasa in May and June 1992 alone, resulting in some fifty arrests. As we have seen, similar outbursts of protest occurred during the screening and investigation campaign in the autumn of 1989, and again after the fortieth anniversary celebration in the summer of 1991. Small-scale protest, with the demonstrators prepared to submit to arrest and imprisonment, no longer occurs just on dates commemorating past Tibetan resistance, but is likely to be at any time when ideological campaigns are mounted.

There is also growing evidence of the spread of protest throughout rural areas of Tibet, including those in the east incorporated into Sichuan and Qinghai provinces, as well as those in the west of the country where protest had not previously been reported.[10] Rural Tibetans are especially suspicious of ideological campaigns, associating them with the collectivization of agriculture during the 1960s and the "class struggles" of the Cultural Revolution. Yet they have been specifically targeted in recent campaigns. In a speech to the annual plenary session of the regional Party on 15 January 1992 launching the socialist ideological education campaign in Tibet, Gyaltsen Norbu

---

[10] Protests resulting in the arrest of a substantial number of monks took place in four monasteries in the Shigatse area southwest of Lhasa in March 1992, as monks put up posters and staged small protests in the monastery compound. In May, similar incidents took place in monasteries in Phempo and Medrokunga, east of Lhasa. Three laymen were also arrested in March 1992 for putting up posters in a village in the Gyama region in Medrokunga county. Other reports of protest come from Ngaba in the Chinese province of Sichuan and Rigong in Qinghai province, where a Tibetan flag was raised on a government building. A Tibetan delegate to the National People's Congress revealed on 30 March 1992, that there had been disturbances in Ngari, 1,000 km. west of Lhasa, during the fortieth anniversary celebrations in May 1991.

called on the Party to recognize the need for "waging an anti-splittist struggle in rural and pastoral areas" in order to "instill ideas of patriotism, socialism, and collectivism into the masses of peasants and herdsmen."[11] Yang Rudai, Party secretary of Sichuan, acknowledged the problem of rural unrest in an address to county Party secretaries from Tibetan areas, admitting that "we must soberly realise that there are still destabilizing factors in those areas."[12] He, too, calls for more ideological education to "enable the broad masses of peasants and herdsmen consciously to resist, in terms of ideology, the reactionary propaganda launched by the separatist forces."

Ideological campaigns remain a permanent feature of the Chinese political system. They may be understood in terms of factional struggles within the Party, but they are also expressions of the chronic legitimacy crisis that underlies Party rule. Cycles of ideological retrenchment, a feature of Chinese politics in the 1980s, are likely to recur for the foreseeable future. In the 1980s there were three such cycles — the campaign against "spiritual pollution" in 1983–4, the campaign against "bourgeois liberalization" in 1986–7, and the post-Tiananmen revival of socialist orthodoxy; each was followed by accelerated economic reforms. In lieu of other political mechanisms, ideology endures as a principal means of periodically shoring up the Party's monopoly of power.

Contradictions in the reform policy

The second strategy for maintaining Party control in Tibet has been to accelerate the pace of economic reforms on the assumption that a visibly improving standard of living will quell Tibetan discontent. Following his 1980 visit, Hu Yaobang's recommendations became the basis for policy in Tibet throughout the 1980s. After 1981 the rural communes were dissolved and commune land and livestock were redistributed among commune members on an equal basis.[13] Under the "responsibility system" for agriculture, land is nominally owned by the state and leased to producers, but individual households engage in

---

[11] Lhasa Tibet Television Network, 15 January 1992, in *FBIS*, 22 January 1992: 57.
[12] Chengdu Sichuan People's Radio Network in Mandarin, 28 March 1992, in *FBIS*, 1 April 1992: 40.
[13] See Goldstein and Beall (1989) and Clarke (1987) for two accounts of the implementation of the economic reforms in rural Tibet.

production and are not subject to collective management. In principle they are free to sell their produce for cash in the market. Tibetan farmers in fact speak of themselves as the "owners" (*bdag po*) of their land. Farmers and herders in Tibet were also exempted from taxes and quota sales to the government — initially for two years — but the exemption has remained in place since it was first instituted and is now regarded as something of a "right" by agricultural producers.[14]

The breakup of the communes and the return to private plots in agriculture, and private management of herds, reestablished traditional household forms of production, including traditional patterns of trade between herders and farmers and between regions, and freed labour previously commandeered by the state. It also opened new opportunities for the direct sale of commodities in the market-place, which did not exist in Tibet during the collectivization of the 1960s and 1970s. The break-up of the communes set loose a transient population, no longer tied to production teams and work units, many of which have migrated to Lhasa and other cities to set up businesses and engage in trade. Independent truck-drivers move goods and people from the Nepali/Indian border in the west to the borders of Sichuan and Gansu provinces in the east and Xinjiang in the north. The growth of a cash economy has meant that consumer goods have become readily available throughout Tibet.

Tibetans will acknowledge that there has been a dramatic improvement in their standard of living with the economic reforms — especially when compared to the harsh conditions during the period of collectivization and the turmoil of the Cultural Revolution. But the negative character of the reforms in the perception of most Tibetans should be recognized. They represent the lifting of an alien and oppressive system, and the reversion to traditional patterns of social and economic life. The government receives no credit for the growth of the market economy, which is regarded as the result of people's own individual efforts. The comparison is not made with the pre-1959 social and economic system,

---

[14] In fact, a variety of "unofficial" taxes and "voluntary" quota sales have been imposed on farmers and nomads since the new agricultural policy was introduced in the 1980s. The onerousness of these seems to vary considerably from area to area (both within and outside the TAR). Particularly since the late 1980s, these exactions have come to be increasingly resented as the government quota prices for agricultural products has not kept up with the market price for these products nor with the rise in prices of other commodities in the market.

with its traditional institutionalized inequalities, but with an idealized "natural" order, where individuals and households are free to pursue their own destinies. Thus, Tibetans take the benefits of the reforms for granted, while resenting continuing government interference in their lives, and remain fearful of a reversion to the policies of the past.[15]

The breakup of the communes meant that intrusive political interference in daily life largely ceased. The state, formerly represented by commune officials and cadres, now exercises administrative functions from the county and sub-county level, and former commune officials have lost their power. However, both rural and urban Tibetans continue to experience a variety of bureaucratic intrusions: unofficial or "voluntary" quotas for sales to government offices remain, herders complain of limits on herd size, officials exercise control over state subsidies and loans, movement is still restricted through registration and permits, and merchants and traders are subject to licences and taxes. The question is not whether these intrusions by the state into economic and social life are necessarily onerous; rather, Tibetans do not trust the state, or its commitment to currently favourable policies, and resent remaining areas of interference. The potential of state officials to call on the security apparatus to deal with discontent is always present. Any changes in policies — e.g. increases in taxation, new licensing restrictions or restrictions on movement — are likely to prompt spontaneous public protest. A heavy-handed response by officials can easily lead to escalation, precipitating overtly nationalist forms of protest. Although the command economy has been partly dismantled, Tibetans are still subject to a wide range of state controls over their freedom of action.

As a result of the reforms, Tibetans have been able to restore much of the traditional culture that had been suppressed during the Cultural Revolution and a wide range of traditional practices and beliefs have come out into the open. Most Tibetan homes, both rural and urban, have altars with religious statues and pictures (including pictures of the

---

[15] Goldstein and Beall (1989: 630) describe the attitudes of Phala nomads toward currently favourable government policies which have enabled them to rebuild much of their traditional culture: ". . . their knowledge (and fear) that the current government could intervene again at any time and impose its alien values has left feelings of vulnerability, anxiety, and anger and has discouraged the development of positive attitudes toward the state. To a considerable extent this accounts for the obvious incongruity between the objective effects of the new policy in Tibet and the Tibetan's often negative reaction to the government that enacted it. It will take a long time for most nomads to forget the first few decades of Chinese rule."

Dalai Lama); the holidays of the Tibetan calendar are publicly celebrated in traditional ways; divination is openly practiced and the services of religious specialists are sought for the performance of beneficial rites. Most important, as we have seen, monasteries have been rebuilt and restaffed with young people, and receive a steady flow of contributions in money and goods.

This revival of traditional Tibetan culture was not a deliberate aim of the reforms, and the strength of the revival was unanticipated by the Chinese government. It has come about spontaneously as economic restrictions have been lifted and political sanctions for the expression of traditional culture ended, leaving households free to make their own choices about the disposal of their wealth. At the same time, continuing interference by the state in religious and cultural life remains a source of frustration and resentment. Restrictions on rebuilding monasteries, on travel for pilgrimage and on religious practice and teaching confirm negative perceptions of the state, which at any time may revoke present freedoms.

With the advent of the reforms, economic development in Tibet has been self-consciously styled by Chinese planners as synonymous with global modernization. In particular, soliciting foreign investment and encouraging contact with the outside world through the tourist industry are expected to overcome Tibetan "backwardness" and draw Tibet into the modern world under Chinese tutelage. At the same time, traditional patterns of production and consumption are perceived by Chinese reformers as an obstacle to economic modernization, and in particular to the development of a market economy linked to China. The reforms thus convey a contradictory message, offering new opportunities and freedoms to Tibetans, while reinforcing negative valuations of traditional Tibetan culture.

Underlying Chinese thinking on economic development in Tibet are abiding assumptions about the backwardness of Tibetans which cut across otherwise important political and ideological differences. For example, these assumptions form the basis for the influential study of development in "backward regions" of China by Wang Xiaoqiang and Bai Nanfeng of the Economic Structural Reform Institute of China, the group which advised Zhao Ziyang on reform policies up till his ouster in 1989.[16] Wang and Bai frame Tibetan cultural backwardness in economic terms, complaining of the "poor quality of human

---

[16] Wang and Bai (1991).

resources" in backward regions. The problem, as they see it, is that the relaxation of controls has led to a resurgence of the "natural economy" rather than market-oriented production and consumption: ". . . relaxing controls in backward regions and developed areas released two kinds of impetus working in different directions, one leading to the development of the natural economy and the other to that of the commodity economy."[17]

As planners they are clearly frustrated with the unwillingness of Tibetans to become dependent on a China-wide market economy for the satisfaction of needs:

A number of industrial goods such as thermos flasks, Mao caps, bicycles and watches have to differing extents been nominally accepted by a proportion of urban dwellers in backward regions, but for the large majority these sorts of commodities which can only be obtained through cash exchange are still far from 'necessities' such as tea has become. Much of the population in backward regions are not only able to do without watches or bicycles, but can also go without vegetables, poultry, fish and even wheat, as in Tibet. The traditional way of life prolongs the traditional modes of production, and moreover sustains traditional concepts of value and leads to contentment with the traditional way. When people are satisfied with the traditional natural economy, there is no demand for commodities that are solely available through exchange . . .[18]

The resurgence of the "natural economy", where Tibetan producers "cling to their self-sufficient ownership of livestock that are never sold, or to their wealth which consists in the consumption of a few hundred kilograms of yak butter every year", is an undesirable outcome of the reform policy of the 1980s.[19] The same is true for the revival of traditional religion, which consumes economic resources and reinforces the traditional way of life and traditional modes of production. The expanding Chinese market economy is thus used as a standard against which Tibetan cultural attitudes are measured. Tibetans are expected to produce for the Chinese market and, in turn, seek goods only available from the Chinese market. The implicit assumption is that modernization and sinicization amount to the same thing.

Wang and Bai's key proposal for overcoming Tibetan backwardness is the development of the tourist industry. This has in fact been the

[17] *Ibid.*: 176.
[18] *Ibid.*: 146.
[19] *Ibid.*: 167.

centrepiece of Tibetan development strategy since the mid-1980s. Tourism, they argue, is an industry high in "information content", communicating modern values and lifestyles, and modern consumption patterns, through exposure to the outside world, thus improving the quality of human resources:

The tourists' eating habits, clothing and jewellry, how they treat people, their appearance and behaviour may become the objects of wonder, admiration and emulation by the local people . . . The consumption patterns of the indigenous population in backward regions can, through emulation and learning, become enriched thus resulting in production for exchange, and from this there emerges the possibility of transforming modes of production.[20]

The fallacy in tourism as a development strategy is the assumption that the modern values and "information" carried in by tourists are consistent with modernization as it is understood in Beijing. Tibetans do not learn the value of political repression and Party control from foreigners; instead, Tibetans and foreigners come to share common perceptions of Chinese regulations and restrictions. As we have seen, Tibetans associate ideas of human rights and democracy with the West, and find that their own understanding of Chinese rule as colonial occupation is reinforced through contact with Westerners. The tendency is also to see Chinese rule in Tibet as a barrier to access to Western goods and services. In fact, the values that Tibetans have come to identify with tourists are the cultural and political values of the West. Tourists have generally shown an appreciation of Tibetan culture and religion, and a sympathy for Tibetan political aspirations. Tourism has thus highlighted the political and cultural "backwardness" of China, not Tibet. Tourists in turn have been an audience for Tibetan protest, relaying information on the situation in Tibet to the West. The Chinese response since the outbreak of unrest in 1987 has been to curtail foreign access to Tibet.

Wang and Bai generally regard the transfer of a foreign urban population into backward regions as a desirable force for cultural transformation, believing that "the influx of a large body of 'immigrants' has brought new learning and culture; and the growth in numbers of indigenous urban dwellers has brought about a fundamental change in the way of life and concepts of value of a considerable portion of

[20] *Ibid.*: 171.

them."[21] But, as their own research in Tibet shows, the massive and accelerating infusion of capital into Tibet during the 1980s has simply subsidized the importation of commodities from China, with no tangible returns in terms of the development of commodity production within Tibet: "The lion's share of the money provided by the central government has been used to pay for goods purchased from the rest of the country."[22] At the same time, administration and management costs have risen dramatically. In effect this means subsidizing consumption for the army of Chinese cadres sent to Tibet to oversee its economic development and staff its administration — almost entirely an urban population, residing in large towns, especially Lhasa. As Wang and Bai demonstrate, Tibet is very much an over-administered society, with a top-heavy and highly articulated governmental superstructure made up of "all the institutions one expects to find in developed regions", consuming more wealth from government subsidies than it generates through increased economic activity.[23] Thus, the "modern urban system" in Tibet is increasingly insulated from the larger Tibetan society, which is primarily rural, and depends on "blood transfusions" from the state for its perpetuation.[24]

Economic development throughout the 1980s under the policy of reform has increased the disparities between Tibet and China, and, within Tibet, between Tibetans and Chinese. The former problem is frequently acknowledged by the Chinese administration in Tibet, whose solution is more rapid development, which leads inevitably to the importation of still more personnel from China. The latter problem has been aggravated by the influx of Chinese — entrepreneurs, construction workers, teachers, technicians, and administrators — who are disproportionately the beneficiaries of increased economic activity. Chinese cadres recruited to fill positions in the administration in Tibet receive a variety of incentives, including housing, special salaries, allowances for travel to their homes in China, and education for their children. Large numbers of Chinese construction workers have also

---

[21] *Ibid.*: 147.

[22] *Ibid.*: 73.

[23] *Ibid.*: 100.

[24] See also Wangchuk (1992: 43–7) for an analysis of the growing subsidization of the bureaucracy and loss-making state enterprises (where most Chinese residents are employed). This produced throughout the 1980s a widening gap in incomes between the Tibetan rural sector and the Chinese urban sector.

been brought in to work on development projects initiated by the Chinese administration.[25] The use of Chinese workers results from a combination of factors, including training, familiarity of Chinese engineers with Chinese workers and recruiters, the availability of Chinese workers for rapid recruitment, and personal relationships (*guanxi*). Finally, a mobile population of Chinese in service occupations — traders, artisans, food-sellers, hairdressers — have taken advantage of economic opportunities in the cities and towns of Tibet. Similar factors are at work here: migrants draw on past business experience, access to capital and sources of goods in China, and personal relationships with the Chinese officials who provide permits and licences.

Tibetans in towns and cities feel excluded from this new economic activity and express fears about the growing number of Chinese in Tibet. Hu's policy of withdrawing Han cadres from Tibet may have been implemented for some older cadres, withdrawn in the early 1980s, but their numbers were rapidly supplanted by a new influx of technical and administrative workers, entrepreneurs, and labourers — partly resulting from government policies and partly a function of the new economic freedoms made possible by the reforms. In the eyes of Tibetans, this influx has continued unabated from the mid-1980s to the present, perceptibly increasing after the suppression of protest in 1989. Most Tibetans continue to work in traditional occupations — farming, herding, and some forms of trade — while Chinese are recruited for non-traditional work in Tibet (mining and lumbering, construction, factory work, and non-indigenous agriculture). To the extent that Chinese development policy demands expansion in these areas, the increasing importation of Chinese workers seems inevitable.[26]

More than 90 per cent of the Tibetan population in the TAR is

---

[25] Clarke (1987) mentions a figure of 60,000 construction workers in 1985 brought in to work on construction projects in Tibetan towns and to provide tourist facilities. Since 1984 cities and provinces in China have sponsored 43 construction projects in Tibet, sending whole work units to Tibet under the banner of a "Help Tibet Prosper" campaign (Xinhua in English, 29 September 1987, in *FBIS*, 2 October 1987: 27).

[26] The massive World Food Program project for developing the Lhasa River area (Project 3357) calls for the importation of large numbers of Chinese workers and aims to produce non-indigenous agricultural products for an urban Chinese market ("Tibet Launches Massive Development Project," *Beijing Review*, vol. 34, no. 3, 21–7 January 1991: 5–6).

rural,[27] the total urban population of the TAR (cities and towns) based on the 1990 census being just 263,792. If the Chinese population of 81,217 is assumed to live exclusively in cities and towns, then more than 30 per cent of urban dwellers are Chinese. However, these official figures refer only to the "registered" population of the TAR, and thus include primarily Chinese employees of state enterprises and government bureaucracies. There are no official figures for the large "floating population" of unregistered Chinese migrants to Tibet's cities and towns. Some Chinese sources have indicated that the floating population in Lhasa alone may be as high as 100,000.[28] An estimate of the total Chinese population of the TAR (excluding the large military population stationed in Tibet) in the range of 150,000 to 300,000 has been suggested.[29] Thus the overall Chinese population in urban areas exceeds 50 per cent, and in Lhasa is probably as high as 60 or 70 per cent.[30] More important, there appears to be no policy to limit or

[27] The urban population of Tibet (cities and towns) based on the 1990 census is 263,792. Assuming that all the Han population of 81,217 live in towns and cities, this leaves a Tibetan urban population of just 182,575 out of a total of 2,096,346 Tibetans in the TAR — or 8.7 per cent. Results of the 1990 census were released on 3 November 1990 (Lhasa Tibet Television Network in Mandarin, 8 November 1990, in *JPRS*, 28 November 1990: 43).

[28] Ngapö Ngawang Jigme referred to the problem of Han migrants to Lhasa in a discussion among People's Congress deputies on 22 March 1989: "The Tibetan People cannot be separated from the support and assistance of the fraternal Han people. However, a large number of labourers, including peddlers and hawkers, have now flowed into Tibet, with a total of at least 100,000 in Lhasa alone" (Beijing Renmin Ribao in Chinese, 23 March 1989, p. 2, in *FBIS*, 24 March 1989: 21). The mayor of Lhasa has also mentioned a floating population of 100,000: "Lhasa currently has a population of 140,000; it has a floating population reaching more than 100,000, which not only brings certain pressure to citizens of Lhasa and to Lhasa itself, but creates some social and ethnic problems" (Beijing Domestic Service in Mandarin, 27 March 1989, in *FBIS*, 30 March 1989, p. 44).

[29] A probable range of 150,000–300,000 Han in the TAR is offered in the report of the delegation organized by the National Committee on US-China Relations that visited Tibet in August 1991 ("Tibet: Issues for Americans," National Committee China Policy Series no. 4, April 1992: 10). It should be added that the military population around cities like Lhasa and Shigatse is a highly visible presence and itself contributes to considerable economic activity by Chinese migrants.

[30] Official census statistics for Lhasa certainly underestimate the number of Chinese. Detailed population statistics for Lhasa were published in the *Tibet Daily* (in Chinese), on 24 November 1990. According to the results of the 1990 census the city of Lhasa has a population of 137,661. The population of the city from the 1982 census was 105,866. The number of Han for the entire Lhasa Municipal Area in 1990 is given

exclude this floating population from Tibet, which is an increasingly visible presence.[31]

Tibetans fear that the pattern of development in areas of eastern Tibet incorporated into neighbouring Chinese provinces will be repeated in central Tibet. Chinese census data indicate that the Tibetan population in designated Tibetan areas outside the TAR (autonomous prefectures and counties) increased by 38 per cent from 1953 to 1982 (from 1,500,000 to 2,080,000), while the Chinese population in these areas increased by 340 per cent (from 426,000 to 1,449,000). In Tibetan areas of Qinghai province (the Amdo region of Tibet) the increase in the Chinese population is dramatic — from 40,000 in 1953 to 504,000 in 1982, or 1,260 per cent. Overall, Chinese comprised more than 40 per cent of the registered population in Tibetan areas in eastern Tibet.[32]

Some Chinese have always lived in these border areas, along with other ethnic groups. But the rapid growth in the Chinese population has been sustained by a policy of urban and industrial development that has brought large numbers of permanent settlers into these areas. New towns and factories have been built in traditionally rural areas. This new urban population is almost entirely Chinese, with Tibetans continuing to work in traditional occupations. Chronic poverty and

---

as 44,539 (about half the total number of Han officially in Tibet). If all these people lived in the city, the Han population of Lhasa would number around 32 per cent of the total. However, the census results indicate that this figure represents an increase of only 1,528 Han over 1982. Thus the 32 per cent increase in the registered population of Lhasa over eight years comes almost entirely from the increase in the Tibetan population. This may not be an unreasonable increase for the Tibetan population, but 140,000 for the total population of Lhasa must therefore be low. Ma Rong, in a study of residential patterns in Lhasa, cites Chinese figures based on "incomplete registration" during June–August 1985 of 52,800 temporary migrants from other provinces, and gives his own estimates of 40–50,000 "temporary" migrants in the summer of 1988, mainly from Sichuan province (Ma 1991: 827–8). The visible evidence of increasing economic activity by Chinese migrants to Lhasa since 1989 suggests that more recent numbers must be substantially higher.

[31] Following the declaration of martial law, the TAR government announced that an estimated 30,000 to 40,000 non-residents of Lhasa would be required to obtain a residence permit (Lhasa Tibet Regional Service in Mandarin, 20 March 1989, in *FBIS*, 21 March 1989: 58). Tibetans in Lhasa subsequently reported that the registration requirement was being applied exclusively to Tibetans.

[32] These numbers are from official statistics, discussed in Rong and Naigu (1988). Since 1982 a large unregistered Han population has certainly also moved into these areas in eastern Tibet.

over-population in neighbouring Chinese provinces push Chinese migrants into these border areas, where they find work in mining, lumbering and new industrial enterprises. Tibetan farmers in Qinghai also complain that Chinese are being settled on agricultural land used by Tibetans. Though industrial development on the same scale has not taken place in the TAR, there is no reason to doubt that it would bring the same results.

Before 1980, Chinese in Tibet were mainly functionaries in the administration, carrying out government-assigned duties. Now those in urban areas are perceived as advantaged competitors for the resources and opportunities opened up by the reforms. The fact that Tibetans and Chinese in Tibet are separate communities, largely living and working apart and not speaking each other's language, lays the basis for ethnic conflict. A multiplicity of linguistic, cultural, economic and physical barriers separate Chinese and Tibetan worlds. Where Tibetans and Chinese do come into contact, as happens in Tibetan cities and towns, friction and hostility are evident. An instance of this was the spate of attacks on Chinese shops during the riots in Lhasa in 1988 and 1989. Ethnic idioms have also begun to make their appearance in Tibetan protest material, stressing the persecution and discrimination that Tibetans face in daily life.

Tibetan cadres, educated in Chinese and trained to staff the Chinese administration in Tibet, have also been beneficiaries of the reforms in Tibet. In line with Hu's recommendations to recruit more Tibetan cadres, a new generation of Tibetans has entered positions within the administration during the 1980s, working alongside newly-arrived Chinese cadres. These young Tibetan cadres are especially well represented in occupations like journalism, broadcasting, the arts and cultural affairs, and tourism. They share with young Chinese cadres a commitment to modernization and reform, and a general disdain for ideological orthodoxy and Party interference. However, they are also almost universally Tibetan nationalists. They complain of the continuing influx of Chinese cadres, with whom they must compete for jobs in state organizations. They find that their own careers are blocked, not because they lack the necessary skills but because they are Tibetan. Since the outbreak of protest, it has become clear to the communist apparatus that Tibetan cadres are untrustworthy, and thus they have become a special target for repeated investigations.

From the beginning of protest in 1987, many of these Tibetan cadres have supported the monks and nuns leading the demonstrations.

Demonstrations by Tibetan students in Lhasa and Beijing in December 1988 after the shooting on 10 December in front of the Jokhang is one indication of this support. When martial law was declared in 1989, underground organizations were formed consisting of Tibetan cadres which have been responsible for much of the subsequent clandestine publication of posters, leaflets, and letters. Literature produced by the cadre underground is markedly more secular in its orientation, focusing on the influx of Chinese as a consequence of the reforms, and on the resulting discrimination against Tibetans in jobs, housing, and education, as well as on the failure of the local government to implement its Tibetan language policy. Tibetan cadres are more sophisticated in their understanding of world events, having greater access to sources of world news, and are thus quick to compare the Tibetan situation with developments elsewhere in the world, e.g. in the former Soviet Union and Eastern Europe.

On 12 May 1992, China announced the creation in Tibet of a "special economic and technological zone", with incentives and preferential tax policies to attract domestic and foreign investment.[33] The significance of this development for the strategy of economic reform in Tibet is made clear in a speech by Chen Kuiyuan on 25 July 1992, four months after his appearance in Tibet as a deputy secretary of the Party. Chen, who was selected to be the new Party secretary for Tibet in December 1992, declares that the "ideological obstacles to reform and opening up come mainly from the left and the old," but singles out the "old" for emphasis, and concludes that the economic revolution in Tibet must be "accompanied by a social revolution."[34] The latter refers to the persistence of traditional attitudes and modes of production and the continuing resistance of Tibetans to incorporation into a market economy.

Outlining the difficulties facing the reforms in Tibet, Chen stresses the "shortage of qualified personnel, particularly managerial personnel,

[33] The "Provisional Regulations of the People's Government of the Tibet Autonomous Region on the Encouragement of Foreign Investment in Tibet" were promulgated on 14 July 1992. They regularize private domestic Chinese business enterprises in Tibet and establish guidelines for the "compensatory transfer of land use right" to non-Tibetans ("Tibet Encourages Foreign Investment," *China's Tibet*, vol. 3, no. 4, Winter 1992: 19–20). One immediate consequence of the new regulations has been the purchase for the first time of Tibetan agricultural land in the Lhasa valley by Chinese farmers.

[34] Lhasa Tibet Television Network in Mandarin, 27 July 1992, in *FBIS*, 3 August 1992: 77.

scientists, technicians, teachers, and those who know how to develop village and town enterprises and a commodity economy" and the "lack of a market system of two-way circulation because of underdeveloped markets and poor connections to the outside."[35] Chen's appraisal of the economic situation in Tibet returns to the same themes voiced by liberal reformers like Wang and Bai. Faced with the competing demands set loose by the reforms for both greater Tibetan participation in the local economy and adminstration, on the one hand, and the rapid incorporation of the local economy into the Chinese commodity economy, on the other, government policy in the 1990s is likely to favour the latter. Chen's words indicate the future direction of Chinese reform policy for Tibet:

To accelerate Tibet's development, we must emphasize opening up and invigorating the market. To do so, we must overcome, as soon as possible, a state of relative seclusion, which is left over from history. We should open Tibet wider to the outside. In other words, we should open Tibet to all countries and regions and open our job market to our fellow countrymen.[36]

This new phase of economic reform, which involves actively recruiting labour and personnel in China for work in Tibet, along with soliciting investment for profit-making enterprises, has provoked a sense of crisis in the thinking of Tibetan cadres. Letters coming from cadre groups in Tibet in 1992 speak with growing urgency of the threat posed by foreign investment in the country, with contracts awarded to Chinese contractors and labour imported from China, while local Tibetans receive no material benefits. In August 1992, a poster appeared in Lhasa denouncing the policy for the further opening up of Tibet:

These days, under the pretext of wanting to expand the economy, they are opening the whole Tibetan region to China. In reality, Tibetans have no rights and are losing their jobs, and it is clear that they plan to make it impossible for us to live in our own land by sending countless Chinese to stay in Tibet.

This poster, from the underground group calling itself "The Unified Committee of the Three Provinces" (*chol gsum mthun tshogs*), refers to the growth in housing for Chinese in Tibet and disputes Chinese claims that money spent by the government benefits Tibetans. The overall number of Chinese in the TAR may remain small compared to the large

[35] *Ibid.*: 76.
[36] *Ibid.*

Tibetan rural population, but the expansion of Chinese-run enterprises in urban areas causes real fear. Tibetan cadres, in particular, see themselves being pushed aside and losing the few advantages they have secured through the reforms. They know they are not trusted by the Chinese administration, and fear that they will be replaced or downgraded as a new wave of Chinese cadres is recruited.[37] The exclusion of Tibetans from the new plans for expanded economic development is likely to generate further calls for protest and resistance.

Weaknesses of the United Front strategy

In his impassioned pleas not to return to a policy of repression after the outbreak of protest in 1987, the Panchen Lama urged that the special characteristics of Tibet continue to be recognized in implementing political and economic policies in the region. He insisted that the relaxation of restrictions on religion should remain in place, and attributed unrest to the legacy of resentment and mistrust engendered by leftist policies. Throughout the 1980s it was politically desirable in Tibet, as in China, to acknowledge the "mistakes" of the Cultural Revolution. The movement to "Redeem Wrongs", initiated after Hu's visit in 1980, attempted to undo the damage of the Cultural Revolution by allowing Tibetans to practise their religion and culture once again. Reformers in the Party, following Deng Xiaoping, were able to use the mistakes of the Cultural Revolution in their attack on entrenched leftism. The relaxation of religious and cultural policy was a way to placate popular discontent while mobilizing support for the economic reforms in Tibet. With a secure commitment from the leadership in Beijing to continuing economic reform, there is no longer the same

---

[37] These fears are expressed in an "open letter" from a group of Tibetan cadres circulated in Lhasa in the winter of 1993. The letter bears the title "A statement concerning the general welfare of Tibet to be distributed among all Tibetan cadres of one flesh and blood, Tibetans who struggle, and the broad masses" (*sha khrag gcig gi bod mi'i las byed pa yongs rdzogs dang bod mi'i 'thab 'dzin pa rgya che'i mang tshogs bcas la bod spyi'i don gsal sgrags spel rgyur*), and is signed "a section of cadres" (*las byed khag gcig nas*). It refers to a report by Hu Jintao in which "he says that he has no confidence [*yid ches*] in Tibetan leaders and cadres." The letter protests the "many tens of thousands of Chinese being sent to live in Tibet," but the Tibetan cadres complain specifically of "many Chinese from China being sent to supervise Tibetan cadres." The cadres affirm their faith in the Dalai Lama's efforts to achieve self-determination for Tibet and indicate that they will continue to work as cadres for the Chinese.

need to draw attention to the wrongs committed during the Cultural Revolution. At the same time, periodic political campaigns to contain expressions of dissent are not helped by comparisons with that event.

Using the Cultural Revolution as a standard against which to measure developments in Tibet, as the Panchen Lama did, has not necessarily increased popular support for the Party. Tibet, unlike China, does not have a decades-long history of popular revolution and resistance to foreign invasion to establish the political legitimacy of the communist Party. Thus the Party there cannot mobilize patriotic national sentiments, as it can in China. In a very real sense, the Cultural Revolution *was* the revolution in Tibet; the suppression of the 1959 uprising was followed in the space of just a few years by the collectivization of the whole society and the wholesale destruction of Tibetan culture under the extreme conditions of the Cultural Revolution. Thus attacks on the Cultural Revolution call into question the basis of Chinese rule in Tibet, while ideological movements defending socialism renew Tibetan fears of a return to a policy of cultural repression. Significantly there has been no public airing — in newspapers, literature, or film — of the hardships and injustices endured by Tibetans during the Cultural Revolution, as there has been in China.

The spontaneous reconstruction of Tibetan religion and culture has had unpredictable and destabilizing consequences — the most significant, as we have seen, being the emergence of a body of politically militant monks and nuns. The United Front apparatus of the Party has attempted to direct and control the revival of religion through the organizations under its control. Thus, the regional Buddhist Association, one of the government-approved "patriotic religious organizations", consists of rehabilitated religious leaders who are prepared to cooperate with the Chinese administration. The designated functions of patriotic religious organizations — which, like the Democratic Management Committees of the monasteries, fall under the authority of the Religious Affairs Bureau — include assisting "the Party and the government to implement the policy of freedom of religious belief" and helping "the broad mass of religious believers and persons in religious circles to continually raise their patriotic and socialist consciousness."[38]

In reality, the United Front has employed a top-down strategy, attempting to coopt the leaders of the religious hierarchy and thereby contain the potential for militancy of the monks and nuns. In line with

---

[38] "Document 19," in MacInnis (1989): 19.

this strategy, the Chinese government has made the search for the reincarnation of the Panchen Lama a state affair. Similarly, in June 1992 the Buddhist Association and the Bureau of Religious Affairs conveyed the official approval of the Chinese government for the selection of the 17th reincarnation of the Karmapa, head of a branch of the Kargyü sect, traditional rivals to the Gelugpas.[39] The boy was located in Tibet by senior monks of his former monastery in Sikkim. In this case, recognition of the incarnation by the Dalai Lama was forthcoming and thus it is unlikely that the legitimacy of the selection will be challenged by the Tibetan community. Another reincarnate lama was installed at a monastery in Amdo in October 1991 with the blessing of the government.[40]

The selection of reincarnate lamas has not been practised in Tibet since 1959, and the aim of current Chinese religious policy appears to be to use the institution as a source of political stability. State recognition of incarnate lamas also serves to foster the Chinese claim that Tibetan religious leaders have, since imperial times, received their titles and exercised power as a dispensation from the Chinese state. Whether the Chinese government will be able to control the selection of incarnate lamas, and whether they will all prove to be compliant agents of state power, remains to be seen.

However, there are sociological reasons to doubt that this will prove an effective strategy. The middle layers of the self-governing monastic hierarchy were destroyed in the 1960s and have not been rebuilt. Instead, the functions of monastic management belong to the Democratic Management Committees, who are subordinate to the Party and the Chinese administration. As we have seen, the young monks and nuns do everything in their power to subvert attempts at control from above, and have little respect for the showcase lamas who cooperate with the administration and defend Chinese rule in Tibet. The Chinese government has not succeeded in generating loyalty among young monks and nuns, and the monasteries are controlled primarily through coercive restrictions. The need to send Work Team cadres regularly to the monasteries indicates the failure of the present system of Democratic Management Committees to exercise effective political control. In

---

[39] Beijing Xinhua in English, 27 June 1992, in *FBIS*, 30 June 1992: 44–5.
[40] The enthronement took place at Rongbo Monastery in Amdo (Huangnan Prefecture, Qinghai) on 29 October 1991, in the presence of Party and government officials ("Living Buddha Xarucon," *China's Tibet*, vol. 3, no. 3, Autumn 1992).

sociological terms, the destruction of traditional ecclesiastical organization, leaving an atomized mass of newly-recruited monks and nuns in conflict with external political control, creates precisely the conditions under which monastic political activism is most likely to occur.[41]

The principal objective of the United Front strategy on religion has been to train a "younger generation of patriotic religious personnel" who "fervently love their homeland and support the Party's leadership and the socialist system."[42] Nevertheless, toleration of religion remains an expedient. Party members are still required to be atheists, accepting the Marxist-Leninist interpretation of religion, which is understood as "a historical phenomenon pertaining to a definite period in the development of human society" and is expected to "disappear naturally . . . through the long-term development of Socialism and Communism."[43]

The attempt to eradicate religion prematurely is described as a leftist error that gained prominence during the Cultural Revolution. According to current thinking, the "religious question" is expected to persist for a long time, "to have a definite mass nature, to be entangled in many areas with the ethnic question, and to be affected by some class-struggle and complex international factors."[44] The "correct" policy — i.e. that of Party reformers through the 1980s — is to avoid alienating the "religious masses" while steering religion in socially constructive directions. There is no doubt that the freedom to practise religion is universally appreciated by Tibetans. The potential for it to be used as a patriotic force in the building of "socialist spiritual civilization" is another question. The hope of United Front strategists has been that religion can be transformed as an ideology and made to assume a form congenial with government aims for political stability and economic progress.

In a propaganda guide for Party cadres issued by the Ganze Prefecture

---

[41] There are some parallels between the situation of monks and nuns in Tibet and the conditions Tambiah describes for monasteries in Burma during and after British colonial rule, where the "domination by a Western colonial power activated Buddhist monks into a tradition of political action" through a vacillating and destructive religious policy that led to the "atrophy of any hierarchical authority exerting control over the monks and monasteries." The "weakened, atomistic nature of sangha organization" contributed in turn to the "politicization of monks and their engagement in militant, anticolonial, nationalist politics". (Tambiah 1976: 461–2).

[42] "Document 19", in MacInnis (1989): 19–20.

[43] *Ibid.*: 10.

[44] *Ibid.*: 11.

Propaganda Department in February 1990, cadres are instructed to "creatively carry out the Party's policy, to mobilize the masses to work harder, to create and improve the material and spiritual conditions, to accomplish our due responsibilities in order to promote the natural extinction of religion."[45] While allowing people to carry on religious activities "within the scope of the permission of the policy and law," cadres are instructed to "propagate and popularize the knowledge of science and opposition to feudal customs".[46] The document calls for the advocacy of "Humanist Buddhism", which will reorient "the masses of religious people and the monks" toward "the reality of the present time", "add new content to the doctrines", and "make new explanations for the development of the cause of socialist construction."[47]

While restrictions and regulations may control the revival of religious activity, the potential of religion to assume new ideological forms is less easily managed. The intellectual ferment that has accompanied protest in Tibet since 1987 has led to the creation of something very much like the Humanist Buddhism advocated by the Party — i.e. a politically aware Buddhism oriented toward the problems of the present. However, it does not draw its inspiration from "socialist civilization" but from currents of ideas originating outside China. Under present conditions, where Tibetans are able to compare their situation under Chinese rule with the contemporary world beyond China, efforts to reshape thinking through ideological education have had consequences unanticipated by the Party, provoking not merely resistance, but the development of intellectual alternatives.[48]

---

[45] Chapter 5 of "Propaganda Speeches on Strengthening National Solidarity and Preserving the Unification of the Motherland", by the Propaganda Committee of the Ganze Prefectural Committee of the Communist Party of China, February 1990, translated from Chinese and reprinted in *Defying the Dragon* (1991: 112). Ganze Prefecture is one of two Autonomous Prefectures in Sichuan province.

[46] *Ibid.*: 110.

[47] *Ibid.*: 112.

[48] Wang and Bai also regard religion as something that can be made use of in promoting cultural and economic change, and discuss the need for "religious reform" in Tibet that will mobilize the "positive side" of religion: "Religion can be separated into rational deliberation and formalised blind superstition. The former is largely the source of the positive impact of religion such as the development of national culture and meeting people's needs, while the negative effects, such as superstition, extravagance, fatalism, and other pernicious concepts, are mainly confined to the latter". (Wang and Bai 1991: 185).

While Article 36 of the 1982 Chinese Constitution guarantees the right to engage in "normal religious activities",[49] the Chinese government distinguishes these from so-called "feudal and superstitious activities", which are not protected. Article 99 of the 1980 Criminal Law of China prohibits "utilizing feudal superstitious beliefs" to carry out "counter-revolutionary activities."[50] These stipulations are meant to apply throughout China, and are aimed at such diverse local practices as fortune-telling, sorcery, folk healing and exorcism, as well as secret societies and underground churches. In Tibet, however, the line separating religion and superstition is by no means clear, and the interpretation of particular practices is an object of political contention. For instance, Tibetan taboos governing the killing of insects and animals, mining, and the desecration of sacred sites are perceived as signs of Tibetan backwardness and obstacles to scientific progress and economic modernization. Yet these attitudes have a strong basis in popular religious belief, as well as being important markers of Tibetan identity. They can readily assume political significance in response to Chinese attempts at suppression, provoking both resentment and resistance.

Other non-institutionalized forms of religious expression, such as oracles, divination, and popular cults, are viewed with suspicion by the authorities, and practitioners may be persecuted. These have the potential for mass mobilization and can easily assume volatile political forms. Similarly, prayers invoking protector deities to come to the aid of Tibet, as well as the long life prayer for the Dalai Lama (*rgyal ba'i zhabs brtan*) and the "Prayer of Truth" (*bden smon*) written by him, have all acquired an explicit political meaning for Tibetans. The authorities have tried to ban the performance of these kinds of rituals since the outbreak of protest in 1987, but Tibetans respond by insisting that these also constitute "religious freedom", and they have carried on with the performance of these rituals in the face of government attempts at suppression. Thus, non-institutionalized expressions of religion are becoming more widespread as well as politicized. Although from the government's point of view the message is clearly a "counter-revolutionary" one, popular religious practices exist in a grey area of interpretation, tempting Tibetans to flaunt restrictions and dare the authorities to do something about it.

---

[49] Article 36, *The Constitution of the People's Republic of China* (1983): 32.
[50] *The Criminal Law and the Criminal Procedure of the People's Republic of China* (1984): 37.

The problem for Chinese religious and cultural policy is that almost every form of Tibetan religious and cultural expression has acquired political significance. Customs that were spontaneously recovered after the end of the Cultural Revolution and the lifting of restrictions in the late 1970s and early 1980s are now self-consciously identified with the cause of Tibetan independence and resistance to the Chinese. Thus, when the Dalai Lama was awarded the Nobel Peace Prize, Tibetans in Lhasa threw tsampa in the air and burned incense around the Barkhor to celebrate, forcing the authorities to prohibit these traditional religious practices on political grounds. Protection cords (*srung mdud*) for wearing around the neck, which have been blessed by the Dalai Lama in exile or other revered religious teachers, were tolerated before 1987 but their possession or distribution has since come to be regarded as "counter-revolutionary". When Dorje Wangdu, the elder brother of Lobsang Tenzin, was sentenced by the Lhasa Municipal People's Court on 26 September 1991, the charges included advocating that Tibetans wear Tibetan national clothes during Chinese National Day celebrations.

The same weakness is evident in other aspects of Chinese cultural policy in Tibet. The language policy announced in 1988, calling for Tibetan to become the primary language of official communication within two years, has yet to be implemented, and Chinese is still used as the working language in government offices. With the influx of new Chinese personnel anticipated as a result of economic expansion it is difficult to see how this policy can ever be implemented. Nevertheless, the formulation of policies designed to promote Tibetan culture have both raised expectations and provided a target for complaints against the Chinese state. In the case of the language policy, there is now widespread discontent about it among Tibetan cadres, who take the failure of the government to implement the policy effectively as evidence of its insincerity.

The deliberate promotion of ethnic culture has been a cornerstone of Chinese nationalities policy in Tibet. The 1982 Chinese Constitution makes special provisions for "minority nationalities", who are entitled "to use and develop their own spoken and written languages, and to preserve or reform their own ways and customs."[51] Official sinicization and the aggressive destruction of Tibetan culture that characterized the Cultural Revolution have been replaced by the state-sponsored

---

[51] Article 4, *The Constitution of the People's Republic of China* (1983): 13.

preservation of Tibetan cultural traditions. "Tibetology" as an academic and cultural enterprise has been appropriated by the Chinese government, which has subsidized the collection and publication of a huge amount of Tibetan literature, both classical and folk, and supported the performance of Tibetan folk arts.[52] The standard phraseology for cultural production of this sort is "Tibet's contribution to China's rich cultural heritage," thus depoliticizing cultural material by subsuming it within the larger category of Chinese folk culture. The emphasis on folk traditions, in particular, reflects not only their "proletarian" origins, but the fact that they are regarded as politically unthreatening. At the same time, where cultural production in art, music, and dance has been allowed to evolve in "modern" directions, these are always heavily influenced by contemporary Chinese styles. In part this reflects the Chinese training of younger Tibetan artists, but it also confirms the equating of modernity with sinicization.

Official cultural policy is sharply different from Tibetan perceptions of longstanding Chinese attitudes toward Tibetan culture. Here, Tibetans are characterized as backward and savage, their religion primitive and superstitious. This view pervades both the popular Chinese imagination and portrayals of Tibetans in Chinese stories, films, and drama, and has been used consistently for several decades to justify the "liberation" of Tibet. It is accepted even by liberal young Chinese as excusing Chinese rule in Tibet, regardless of what they may otherwise think of communism and the Communist Party. Although official propaganda attacks only the "feudal customs" of the old society before "liberation", Tibetans understand these as attacks on Tibetan culture and the Tibetan people. Jigme Ngagpo, a Chinese-educated Tibetan now in exile in the United States, writes:

People from mainland China know that since 1949 all the literary works on Tibet are filled with the theme of the backwardness of Tibetan customs — the country's brutality and darkness. In these works about Tibet, children are buried alive, hands and feet of people are chopped off, daughters and nieces are raped by their fathers and uncles, people are skinned and their eyes dug out. All the ugly things that can be imagined are attributed as customs of the Tibetan people. The image of the Tibetan people has been ruined by these

[52] A survey of officially sanctioned cultural studies is in the "White Paper", issued by the Information Office of the State Council of the PRC: "Tibet — Its Ownership and Human Rights Situation," in *Beijing Review*, vol. 35, no. 39, 28 Sept.–4 Oct. 1992: 9–42.

unrealistic works. Those who are from mainland China are indoctrinated with this distorted image of Tibet. If they were asked about their impression of Tibetans, even though they may not have been to Tibet or ever met any Tibetan people, their answer would be "savage and backward."[53]

The pervasive denigration of Tibetan culture thus provides another source of discontent and grounds for protest. One indication of the direction this kind of protest may take was a large demonstration on 8 October 1992 in Labrang, a town in a part of eastern Tibet incorporated into Gansu province. About 500 monks from Labrang Tashikyil monastery, along with as many schoolchildren and laypeople, marched up and down the main street of the town for two hours, shouting slogans and distributing leaflets. The monks claimed that the demonstration was organized to protest a magazine article by a Chinese scholar denigrating Tibetan religion.[54] Posters in both Tibetan and Chinese characters had been put up the previous day announcing that it would take place and asking local people to take part. The local police, who are Tibetan, were cooperative and friendly toward the demonstrators. No Tibetan flags were displayed, and the posters, leaflets, and slogans demanded only that Tibetan culture be respected — in line with official policy. The leaflets, printed at the monastery, read simply: "We must oppose those who scorn and belittle our race and religion."[55] Four days after the demonstration Chinese PSB officials arrived, reportedly to investigate the failure of the local police to prevent the demonstration. No demonstrators were arrested.

Official cultural policy, particularly to the extent that it is incompletely implemented or subverted by the local Chinese administration, focuses Tibetan resentment of Chinese attitudes toward Tibetan culture. Under these conditions, folk culture and traditions, along with language and religion, have the potential to become further politicized. The explicit formulation by the government of a cultural policy provides a target for a broad range of demands and complaints, and offers Tibetans another opportunity for collective mobilization and protest, again testing the limits of Chinese tolerance.

[53] Ngagpo (1988): 27–8.

[54] The offending article, of which the monks had obtained a copy, was written by Zhao Lu and appeared in the series *Studies on Xizang* (Xizang Yanjui), no. 3, 1992. The monks complained that it presented a distorted sexual interpretation of the Triple Gem in Tibetan Buddhism.

[55] *mi rigs dang chos lugs la dma' 'beb dang mthong chung byed mkhan rnams la ngo rgol byed dgos.*

8

THE DIMENSIONS OF TIBETAN NATIONALISM

This book focuses on one important facet of the current situation in Tibet — the emergence of new non-violent forms of political protest since 1987. Demonstrations around the Jokhang in the centre of Lhasa offer Tibetans a model for the expression of resistance to Chinese rule. Protest in this form has not merely come to signify opposition to Chinese rule, but it also represents for Tibetans a means of articulating national identity. It has spread from Lhasa to other towns and villages throughout Tibet, posing a constant challenge to the Chinese administration, and through it Tibetans have been able to continue a process of nation-building and political development in the face of overwhelming Chinese power. In turn, the rituals of nationalist protest are sustained by the conditions of Chinese rule in Tibet. Ongoing resentment and fear produced by the system of political control, uncertainty and frustration as Tibetans find themselves excluded by Chinese economic development strategies, and the inability of religious and cultural policy to satisfy Tibetan aspirations, guarantee that the potential for unrest will remain for the foreseeable future.

Ideology remains a central feature of Chinese rule in Tibet. The communist party/state, obsessed with threats to its power, needs to maintain a constant hold over people's thoughts — even more so when its authority is challenged. Thus Tibetans are locked in an ideological struggle with the Chinese state. Nationalism has developed as the Tibetan response, giving form and constancy to Tibetan aspirations. Tibetan protest does not arise from a feeling of minority status. It is overtly political, targeting the Chinese state and the apparatus of social control that maintains state power. As we have seen, protest is periodically renewed in direct response to efforts by the Chinese state to suppress dissent. These are the conditions under which Tibetans assert themselves to be a nation and define themselves in political terms.

Nationalism in this political sense is a modern phenomenon among Tibetans, an outcome of their recent experience with the Chinese communist state. Thus, the definition of nationalism as "a theory of political legitimacy, which requires that ethnic boundaries should not cut across political ones,"[1] must be qualified to reflect the Tibetan experience of the Chinese communist state. For Tibetans the political dimension takes precedence, while ethnic opposition is a by-product of political domination. Resistance to Party control spills over into general antagonism toward the Chinese. Thus Tibetan informants frequently used the term for "Chinese person" (*rgya mi*) to refer to both Tibetan and Chinese political cadres (*rgya mi'i las byed pa*) when providing accounts of political meetings and interrogation sessions.

Concepts developed to explain the rise of nationalism in European societies during the 19th and 20th centuries must be used with caution. One finds little evidence in Tibetan protest of the romantic glorification of the *Volk* that characterized European nationalist movements in their opposition to alien high cultures.[2] Tibetan nationalism is not the outcome of centuries of foreign domination. Tibetans are not revitalizing a local folk culture to forge a distinct national culture. Traditionally, Tibet had no *comprador* class who represented Chinese interests and adopted Chinese culture. Chinese social institutions never penetrated the country, nor had most Tibetans had much experience or contact with the Chinese before 1950. The only Chinese social institutions with which Tibetans are familiar are those of the communist Chinese state. Although its neighbours have sometimes played a role in its divisive political conflicts, throughout most of its history Tibet has not been an arena for competing religions, cultures, and social institutions. When ordinary Tibetans speak of the pre-1959 Tibetan "government" (*sde pa gzhung*), they attach no qualifications to the term; it was for them the only government of Tibet, headed by the Dalai Lama, with all the appurtenances of a government. The fact that

---

[1] Gellner (1983): 1.

[2] Gellner, who stresses the mediating role of nationalism in the transition to modern industrial society, notes with irony: "Nationalism usually conquers in the name of a putative folk culture. Its symbolism is drawn from the healthy, pristine, vigorous life of the peasants, of the *Volk*, the *narod*. There is a certain element of truth in the nationalist self-presentation when the *narod* or *Volk* is ruled by officials of another, an alien high culture, whose oppression must be resisted first by a cultural revival or reaffirmation, and eventually by a war of national liberation. If the nationalism prospers it eliminates the alien high culture, but it does not replace it by the old local low culture; it revives, or invents, a local high (literate, specialist-transmitted) culture of its own, though admittedly one which will have some links with the earlier local folk styles and dialects." — Gellner (1983): 57.

Tibetans of different regions and different interests may have resisted the encroachments of that government does not lessen the sense of their having belonged to a single, distinct political community.

The Chinese response to Tibetan nationalism has been constant repetition of the same propaganda themes: Tibet has "always" been part of China (or at least since China was "unified" by the Mongols in the thirteenth century); the idea of Tibetan independence is an imperialist plot orchestrated by the "Dalai clique" and "reactionary enemies of China"; Tibetans have welcomed the Chinese as "liberators". These themes have remained unchanged throughout forty years of Chinese rule.[3] An enormous propaganda effort is expended attempting to legitimize the Chinese claim to "ownership" of Tibet. At the same time, the official political culture and political symbolism are exclusively Chinese. Tibetans find themselves included within Chinese national culture and thus obliged to regard the ceremonies of state patriotism as their own — celebrations of the victories of the People's Liberation Army and the establishment of the People's Republic of China, military parades and patriotic anthems, eulogies of revolutionary heroes. These are the stock-in-trade of the modern nation-state, which, in Hobsbawm's words, "invents tradition" in the form of symbols and ceremonials that bind the citizen to the emergent state and generate more inclusive kinds of loyalty and commitment than existed previously.[4]

This construction of Chinese national culture makes Tibetans merely one of many ethnic groups. In official speeches and publications the Tibetan transliteration of the traditional Chinese word for "China" (*krung go*) now refers to both China and Tibet, while the Tibetan word for "Tibet" (*bod*) indicates merely a region and an ethnicity. There has never been a word in the Tibetan language to refer to an entity subsuming both Tibet and China. Both were "nations" (*rgyal khab* — literally, "kingdom"), a term in Tibetan now used officially only to refer to China. The 1982 Constitution defines the People's Republic of China as a "unitary multinational state built up jointly by the people of all its nationalities."[5] The term "Han", historically synonymous with "Chinese", is now used to mark the Chinese as an ethnic group,

---

[3] See page 216 above, note 52.

[4] Hobsbawm (1983).

[5] "Preamble" to the *Constitution of the People's Republic of China* (1983): 7.

enabling the term "Chinese" to encompass Tibetans along with other minorities. In this formulation of the ethnic composition of China there are Hans, Tibetans, and other nationalities, all of whom are Chinese. Tibetans may be allowed — even encouraged in some circumstances — to display the ethnic characteristics of a minority group, but they are also expected to participate in the national culture, the "Chineseness" of which goes unacknowledged. Contemporary Chinese national culture is also very much a political culture; thus, to reject Chinese national culture is to challenge the power of the state. Ethnic culture, on the other hand, must remain unpolitical, little more than a collection of colourful traditions and customs.

Under these conditions the cultural and religious forms that define "Tibetanness" have assumed their current political significance. Tibetans respond with growing confidence to Chinese attempts to obliterate their past, but it is the Chinese who have turned historical memory into a battlefield, not Tibetans. The rituals of nationalist protest build continuities between the recollected Tibetan past and contemporary political experience. The Jokhang temple in the centre of Lhasa has become the symbolic focus of political protest precisely because it exemplifies these continuities, linking Tibetan identity to its remembered past. The legends of Songtsen Gampo and the ancient kings likewise reinforce a collective political identity and sustain a sense of political agency in the face of Chinese political domination. The Dalai Lama as a symbol and rallying-point of Tibetan protest exemplifies these continuities best of all, since he epitomizes both the Tibetan religious and political past and a bridge to the modern world. The sense of constituting a political community is condensed into the figure of the Dalai Lama, who represents not only the pre-1959 government in Lhasa, which continues in exile in India, but a remembered political history stretching back to the time of the ancient kings.

Monks and nuns have played a leading role as organizers and initiators of demonstrations, drawing on Buddhist religious ideas and practices to oppose the power of the Chinese state. This role is in keeping with the traditional monastic roles of political and spiritual leadership. The rebuilding of Buddhist institutions has, more than anything else, been an opportunity to reassert an independent Tibetan identity and restore the integrity of Tibetan social institutions. Religion, which has always had political salience for Tibetans, has acquired a new self-conscious political significance under Chinese rule. However, the politically active Buddhism developed by young monks and nuns in Tibet does not represent a retreat into religious orthodoxy. Religion in Tibet is itself conditioned by the development of a nationalist political consciousness, assuming here an outward-looking and progressive form in response to the ideological claims of the Chinese state.

Buddhism has figured prominently in national independence movements opposing colonial rule in a number of Asian countries in the twentieth century, and has undergone a variety of ideological transformations in adapting to the modern world. Interpretations of doctrine are shaped by the political exigencies of nationalist practice, even as religion in all its popular forms continues to provide meaning and purpose to people's lives. The situation in Tibet under Chinese rule can be compared with political developments in the Theravadian Buddhist countries of Thailand, Burma, and Sri Lanka. Bruce Kapferer, writing of religion and nationalism in Sri Lanka, describes the process of ideological transformation through which Buddhism acquires a nationalist political form:

While Sinhalese nationalism may be Buddhist, the Buddhism which is brought to consciousness is that conditioned within the nationalist process. The Buddhist ideas practised by Sinhalese and to which they refer are wide and various. Sinhalese nationalism selects within the many possibilities of Buddhism in practice and realizes a particular logic, a logic made integral to Sinhalese nationalism and forceful to its process.[6]

This selection and reinterpretation of cultural traditions in the formation of nationalist political consciousness is never a matter of pure expediency. Cultural traditions are "chosen because of what they distil ontologically; that is, they make sense and condense a logic of ideas which may also be integral to the people who make the selection although hidden from reflective consciousness."[7] Kapferer is writing in the context of the tragic conflict between Sinhalese and Tamils in Sri Lanka, and thus identifies the totalizing form of Sinhalese nationalism with those aspects of Buddhist tradition which stress hierarchical subordination and the violent subjugation of the threatening "other." Thus, it is all the more striking that Tibetan nationalism has taken a different path, selecting Buddhist values and practices that sustain a symbolic dialogue with the "other" — however one-sided it may be. Tibetan

[6] Kapferer (1988): 8.
[7] *Ibid.*: 211.

protest, while drawing its strength from religious passions, remains morally and politically "rational", committed to universalistic values and appealing for human rights and democracy. But the human cost of non-violent protest has been high, since it calls for a constant supply of heroes and martyrs prepared to accept death or imprisonment. Here again, Buddhist values of meritorious action and self-sacrifice, exemplified in the monastic vocation, provide the inspiration.

Chinese communist rule in Tibet has clearly been a modernizing force. Tibetans have been exposed to, and incorporated into, a range of modern administrative and economic structures, albeit in their Leninist/socialist variants. These changes are irreversible; modernization continues to be positively valued in Tibetan nationalist thinking precisely because under Chinese tutelage it is perceived to be incomplete. The idea of Tibetan independence — broadly conceived of as the departure of the Chinese, the return of the Dalai Lama, and an independent democratic Tibet — aims to continue this process. Thus Tibetan nationalism situates Tibetans in the modern world, and non-violent forms of protest will continue as long as they remain locked in a symbolic competition with the Chinese state, and are able to overcome the realities of powerlessness and isolation through symbolic "victories." The symbols of Tibetan protest, linking Tibetan nationhood to universalistic values, enable Tibetans to leap over the ideologies of Chinese domination and build a bridge to the modern world. Paradoxically, then, the persistence of ideology in the exercise of Chinese control over Tibet sustains Tibetan protest in its present form.

The potential remains for Tibetan protest to assume other forms besides non-violent demonstrations. One such possibility is acts of violence targeting the Chinese administration in Tibet or Chinese persons and property. Even during the riots in 1988 and 1989, Tibetans were generally reluctant to attack individual Chinese. Although Tibetan demonstrators can be provoked into violence, it has no place within the symbolic construction of Tibetan protest; the Dalai Lama, speaking from exile, has repeatedly called on Tibetans to refrain from it and has emphasized the need for the Tibetan struggle to be perceived as non-violent.

A recurrence of the armed insurrections of the 1950s and 1960s is possible. However, the conditions that produced them in the past — including social breakdown on a mass scale and the possibility of arming and mobilizing large populations — are not likely to recur. More likely forms of violent action are acts of sabotage by organized underground resistance groups. A high level of frustration has led some Tibetans to think increasingly of direct action against the Chinese. After the execution in May 1990 of two Tibetan prisoners for attempting to escape from Drapchi prison, printed posters appeared in Lhasa threatening violence against government officials:

If directly or indirectly any harm comes to the life of one of the patriotic Tibetan heroes presently in prison, then we will not be able to forsake the unity of the Tibetan race, and the Chinese who are chiefly responsible will receive retribution without hesitation. This is a warning to the communist Chinese invaders that they will have to bear complete responsibility.

Poems and leaflets have circulated in Lhasa since 1990 warning Tibetans collaborating with the Chinese administration that they too face retribution. Some militant university students have also discussed violence against the Chinese, arguing that the predominance of religion in the country has prevented Tibetans from mounting an effective independence movement.

On 6 March 1992, two days after the United Nations Human Rights Commission voted against a resolution directly criticizing China for human rights violations in Tibet, a Tibetan underground organization calling itself the Tiger-Leopard Youth Association (*stag gzig gzhon nu tshogs pa*) issued a letter through Western contacts indicating that Tibetans were reconsidering the place of violence and sabotage in their struggle. The letter, addressed to the Secretary-General of the United Nations, the United States President, and the Tibetan government-in-exile, clearly reveals the sense of bitterness and isolation felt by Tibetan dissidents:

Our non-violent methods have been taken as a sign of weakness. We are determined to regain our freedom, and the recent UN vote clearly shows us that without bloodshed, sabotage and aggressive acts, we will not gain publicity, sympathy and support. No one is independent. Everyone is interdependent. So why should we not follow the destructive path? The UN liberated Kuwait within 48 days. We have been fighting for 40 years to get free from the rule of the Red Chinese. The world bodies are taking a keen interest in Yugoslavia, Burma, Palestine and Africa. Thousands of human lives have been lost in the struggle in these countries through acts of sabotage and violence. Hijacking and sabotage are tactics used by Palestinians, and still world bodies support them. Now we feel that if these acts of aggression bring results, why should we not do the same? The world believes in these acts. Therefore, if no action is taken against the Chinese promptly by the UN, we will not hesitate to go ahead with modern destructive measures.

The authors of the letter add that they are aware that violence is "against our religion and beliefs," and that the Dalai Lama "will never allow us to carry out inhumane acts," but they feel they have no other available options.

It is difficult to ascertain how widespread these sentiments are, or how likely they are to be translated into action. Certainly the Dalai Lama's rejection of violence continues to have influence inside Tibet. But there is a long history of underground organization and resistance by Chinese-educated students and cadres, dating back to the first recruitment of Tibetans for training as cadres in the mid-1950s.[8] The authors of the letter claim that the group they represent is descended from an earlier resistance group with a similar name, the Tiger-Dragon (*stag 'brug*) Group, which carried out clandestine operations in the late 1970s and early 1980s.

One of the consequences of the suppression of public protest and the tightening of the security apparatus during and after the imposition of martial law has been the resurgence of small, tightly organized underground cells. These groups, composed of Chinese-educated Tibetan cadres, are familiar with the workings of the Chinese administration. They have also been inculcated with Marxist ideas of revolution and are aware of Chinese support for liberation movements throughout the world. Their commitment to non-violent protest is correspondingly more pragmatic and less based in religion; thus they are prepared to consider other models for national liberation.

Tibetan university students and Chinese-educated Tibetan cadres are an important group for the future political development of Tibet. They have the potential to develop a pluralist alternative to the Chinese communist system. Under current conditions of repression, however, the kind of political discourse needed to generate new ideas has become extremely difficult. Tibetans inside Tibet have less sense of participating in a global political movement for democracy and self-determination than was the case a few years earlier. Contact with Westerners has been largely curtailed. Thus, the intellectual ferment that followed the outbreak of protest in 1987 has been replaced by an entrenched resistance movement, focused on building an underground organization that will be in position when the political climate changes. Suggestions

---

[8] The history of these underground organizations of Tibetan cadres remains largely undocumented. For one account of cadre resistance during the 1950s and 1960s, see Tsering (1980).

that violence and sabotage replace non-violent forms of protest, whether or not they are realistic means of achieving political goals, are an indication of the isolation and frustration experienced by the relatively privileged group of educated Tibetans working within the Chinese administration.

Another possible direction for Tibetan resistance to Chinese rule lies within popular religion. A striking characteristic of protest since 1987 has been the extent to which rational-ethical elements in Buddhism have been in the foreground. These are the elements stressed by the young monks and nuns, whose role as intellectual leaders is largely responsible for their continuing prominence. Magical signs and omens, and millenarian hopes for salvation, are also elements of Tibetan popular religion. These elements have not been conspicuous in current protest, remaining in the background, where they provide a kind of supernatural gloss to current political developments. A typical example: Tibetans in Lhasa related at the time of the first demonstration on 27 September 1987, that on the 25th a rainbow had been seen over Drepung monastery and the following day earth tremors had been felt; these were interpreted afterwards as signs of impending political upheaval.

Under other conditions these elements may come into the foreground, producing a religious revival along millenarian lines, where the political content is expressed through religious themes, and religious longing becomes a substitute for effective political power. Popular religion preserves the hope that the deities will intervene, that prayers will be answered, and that calamity will befall the enemies of the Dharma. Increasingly, in the period since the declaration of martial law, expressions of this kind of popular religion have reappeared, with reports of spirit-possessions and "manifestations" of deities.

In one account circulating in Lhasa in the spring of 1990, some 200 people attending the ritual consecration of a temple in Kongpo in the autumn of 1989 reported seeing a rainbow, followed the next day by appearances of the deities Amitabha (*'od dpag med*), Avalokiteśvara (*spyan ras gzigs*), and Padmasambhava. The Panchen Lama is the worldly incarnation of the first, the Dalai Lama of the second, and the third is the magician-saint-hero who propagated Buddhism in Tibet in the eighth century. Such accounts, which spread quickly among Tibetans, are sanctioned by traditional religious beliefs and have credibility as indications that the deities and protectors of Tibet have not abandoned them.

Goldstein and Beall report the case of a nomad "medium" among

Phala nomads in the winter of 1987.[9] The medium spontaneously entered a trance and, while possessed by the spirit of a deity, offered an explanation for another man's illness. When district officials did not move to suppress the practice, the nomads fashioned the traditional costume for mediums and now seek the deity's aid in cases of illness. Goldstein and Beall interpret the phenomenon as part of a spontaneous and diffuse process of "cultural revitalization" following the lifting of prohibitions on expressions of traditional culture. On 9 July 1992, during a celebration at Nechung monastery near Lhasa, a Tibetan woman in her fifties went into a trance and was, according to Tibetan reports, possessed by the "Drapchi Lhamo." While possessed by the deity, she is reported to have spoken in Chinese. In this case, the authorities acted quickly, and the woman was taken away by the police.

Mediumship of this kind has a long-standing basis within Tibetan religious practice, persisting as part of popular religion, as well as being incorporated into institutionalized Buddhism.[10] It is not protected under the Chinese policy of freedom of religious belief, however, which applies only to state-sanctioned religion, and is considered a form of "feudal superstition", which is prohibited. As a spontaneously recovered folk practice it lies outside the scope of state control. The medium may offer magical advice on the conduct of personal affairs and prescriptions for dealing with illness and misfortune, but the potential of such practices for mass mobilization remains a threat. Speaking through the medium, the deity is able to interpret the plight of Tibetans in terms of religious themes and promise divine intervention to overcome evil and drive away enemies.

One account of a religious movement organized around spirit-possession and magical practices with millenarian overtones comes from official Chinese sources. A report was distributed among Party officials in 1982 documenting the suppression of the "Heroes of Ling" (*gling gi dpa' brtul*) movement in Amdo county, a nomadic area 300 km. north of Lhasa.[11] The leader of the group, Sonam Phuntsog, claimed to be a

---

[9] Goldstein and Beall (1989): 627.

[10] See Nebesky (1956).

[11] The report, entitled "On the Illegal Establishment of the 'Heroes of Ling' in Amdo County and Their Elimination" (*a mdo rdzong du khrims 'gal gyis "gling gi dpa' brtul" btsugs pa dang de med par bzos pa'i skor*), is contained in Volume 9-10-11 of the "Tibet Information Book" (*bod ljongs 'phrin deb*), issued by the Bureau of the TAR Party Committee on 2 July 1982, pp. 39–48 (numbered for internal circulation).

reincarnation of the legendary warrior-hero King Gesar of Ling, whose deeds comprise a huge epic narrative familiar to most Tibetans. Under his instruction, the members of the group learned magical procedures for inducing trance by "opening the primal veins" (*rtsa sgo phye ba*) and becoming possessed (*lha phab pa*) by a deity referred to as Gyatsa (*rgya tsha*), enabling them to make prophecies and perform cures for illnesses. According to the Chinese report, the group consisted of altogether thirty-six people, including two members of the Youth Association and a woman deputy leader of the commune. The report notes that the participants were mostly young people with an average age of twenty-seven.

Following the suppression of the movement, public meetings were held to denounce the participants. The leaders reportedly confessed that they had no supernatural powers and had "only spread lies and deception." They are portrayed as ordinary swindlers who "pretended to give medical treatment and defrauded the public of wealth," frightening them by spreading "baseless rumours," and thus "sabotaged collective production." The Chinese account of the suppression of the movement conforms to the definition of feudal superstition as exploitative practices preying on the ignorance of the masses. According to the report, commune members willingly denounced the movement, rising up "one after another" to confess: "We deeply regret being deceived and believing in these so-called Heroes of Ling." Thus, the solution to controlling these expressions of popular religion is public education through ideological and political campaigns. The report attributes the spread of the movement to the erosion of the authority of commune leaders and the lapse in political education following the introduction of the "responsibility system" in agriculture to the area.

As the report indicates, however, the real political threat posed by the movement lay in its potential for mass mobilization against the Chinese. Yin Fatang, Party Secretary for Tibet from 1980 to 1985, attached a preface to the report expressing concern that "if effective measures are not taken at the time problems of this type appear, it is possible they will continue to spread." He remarked that similar disturbances had also occurred in neighbouring Nagchu county, another nomadic area. The movement demonstrated how "reactionaries" would use religion "from beginning to end" to "protect, conserve, and expand their reactionary power;" the answer, as Yin indicated, lies in "consolidating the democratic dictatorship."

These concerns seem to have been prompted by millenarian themes running through the movement, identifying the Chinese with demonic forces and calling on the deities to protect the virtuous and overcome the power of evil. During one meeting in July 1981, according to the report, a member of the group while in trance was asked whether it was possible for the Gyatsa to harm the Chinese. The deity replies through the medium: "Now is the time when the deities of the 'white side' (*dkar phyogs kyi lha rnams*) hold their heads high and the demons of the 'dark side' (*nag phyogs kyi bdud rnams*) are defeated." For the Chinese officials investigating the movement this was evidence that its leaders "have openly instigated rebellion against the revolutionary struggle and are destroying the relationship between the nationalities." The political challenge to Chinese authority is clear enough, but the millenarian expectations of the participants, hoping to overturn the existing order through divine intervention, are beyond the range of official discourse, which is unable to acknowledge the psychological and cultural reality of religious motives. Movements like the "Heroes of Ling" aim to restore a social world that has been violently disrupted. The participants are able to recover a sense of both individual and collective integrity by aligning the Tibetan experience of Chinese rule with the conflict between spiritual powers of good and evil.

Millenarian religious movements of this kind may be more likely to occur in rural areas, particularly among isolated nomadic groups, although the practice of spirit possession has wide currency among Tibetans. The extensive rebuilding of orthodox monastic institutions throughout Tibet during the 1980s eclipsed this aspect of popular religion. This in turn has favoured rational-ethical forms of protest under monastic leadership, reducing the potential for millenarian expressions of resistance. On the other hand, the increasing scale of restrictions on state-sanctioned monastic Buddhism since the outbreak of protest in 1987 may lead to a resurgence of heterodox forms of popular religion. Likewise, the increasing marginalization of the rural Tibetan population resulting from urban economic development and the influx of Chinese may also create conditions favouring millenarianism.

Millenarianism is just one expression of the challenge posed by the destruction of traditional Tibetan society and culture to Tibetan religious beliefs. The problem of finding meaning in the calamity of the Chinese occupation, and some basis for hope for the future, is one that is felt by all Tibetans.[12] They ask what they have done to bring this fate upon themselves. The Buddhist doctrine of "karmic retribution" (*lan chags*) explains present misfortune as the fruit of past misdeeds. This doctrine situates individuals within a hierarchy of merit, where differences in wealth, social position, and life circumstances are accepted (and legitimized) as the reward or punishment for good and bad actions in former lives. But it cannot satisfactorily explain collective misfortune. How can karmic retribution apply to a whole society, regardless of individual actions? What kind of collective sin accounts for the common fate of Tibetans under Chinese rule? The whole system of religious values that gives meaning to life is called into question by the Chinese occupation.

Perhaps the explanation most frequently heard from Tibetans for the catastrophe which has befallen their country is that they failed to heed prophecies and warnings in the past, and thus provided an opportunity for the triumph of demonic forces. But collective guilt assigned in this way is not guilt at all; history has an inevitable and predetermined end from which there is no escape. The fate of Tibet confirms a shared Buddhist picture of historical process that uses the concept of an "evil era" (*dus ngan pa*) to account for the increasing violence and strife in the contemporary world, and the deterioration of religion. The levelling of the social order, envy, greed, corruption, and the despoiling of nature are all characteristics of the evil era. The collective failure of Tibetans to heed past prophecies is itself symptomatic of the evil era — thus transferring collective responsibility to the historical process itself.

A collective destiny, however, contains the possibility of collective salvation. The fact that Tibetans suffer collectively rather than individually holds the promise of collective deliverance. This shared Tibetan predicament translates into a political identity that transcends the traditional divisions within Tibetan society. Stan Mumford notes that the theme of evil-era decline contains its utopian counter-image: the reconstruction of the world and a return of the good era.[13] These possibilities are preserved in a variety of mythologies that inform Tibetan religious thought — the return of King Gesar, the reign of Shambala over the world following a final battle between

[12] See Appendix C for a moving statement of these themes in an "urgent appeal" (*drag bskul*) to the protector deities of Tibet, distributed in Lhasa on 27 September 1989.
[13] Mumford (1989): 236.

the forces of good and evil, the coming age of the Buddha Maitreya.[14]

For Tibetans these utopian expectations are now expressed through the more immediate and tangible possibility of the return of the Dalai Lama to Tibet. The Dalai Lama's exile and the common fate of Tibetans are inextricably linked in Tibetan thinking. The fact of collective suffering gives meaning to history and provides grounds for faith. Anticipation of the return of the Dalai Lama justifies patience, and preserves the hope of deliverance. Out of this narrative of exile and return emerges the deepest sense of Tibetan political identity. The most widespread conviction among Tibetans — expressed in countless prayers, letters, and appeals — is simply that one day the Dalai Lama will return. Individual acts of resistance and self-sacrifice are sustained by the certainty that the political destiny of Tibet is part of a larger story in which suffering will finally be vindicated and good will finally triumph.

[14] Belief in a coming age is extremely widespread among adherents of Tibetan Buddhism. Humphrey (1983): 430–2, describes the cult of Maidari (Maitreya) among Buryat Mongols, where it is the most persistent surviving element of Lamaist religion. Here Buddhist themes have intermingled with Christian and Marxist themes, resulting in the utopian idea of a "society which governs itself" following the apocalyptic destruction of civilization.

APPENDIXES

A

THE MEANING OF THE PRECIOUS DEMOCRATIC CONSTITUTION OF TIBET[1]

Although it is difficult to describe what our future situation will be, it is the responsibility of everyone to prepare for the future. If Tibetans continue to struggle with a courageous determination based on the force of established truth, we will not always have to remain under the foreign Chinese invaders; possessing the right to self-determination in accordance with international law, there is no doubt that we will be able to enjoy the splendour of all religious and political freedoms. Having completely eradicated the practices of the old society with all its faults, the future Tibet will not resemble our former condition and be a restoration of serfdom or be like the so-called "old system" of rule by a succession of feudal masters or monastic estates. Understanding that a democratic government embodying both religious and secular principles is necessary, and for the purpose of demonstrating the future way forward for the Tibetan people, His Holiness the Dalai Lama has bestowed a national law for a future Tibet that accords with the general practice of the contemporary world. This constitution is based on the sacred teachings elegantly spoken by the Buddha, as well as the United Nations Declaration of Human Rights, the right to self-determination, and the proclaimed authority to exercise the right to self-determination.

In this constitution there is equality without discrimination between clergy and laypersons; there is no discrimination on the basis of sex, language, religion, social origin, race, wealth, region, or any other status [Article 8]. The inhumane treatment of subjects will cease; slavery, exploitative labour,

[1] This document was originally printed as an 11-page pamphlet using wood-blocks by a group of Drepung monks sometime in the summer of 1988. The monks produced several hundred copies, intended for distribution among villagers on visits home to their families. The document cites a number of provisions from the *Constitution of Tibet* (1963), promulgated by the Dalai Lama's government-in-exile. Where the provisions of specific Articles of the *Constitution* are recognizable, their corresponding numbers have been indicated in brackets. See Chapter 5 for a discussion of the significance of this document.

232

and child labour are not permitted [Article 17]. Furthermore, the constitution clearly proclaims that each Tibetan has an equal right to freedom of thought, conscience, and religion [Article 17], freedom of assembly, the right to life, to vote, freedom of movement, freedom of employment, freedom of expression, and the right to form associations [Article 18, 20]. A broad and democratic path for developing society through the freedom and free choice of the people has been settled on.

In order to practise democracy embodying religious and secular principles, it is necessary to understand well the meaning of the term "democracy" [*dmangs gtso*].[2] For example, the first syllable, "people" [*dmangs*], refers to the broad masses, not to a few people, and does not differentiate on the basis of heredity, power, or wealth. Their thoughts are paramount; or, in other words, the broad masses are held to be the final authority. Also, speaking from another point of view, if we take the case of our Tibetan people, the term "people" [*dmangs*] refers to the broad masses of the three provinces of Tibet. As for the second syllable [*gtso*], it should be understood to mean regarding the thoughts and wishes of the people as paramount. Reasoning thus, "democracy" [*dmangs gtso*] refers to a popular system which fundamentally accords with the needs, wishes, and choices of the broad masses. Under the broad framework provided by the democratic constitution, people with different individual views of what course of action to follow, by exercising their democratic prerogatives, will also be able to practise what they think and speak without need of fear, hypocrisy, and concealment.

As for the means for progress in the future, it is necessary to build political and social organization on the basis of the cooperation and consent of the broad masses of Tibet. This kind of organization must be constructed by the broad masses or by their representatives whose powers are limited by the people. Apart from that, an organization built on the rule of force and coercion can never be justified. With regard to the representatives, both the nomination of the representatives and their election must be decided according to the wishes of the masses. Such a system of government is a democratic system. [Taking the government-in-exile as an example] the Assembly of [Tibetan] People's Deputies plays the leading role in the conduct of the highest [National] Working Committee for the purpose of the Tibetan government deciding vital important decisions. Likewise, if we take the example of the cooperative settlement societies [in India], the representatives elected by the people of that area make important decisions on a majority basis.

Not only is this democratic system in accordance with contemporary conditions, it is also in accordance with the philosophy of Buddhism. Only if the

---

[2] The analysis in this paragraph is typical of monastic exegesis. The two syllables of the Tibetan term for "democracy" (*dmangs gtso*) are explained separately. Finally, a definition of the term is offered based on the explanation.

future government of Tibet is a government formed by the people, embodying religious and secular principles, can such a government be accepted as being a people's government. A constitution for a future Tibet should be based on the contemporary system of democracy and should also accord with the actual situation in Tibet.

In order to exercise equality, freedom, and democratic rights, it is necessary to understand clearly the fundamental nature of democracy. Democracy does not mean being allowed to do whatever one feels like doing without any respect for order. Neither do democratic rights excuse pursuing selfish interests without the need to fulfill corresponding democratic responsibilities.

In summary, in order for Tibet to be administered in the future by Tibetans, and for Tibetans to decide Tibetan affairs, and in order for Tibetans to be able to exercise for themselves the rights intended by the precious constitution, we must remind ourselves that everyone, young and old, must steadfastly do whatever they can in every way, directly and indirectly, for the movement to restore Tibetan freedom.

B

WORK PLANS OF THE REGIONAL PARTY AND THE REGIONAL PEOPLE'S GOVERNMENT FOR RESOLUTELY STRIKING SPLITTISTS AND OTHER SERIOUS CRIMINALS THROUGH SCREENING AND INVESTIGATION[1]

To: Residential and Municipal Committees, Prefectural Administrative Offices, the Lhasa Municipal Government, departments of the Regional Party Committee, Tibet Autonomous Region Bureau [*thing*] Committees and County-level Administrative [*cus*] Committees, and the various people's associations.

The notice of the Central Committee of the CPC and the State Council (China-wide document no. 3, 1989) concerning the dissemination of the CPC Committee of Beijing City and the Beijing Municipal Government's document "Report on Work Plans for Resolutely Suppressing Those who Incite Counter-Revolutionary Rebellion through Screening and Investigation" is extremely timely and important. Sometimes in the past, influenced by the disturbances throughout the country, a few people harbouring evil intentions have devised many political conspiracies and formed illegal organizations, planning to start disturbances. During the last two years in the Lhasa area 18 disturbances have occurred. Having been defeated again and again, not only are the actions of the splittists becoming ever more secret, but their strategy has changed, and they are trying to accomplish their conspiracy of "Tibetan independence" using the means of "democracy, freedom, and human rights." They hold the evil hope of using the opportunity to start even bigger disturbances and to propagate evil splittist actions in the farming and nomad regions.

---

[1] This document was distributed to Party members by the Organization Department of the TAR Party Committee. It is referred to as "Document no. 13" and dated 27 July 1989. It appeared in "Selected Study Documents for Discussion by Party Members" (*dmangs gtsos tang yon la dpyad gleng byed pa'i slob sbyong yig cha 'dems bsgrigs*), Organization Department of the TAR Party Committee, March 1990, pp. 78–98 (for internal circulation). See Chapter 6 for a discussion of the significance of this document. Presumably it was first prepared in Chinese, then translated into Tibetan. It is written in a style typical of the genre of Tibetan language communist political essays. Many of the expressions are newly invented Tibetan compound words that bear a one-to-one relationship to Chinese political terms. Tibetan phonetic renderings of some Chinese administrative terms have been included as they appear in the document.

It will be impossible to bring peace to Tibet unless through screening and investigation we resolutely strike the splittists whose aim is to split the unity of the motherland, to overthrow the Party, and to undermine the People's Government, as well as other serious criminals, thereby eliminating these incidents in the future.

Therefore, in order to stabilize the Tibetan situation by mobilizing the entire Party, with the leaders assuming responsibility and broad-mindedly mobilizing the masses, the splittists taking part in the unrest and those deserving serious punishment taking part in disturbances and riots, must be screened and investigated and punished according to the law. The work of internal screening and investigation of the leading offices of the Party and State and the key departments must be done firmly. The work plans to accomplish this are shown below.

I. *Guiding ideology, aims, and requirements*

Resolutely practising the Central Committee's Document no. 3, the crimes of splittists and serious criminals must be screened and investigated. The behind-the-scenes conspirators must be exposed and sentenced according to the law. Dedicating sufficient time and much energy, we must persist in the present struggle because it affects the future prospects and destiny of the Party and the State, and will determine whether or not the Tibetan situation will be stabilized in the long term and what will become of Tibet in the future. Therefore we can show no pity, and we cannot just make a pretence, and we cannot stop half way. By distinguishing between the two types of opposition, we must unite those who are able to be united and save those who can be saved; we must strike the few splittists and similar serious criminals and leave them friendless and alone.

One by one the evidence of the crimes of the planners and organizers of the unrest must be investigated. One by one the types of serious law cases of beating, smashing, plundering, burning, and murder must be screened and investigated, and criminals who have fled elsewhere must be apprehended and prosecuted. Those who continue to collect guns and ammunition, and writers, printers, and distributers of reactionary wall posters, posters for pasting, etc., must one by one be screened and investigated. Splittists who remain in hiding must be resolutely exposed. Through screening and investigation, we must sentence the few splittists and other serious criminals according to the law, and we must deeply educate the entire Communist Party membership, cadres of different nationalities, and the masses in the struggle against splittism and in preserving the Four Cardinal Principles; then, while we undergo reform and opening up, we must improve the self-conscious understanding of opposing bourgeois liberalism, preserving the Four Cardinal Principles, protecting the unity of the motherland, and emphasizing the unity of the nationalities.

II. *Targets for striking*

1. Those who plan behind the scenes to cause disturbances, those who command the organizations, and the ringleaders and principal members of secret counter-revolutionary organizations.
2. Instigators of evil counter-revolutionary propaganda, fabricators of reactionary rumours, writers of reactionary posters, people who put up and distribute reactionary posters, people who make and display "Tibet Independence" flags, criminals who deserve serious punishment.
3. Not only the core who enthusiastically take part in the disturbances, and those who have participated in the disturbances many times, but also those who coerce others into participating in the disturbances.
4. Those with whom we have been lenient after they have participated in the disturbances, and who then once again engage in splittism, or those criminals who once again commit crimes.
5. Those criminals who in disturbances, break, plunder, burn, kill, etc., and cause great harm to social tranquillity.
6. Those who incite disturbances and, in addition, those who shelter and hide criminals.
7. Those who retaliate against and harm those who expose the above-mentioned criminals.

III. *Reorganizing and strengthening the management of the monasteries*

Because those monks and nuns in a few monasteries and nunneries who are not law-abiding are among the principal reasons for not being able to stabilize the situation, screening and investigation of the monasteries and their reorganization cannot be postponed. Not only have we presented a report to the Central Committee of the CCP, "Suggestions for the Reorganization and Management of the Monasteries by Practising the System of Democratic Management of the Monasteries"; but the Central Committee also has basically agreed to this. On this basis we must draw up plans for carrying out the investigation and seriously implement them.

IV. *Seriously doing internal screening and investigation to purify cadres and units of staff and workers*

From the unrest in Lhasa, and from the current disturbances and the rebellion, we can see the lack of purity of the leading offices of our Party and State, and some important departments. Because this great problem remains hidden, it is very important to do the screening and investigation well.

Not including the above-mentioned targets, the object of internal screening and investigation is furthermore: (1) the planners and organizers of disturbances and those who plan evil; foreign countries, and powerful enemies and evil conspirators within foreign countries; those who support the disturbances, those who propagate speech and action to split the motherland, singers and disseminators of "Tibetan independence songs," those who vigorously aid those who start riots; (2) those who participate in illegal organizations, those who support disturbances and rebellion, those who propagate speech and action that opposes the Party and socialism; (3) those who give Party and State secrets to the outside, and likewise those who are suspicious of the need for investigation.

The most important responsibility of the internal screening and investigation is the screening and investigation of thought. It is necessary to investigate what all cadres and workers, and in particular all Party members and leading cadres, have self consciously done themselves to halt the spread of bourgeois liberal ideas and splittist ideas, and how they have handled themselves in the face of this great question of right and wrong. We must investigate whether they have engaged in speech and action providing support and sympathy to the riots and the disturbances, and whether or not they have vacillated on this occasion so vital to the destiny of the Party and the State. Using each person's investigation of himself as a basis, we must try to increase the level of understanding.

The focus of the work of internal screening and investigation, based on the actual situation in Tibet, is the spread of the influence of the disturbances occurring in the region, district, and city, in the offices, schools, state enterprises, and departments of the region; the levels of the leading departments and the important departments of the Autonomous Region and Lhasa City are the focus of the internal screening and investigation. For this reason, Party and State leaders of these departments must take control; they should not check with all and sundry. The work of the internal screening and investigation and the work of investigating the cadres must be combined. Within this struggle it is necessary to observe and encourage those comrades who are clear and steadfast. At the same time, it is necessary to uncover the ones who have problems. We must emphasize the high expectations we have of Communist Party members and of leading cadres above the county administrative (*cus*) level. If the investigation discloses someone who has made a serious error, then, depending on the situation, a decision must be made through Party and administrative discipline; those who are not bearing the appropriate responsibility of leadership, or who are not properly performing the work of important departments, must resolutely be transferred or recalled.

The important departments of administrative discipline etc., must definitely carry through to completion screening and investigation on the basis of this plan. While we are dealing with problems that arise from screening and investigation, we must give greater emphasis to general offices and departments. Those who advocate bourgeois liberalism, those who do not maintain the Four Cardinal Principles, and those who protect and sympathize with the splittists and the ones who cause disturbances, must definitely be transferred. Departments with serious problems must coordinate with leading departments in order to develop capabilities they themselves lack.

V. *Steps and means*

(I) We must strengthen propaganda education. Combining the study and practice of the thoughts of the fourth plenary session of the Central Committee of the CCP, we must expose the facts of the violent counter-revolutionary rebellion in Beijing and the nauseating true nature of the occurrence of violent counter-revolutionary rebellion. We must expose the evil crimes of those who initiate disturbances, thereby destroying the unity of the motherland and the unity of the nationalities, and beating, smashing, plundering, burning, and killing. We must expose the evil conspiracy of foreign countries and powerful enemies within foreign countries who intervene in our internal affairs to split Tibet from the motherland. We must expose politically inflammatory rumours that start disturbances. We must refute those who defame the Party and the State. Through good education and propaganda, the people of different nationalities will correctly understand the damage done by the disturbances and their true nature, and through their own understanding will take the side of the Party and the State. At the same time, we must declare war on those who initiate disturbances and violent rebellion.

(II) Mobilizing the masses with a broad mind, we must expose the criminals who initiate disturbances. Protecting the unity of the motherland throughout the region and deepening the unity of the nationalities are essential for deepening education in patriotism; stressing the Four Cardinal Principles and opposing bourgeois liberalism are essential for deepening education in socialism; self-control and tolerating hardship are essential for deepening education in revolutionary traditions and the law. Relying on hard and detailed political-ideological work, and taking the heightening of the consciousness of the broad Party members, cadres of different nationalities, and the masses as our basis, we must mobilize the masses using various methods to expose the criminals. All counties (and administrative districts [*chus*]) and all village administrations [*shang*], streets, offices, and branches of state enterprises, must have administrators for the work of exposing. They must record piece by piece the information and documents exposed by the masses, carrying screening and investigation through to completion. At the same time, guaranteeing the secrecy of those who expose, they must provide them with protection and support.

(III) Through a profound examination we must make it possible to get to the bottom of the situation. The basic levels of Party and State organization and related departments, bearing absolute responsibility, must thoroughly do the work of screening and investigation, beginning by investigating the problems of the principal people and incidents in the riots and unrest. Thoroughly investigating people who have been released from prison after serving sentences and who have not reformed, people who have been released from reeducation through labour, and in addition criminals who have broken the law and those who are suspected of spying, we must clearly screen and investigate what they have done within the disturbances. The different localities must forcefully screen and investigate criminals who have participated in the disturbances in the different localities. At the same time, we must strengthen mutual assistance to conscientiously supplement the work of screening and investigation in Beijing, Lhasa, and other regions. As soon as we come to know of people and actions associated with the violent counter-revolutionary rebellion in Beijing and people and actions associated with the disturbances in Lhasa, we must jointly investigate and communicate with the cities of Beijing and Lhasa. We must carefully handle the information and people that we expect the investigation in the different localities to reveal.

(IV) Strengthening our control over the whole society, we must promptly strike the criminals who continue to propagate their evil actions.

1. We must resolutely practise the different methods of curfew in Lhasa. All departments and divisions must do whatever they can to protect the social discipline of Lhasa, closely supplementing the army units who are enforcing the curfew, patrolling and inspecting important regions and key places, and safeguarding important residences. We must immediately arrest those who put up and distribute posters and translations of reactionary literature, those who continuously instigate counter-revolution, and those criminals who propagate evil criminal actions. To those who consistently resist arrest, in accordance with the law, army units enforcing the curfew and the police have the power in their respective jurisdictions to use force to execute the law. We must increase our vigilance toward guns, ammunition, explosives, and other dangerous materials; and, gathering up guns and ammunition distributed throughout society, we must eliminate this source of injury to our security.

2. Offices of the Public Security Bureau and State Security, the People's Armed Police, and related departments, resolutely doing the work of supervision and surveillance of criminals engaged in evil actions, must help Beijing and other provinces or autonomous regions to arrest those wanted criminals who have initiated violent rebellion and are fleeing arrest. By checking the borders and putting up roadblocks etc., we must prevent those who start disturbances from escaping across international borders to foreign countries.

3. When those who have been exposed by the people are initially questioned, we must investigate the evidence provided by criminals of those initiating disturbances, and make searches and arrests. Through interrogation we will achieve great results in this work.

4. In conjunction with the registration of foreigners and the renting of

accommodation, by frequently screening and investigating places with big difficulties, such as hotels, bus and railway stations, the residences of units of contract workers coming from outside, rented houses, and the residences of pilgrims etc., we will be able to detain suspicious people and investigate criminals.

5. Quickly and strictly putting this policy into practice, we must punish according to the law criminals from the disturbances and other criminals. Closely assisting the Procurator's Office, the courts, and the Public Security Bureau, we must persist in the investigation and prosecute according to the law. In addition, by holding public meetings to decide sentences, the masses will be motivated and educated, and we will terrify the criminals.

(VI [*sic*]) We must resolutely practise this policy and do this work in accordance with the legal system. We must practise this policy of striking the criminals; the unity of the majority will render the minority of splittists and other serious criminals friendless and alone. We must combine leniency and severity when we make decisions, emphasizing the distinction between the nature of the two types of opposition. We must definitely take facts as our starting point and hold to the law; we must have a basis in reliable evidence and clear facts. We must make a clear distinction as to whether or not a crime has occurred; we must be absolutely certain of this. We must deal with different situations differently: dealing leniently with those who submit to accusation, while sentencing severely according to the law those who hide, those who flee, and those who continue to commit crimes. We must give rewards to those who contribute to exposing people who initiate disturbances, while sentencing harshly according to the law those who conceal and hide criminals. We must distinguish between those who say a few things that harm the unity of the nationalities because they lack a clear understanding and those who propagate evil conspiratorial actions because they are in the grip of reactionary thinking and are committed to the standpoint of "Tibetan Independence." We must distinguish between people who generally believe or spread rumours and speak what they don't wish for, and those who fabricate rumours and instigate counter-revolutionary propaganda. We must distinguish between those who participate in disturbances because they are deceived or are forced by others, and those who are the ringleaders of disturbances and beat, smash, plunder, burn, and kill. We must distinguish between those who distribute and put up documents of reactionary propaganda because of the lies and deceptions of others, and those who make these reactionary documents and organize their dissemination. With regard to the former type of above-mentioned person, if they accept advice and achieve a higher level of understanding through education, then in general it is all right not to hold them criminally responsible; depending on the situation, you may decide whether or not to deal with them through disciplinary action by the Party or State. The latter type of person should receive heavy punishment in accordance with the law.

Having been criticized and having engaged in self-criticism, those who have participated in the demonstrations and given verbal support without really understanding the current situation must increase their level of understanding and accept the lessons of experience. It is all right not to hold them criminally responsible. The meeting of cadres of the Party, State, and Army of the capital [Beijing] on the evening of 19 May concluded that people who have made serious mistakes and who continue to take a mistaken standpoint and support the disturbances are to be dealt with according to Party, State and school discipline. After a full investigation of the circumstances of participants in the disturbances and violent counter-revolutionary rebellion in Beijing and other places, each case is to be dealt with according to the situation.

VII (sic). *Organization and leadership*

Members of the Autonomous Region Party Committee, comrades Hu Jintao and Raidi, are both to take the main responsibility, and the Party Committee Leading Work Group for Stabilizing the Situation is to organize the practice. In addition, comrades from the Advisory Committee, the Discipline and Inspection Committee, the Organization Department, the Propaganda Department, the Political and Legal Affairs Committee, the United Front Work Department, the Education Commission, the Bureau of Nationalities and Religious Affairs, and responsible related departments are to participate in this. Two government offices to do the work of screening and investigation are to be established. The first is to be established by the Political and Legal Affairs Committee, summoning people from related departments, and it will do special investigation work. The second will be established by summoning people from the Regional Discipline and Inspection Committee and the Organization Department, and it will do the work of internal screening and investigation. The responsibilities of these two government offices are to collect information, apply the policy, and supervise the investigation. Lhasa offices, city committees, associations, schools, and divisions of state enterprises, village administrations [shang] and town administrations, businesses, factories, and private enterprises, must all establish Leading Work Groups for screening and investigation, one after another, under the leadership of the Party Committee (Party teams [tang tsu'u]); furthermore, the principal leading comrades must themselves actually exercise strict control. The Leading Work Groups for comprehensively repairing and caring for the stability of the situation in the regions are to bear the responsibility of leading the work of screening and investigation in these regions. The different levels of the Leading Work Group to Stabilize the Situation and the Leading Work Group for Screening and Investigation must both begin to do their work quickly making detailed plans, taking into account their actual individual situations. For offices which have a number of problems, it is all right if they establish departments for special work, and similarly, by mobilizing the people, problems will be exposed.

In accordance with the principle of "in one's own jurisdiction take charge oneself," the Party committees of the respective regions are to bear the leading responsibility for the work of screening and investigating society, and the Party committees of the various departments and offices are to bear the leading responsibility for the screening and investigation of departments of offices, schools, and state enterprises. In Lhasa the different departments of the Autonomous Region are to bear the responsibility for leading the work of screening and investigation in the departments of the Autonomous Region stationed in Lhasa.

The Autonomous Region Political and Legal Affairs Committee is to bear the leading responsibility for the work of investigating and striking serious criminals who have started disturbances and splittists within disturbances. The Autonomous Region Discipline and Inspection Committee together with the Organization Department are to bear responsibility for directing the work of internal screening and investigation.

The work of screening and investigation is a political struggle, and the deployment of this strategy will determine whether or not Tibet remains safe for a long time. As for the key to whether we will be able to accomplish this responsibility well: because we depend on the different levels of Party committees, we must make their responsibilities explicit and they must bear their responsibilities accordingly. In offices where the work of screening and investigation is not going well, schedules must be made for putting the leading departments in order. When the necessity arises, the higher level offices are to send special Work Groups to help.

The Regional Party Committee, the different levels of the Party and the State, and in particular the different levels of leading cadres, taking the standpoint of carrying through to completion without wavering the Four Cardinal Principles, protecting the unity of the motherland without wavering, and opposing splittism, are to struggle resolutely against splittists and other serious criminals. Furthermore, within the current struggle they are to show that they can proceed through self-understanding, by experiment and trial.

Tibet Autonomous Region Committee of the Communist Party of China
and
The Tibet Autonomous Region Government

27 July 1989

C

AN URGENT APPEAL FROM OUR
ANGUISHED HEARTS[1]

The great Protector Deities long ago commanded by Padmasambhava have not
lost their power.[2]

Though we have brought this fate upon ourselves, it is not time for the end
of the aeon.[3]

Are we not under the domination of misfortune and demonic hindrances?[4]

Look with your eye of wisdom and see if it is time now for the forces of power
to rise up.[5]

---

[1] The title in Tibetan is *drag bskul snying gi gdung 'bod*. A *drag bskul* is the most
urgent form of request for supernatural intervention. This "political prayer" was
distributed in Lhasa on 27 September 1989, while martial law was in effect in the city.
It is written in a traditional metrical style characteristic of prayers of this type. It contains phrases reminiscent of the *bden smon*, a prayer composed by the Dalai
Lama in 1960 and familiar to most Tibetans. The author of this *drag bskul* is unknown,
but the style and choice of words suggest that he is an older individual with a
traditional education, familiar with the religious curriculum in Gelugpa monasteries.
The "urgent appeal" was copied and distributed by an underground group of independence activists — the Tiger-Leopard Group (*stag gzig*) — who has been responsible for
distributing a number of political tracts in Lhasa.

[2] This "urgent appeal" is directed to the protector deities of Tibet, requesting their
aid in bringing a speedy end to the Chinese occupation of Tibet and in facilitating the
return of the Dalai Lama. The "protector deities" (*bstan srung ma*) are the dharmapāla,
an important class of deities in Tibetan Buddhism. Generally portrayed as fierce and
wrathful, the protectors are supernatural entities who have been subdued and tamed
by great religious teachers (such as the magician-saint-hero Padmasambhava) and
charged with the protection of the Buddhist faith against its enemies. See Nebesky
(1956) for a description of the cult of protector deities in Tibet.

[3] The "eon" (*bskal pa*) referred to in this line is the present existence of the world,
which has not yet come to an end; therefore, it is reasonable to request help from the
protector deities in overcoming the obstacles and misfortunes that characterize worldly
existence.

[4] The "misfortune" (*rkyen ngan*) and "demonic hindrances" (*bar chad*) in this line
refer to the Chinese occupiers of Tibet, who are generally described as the instruments
of demonic forces.

[5] The "arising" of the "forces of power" (*mthu dpung skyed pa*) is a standard phrase
in prayers of this type referring to the supernatural forces under the command of the
protector deities, who are able to defeat the enemies of the Buddhist faith and dispel
demonic influences.

One deity of this land of snow mountains incarnates the compassion of all
the Buddhas and Bodhisattvas.[6]
A pure unmistaken line of incarnations has come to Tibet.
Now, when the melodious sound of the wheel of Dharma is spoken everywhere in foreign lands,
Look with your eye of wisdom on those who have stayed behind, like the
corpse of a dead lion.[7]

In the midst of the ruins of the great monasteries, magnificent places of
pilgrimage, blades of grass sing a sad song.
The disputations of the monks arguing the five bundles of Sutras are not heard;
a foreign song is sung.[8]
Wild animals dwell in the hermitages and caves of practitioners of Tantra and
Mantra.[9]
Look with your eye of wisdom, you gods, how have we erred to make this
happen?
Although the Buddha's wisdom is always as close to the faithful as a body
and its smell,
Because of the two obstructions, I and those like me are deprived of the
Buddha's words and commentaries.[10]
Like the agony of a baby bird whose training is not yet complete,
Look soon with your eye of wisdom upon the suffering of these sentient beings
so we may see his face.[11]

[6] The "one deity of the land of snow mountains" is Avalokitśvara (*spyan ras gzigs*),
the bodhisattva of compassion, who incarnates in the line of the Dalai Lamas.
[7] The phrase "those who have stayed behind" refers to Tibetans inside Tibet. This
stanza complains that people throughout the world can hear the teachings of the Dalai
Lama while those in Tibet have no such opportunity.
[8] This line suggests that the author of the "urgent appeal" is familiar with the
curriculum in the large Gelugpa monasteries. The "five bundles of Sutras" are
Pramana (*tshad ma* = logic), Prajñāpāramita (*phar phyin* = "perfection of wisdom"),
Madhyamika (*dbu ma* = philosophy of the "middle way"), Abhidharma (*mdzod* =
phenomenology), and Vinaya (*'dul ba* = discipline).
[9] Tantra and Mantra here refer to the esoteric practices of yoga and meditation
pursued in each generation by a highly respected minority in isolated retreats.
[10] This line also suggests the familiarity of the author with the monastic curriculum. The "two obstructions" (*sgrib gnyis*) are the "afflictive obstructions" (*nyon
sgrib*) preventing liberation from cyclic existence and the "obstructions to the omnis-
cience of a Buddha" (*shes sgrib*). The wisdom of the Buddhas is present everywhere,
but ordinary beings are unable to perceive this.
[11] Here the protector deities are being asked to aid in bringing the Dalai Lama back
to Tibet.

Because Tibetans are a people with great compassion and faith in Dharma,
The precious life and warm blood of our heroes and heroines is flowing in
the streets of Lhasa.
Look soon with your eye of wisdom upon the torment of our friends in the
struggle,
Held in the court of the Lord of Death, brought by inhuman foreign enemies
to the land of men.[12]

Unexcelled, most powerful Protectors of Tibet,
Were we not like mother and child, we could not ask this of you.
This is the anguished appeal of a child separated from its mother.
Though unbidden, we are powerless not to speak out, please be patient.
Though the ripening of our sins is relentless, there must be an end.
The Dalai Lama has said the great star of the dawn has already risen.
If we hold fast to the words of truth of the Tibetans,
There is no doubt we will soon be victorious.

From all the friends in the struggle of the Lhasa Tiger-Leopard Group

27 September 1989

---

[12] Yama (*gshin rje*) is the Buddhist "Lord of Death". His "court" takes place in the afterlife, where one is condemned without mercy to punishment for one's sins in this life. This line compares the suffering of Tibetans under Chinese rule to the scenes of torture in the "court of the Lord of Death".

BIBLIOGRAPHY

English-language publications

Ackerly, John, and Blake Kerr. 1989. *The Suppression of a People: Accounts of Torture and Imprisonment in Tibet.* Somerville, MA: Physicians for Human Rights.

Anderson, Benedict. 1983. *Imagined Communities: Reflections on the Origin and Spread of Nationalism.* London: Verso.

Avedon, John F. 1986. *In Exile from the Land of Snows.* New York: Vintage Books.

Background Papers on Tibet. 1992. Tibet Information Network, September 1992. London: Tibet Information Network.

Beijing Review. 1991. "Tibet Launches Massive Development Project." *Beijing Review*, vol. 34, no. 3, 21–27 January 1992: 5–6.

———. 1992. "Tibet — Its Ownership and Human Rights Situation." *Beijing Review*, vol. 35, no. 39, 28 September–4 October 1992: 9–42.

Bullard, Monte R. 1985. *China's Political-military Evolution.* Boulder, CO: Westview Press.

Burridge, Kenelm. 1969. *New Heaven New Earth: A Study of Millenarian Activities.* Oxford: Basil Blackwell.

China's Tibet. 1992. "Tibet Encourages Foreign Investment." *China's Tibet*, vol. 3, no. 4, winter 1992: 19–20.

———. 1992. "Living Buddha Xarucon." *China's Tibet*, vol. 3, no. 3, autumn 1992.

Clarke, G.E. 1987. "China's Reforms of Tibet, and Their Effects on Pastoralism." Discussion paper 237. University of Sussex: Institute of Development Studies.

Connerton, Paul. 1989. *How Societies Remember.* Cambridge University Press.

[*The*] *Constitution of the People's Republic of China.* 1983. Beijing: Foreign Languages Press.

Constitution of Tibet. 1963. New Delhi: Bureau of His Holiness the Dalai Lama.

[*The*] *Criminal Law and the Criminal Procedure of the People's Republic of China.* 1984. Beijing: Foreign Languages Press.

Defying the Dragon: China and Human Rights in Tibet. 1991. LAWASIA and Tibet Information Network, March 1991 (London: Tibet Information Network).

Ding, Xue-Liang. 1988. "The Disparity Between Idealistic and Instrumental Chinese Reformers." *Asian Survey* 28(11): 1117–39.

Dorje Gashi, Tsering. 1980. *New Tibet: Memoirs of a Graduate of the Peking*

Institute of National Minorities. Dharamsala, India: Information Office of His Holiness the Dalai Lama.

Ekvall, Robert B. 1964. *Religious Observances in Tibet*. University of Chicago Press.

Forbidden Freedoms: Beijing's Control of Religion in Tibet. 1990. Washington, DC: International Campaign for Tibet.

Freedom of Religion in China. 1992. Asia Watch, January 1992. New York: Human Rights Watch.

Gellner, Ernest. 1983. *Nations and Nationalism*. Oxford: Basil Blackwell.

Goldstein, Melvyn C. 1989. *A History of Modern Tibet, 1913–1951: The Demise of the Lamaist State*. Berkeley: University of California Press.

—— and Cynthia M. Beall. 1989. "The Impact of China's Reform Policy on the Nomads of Western Tibet." *Asian Survey* 29(6): 619–41.

Grunfeld, A. Tom. 1988. "Developments in Tibetan Studies in Tibet Today." *China Quarterly*, no. 115 (September): 462–6.

Gyatso, Janet. 1987. "Down with the Demoness: Reflections on the Feminine Ground in Tibet." *Tibet Journal*, 12(4): 38–53.

Havnevik, Hanna. 1990. *Tibetan Buddhist Nuns*. Oslo: Universitetsforlaget.

Hobsbawm, Eric and Terence Ranger (eds). 1983. *The Invention of Tradition*. Cambridge University Press.

Humphrey, Caroline. 1983. *Karl Marx Collective: Economy, Society and Religion in a Siberian Collective Farm*. Cambridge University Press.

Kapferer, Bruce. 1988. *Legends of People, Myths of State*. Washington, DC: Smithsonian Institution Press.

Kapstein, Mathew. 1992. "Remarks on the Mani bKa'-'bum and the Cult of Avalokiteśvara in Tibet" in Stephen D. Goodman and Ronald M. Davidson (eds), *Tibetan Buddhism: Reason and Revelation*. Albany: State University of New York Press: pp. 79–93.

The Long March: Chinese Settlers and Chinese Policies in Eastern Tibet. 1991. Washington, DC: International Campaign for Tibet.

Ma Rong. 1991. "Han and Tibetan Residential Patterns in Lhasa." *China Quarterly*, 128 (December): 814–35.

—— and Pan Naigu. 1988. "Tibetan-inhabited Areas: Demographic Changes." *Beijing Review*, vol. 31, no. 14 (4–10 April 1988): 21–4.

MacInnis, Donald E. 1989. *Religion in China Today: Policy and Practice*. Maryknoll, NY: Orbis Books.

Merciless Repression: Human Rights Abuses in Tibet. 1990. Asia Watch, May 1990. New York: Human Rights Watch.

Mirsky, Jonathan. 1990. "The Secret Massacre." *The Observer* (London), 12 August 1990: 17.

Mumford, Stan Royal. 1989. *Himalayan Dialogue: Tibetan Lamas and Gurung Shamans in Nepal*. Madison, WI: University of Wisconsin Press.

Nebesky-Wojkowitz, René de. 1956. *Oracles and Demons of Tibet: The Cult and Iconography of the Tibetan Protective Deities*. The Hague: Mouton.

Ngagpo, Jigme. 1988. "Behind the Unrest in Tibet." *China Spring Digest*, January/February 1988: 22–32.

Norbu, Dawa. 1985. "An Analysis of Sino-Tibetan Relationships, 1245–1911: Imperial Power, Non-coercive Regime and Military Dependency." In Barbara Nimri Aziz and Matthew Kapstein (eds), *Soundings in Tibetan Civilization*. New Delhi: Manohar.

——. 1991. "China's Dialogue with the Dalai Lama 1987–90: Prenegotiation Stage or Dead End?" *Pacific Affairs* 64(3): 351–72.

Nowak, Margaret. 1984. *Tibetan Refugees: Youth and the New Generation of Meaning*. New Brunswick, NJ: Rutgers University Press.

Ortner, Sherry B. 1978. *Sherpas Through Their Rituals*. Cambridge University Press.

People's Republic of China: Repression in Tibet 1987–1992. 1992. London: Amnesty International.

Political Prisoners in Tibet. 1992. Asia Watch and Tibet Information Network, February 1992. New York: Human Rights Watch.

Richardson, Hugh E. 1984. *Tibet and its History*. Boulder, CO: Shambala.

Schwartz, Ronald David. 1991. "Travelers Under Fire: Tourists in the Tibetan Uprising." *Annals of Tourism Research* 18(4): 588–604.

Shakabpa, Tsepon W.D. 1984. *Tibet: A Political History*. New York: Potala Publications.

Southwold, Martin. 1983. *Buddhism in Life*. Manchester University Press.

Spiro, Melford E. 1982. *Buddhism and Society: A Great Tradition and Its Burmese Vicissitudes*. Berkeley: University of California Press.

Stein, R.A. 1972. *Tibetan Civilization*. Stanford, CA: Stanford University Press.

Tambiah, S.J. 1976. *World Conqueror and World Renouncer*. Cambridge University Press.

Tibet: Issues for Americans. 1992. National Committee China Policy Series, vol. 4, April 1992. New York: National Committee for US-China Relations.

Tucci, Giuseppe. 1980. *The Religions of Tibet*. London: Routledge and Kegan Paul.

Turner, Victor. 1977. *The Ritual Process*. Ithaca, NY: Cornell University Press.

Wang Xiaoqiang and Bai Nanfeng. 1991. *The Poverty of Plenty*. London: Macmillan.

Wangchuk Sharlo, Tseten. 1992. "China's Reforms in Tibet: Issues and Dilemmmas." *Journal of Contemporary China* 1(1): 34–60.

Whyte, Martin King. 1974. *Small Groups and Political Rituals in China*. Berkeley, CA: University of California Press.

Tibetan language party and government documents (in order of citation in the text)

Document no. 13 (27 July 1989), "Work Plans of the Regional Party and the Regional People's Government's for Resolutely Striking Splittists and Other Serious Criminals through Screening and Investigation" (*ljongs tang 'ud dang ljongs mi dmangs srid gzhung gi kha phral ring lugs pa dang de min tshabs che'i nyes gsog par gtsang bsher dang 'brel sems thag gtsang bcad kyis rdung rdeg gtong rgyu'i skor gyi las ka'i jus gzhi*), in "Selected Study Documents for Discussion by Party Members" (*dmangs gtsos tang yon la dpyad gleng byed pa'i slob sbyong yig cha 'dems bsgrigs*), Organization Department of the TAR Party Committee, March 1990 (for internal circulation), pp. 78–98.

Document no. 3 (30 June 1989), issued by the Central Committee of the CPC, "Report on Work Plans for Resolutely Suppressing Those who Incite Counter-Revolutionary Rebellion through Screening and Investigation" (*gsar brjer ngo rgol gyi gdum spyod zing slong bar gtsang bsher dang 'brel sems thag gtsang bcad kyis drag gnon bya rgyu'i las ka'i jus gzhi'i skor gyi dgongs skor snyan zhu*), in "Selected Study Documents for Discussion by Party Members" (*dmangs gtsos tang yon la dpyad gleng byed pa'i slob sbyong yig cha 'dems bsgrigs*), Organization Department of the TAR Party Committee, March 1990 (for internal circulation), pp. 68–77.

"Propaganda Program for Socialist Ideological Education" (*spyi tshogs ring lugs kyi bsam blo'i slob gso gtong rgyu'i dril bsgrags rtsa 'dzin*), Work Committee of the Bureau Office of the Regional Government (*ljongs srid gzhung don gcod khang gi las don ru khag*), undated (list of directives distributed to local cadres in April 1992).

Gyaltsen Norbu, "Speech to a Work Meeting of Regional Party Members" (*'dzongs tang ud las don tshogs 'du'i thog gi gsung bzhad*), 30 October 1991 (marked "secret" [*gsang ba*] and internally distributed in numbered copies), p. 28.

"On the Illegal Establishment of the 'Heroes of Ling' in Amdo County and Their Elimination" (*a mdo rdzong du khrims 'gal gyis "gling gi dpa' brdul" btsugs pa dang de med par bzos pa'i skor*), in vol. 9-10-11 of the "Tibet Information Book" (*bod sjongs 'phrin deb*), issued by the Bureau of the TAR Party Committee, 2 July 1982 (numbered for internal circulation), pp. 39–48.

Other sources

Tibet Daily, in Tibetan (*bod ljongs nyin re'i tshags par*).

Foreign Broadcast Information Service — China (referred to in the text as *FBIS*).

Joint Publications Research Service — China (referred to in the text as *JPRS*).

INDEX

Abbots of monasteries (*mkhan po*), 60; and administration of nunneries, 100
Academy of Social Sciences, 47
Ackerly, John, 6n
administrative detention. *See* Reeducation through Labour
Africa, 224
agricultural policy, 196–8
All India Radio, 172
altruism, 71–3
Amdo, 9, 10, 14, 59, 63n, 100, 211, 211n; number of Chinese settlers in, 205–6
Amdo county, 227, 227n
Amitabha (*'od dpag med*), 226
Amnesty International, 6, 6n
Anderson, Benedict, 29n
Ani (nun), 101
Ani gompa (*a ni dgon pa*), 101n; *see* nunneries
anti-splittist campaign: 144, 175, 183; announcement of, 43–4, 44n; in the monasteries, 56–8; and neighbourhood committees, 50–6; phases of, 45; *see also* political campaigns
armed resistance: 32, 223; during 1950s, 11–12; during Cultural Revolution, 13, 99n
arrests: 2, 3, 21, 37, 45, 74, 110, 111, 132, 193, 195; of demonstrators, 24–5, 31, 188; detention without charges, 76n; following 1988 Mönlam festival, 85–6, 93–5; of foreigners, 4, 38, 40; at Ganden in 1983, 59; of monks, 38, 57, 61, 82–3; number of, 186–7, 186n; of nuns, 74, 97, 99, 171; at Ratö, 118; of students, 146
Article 102 (of Criminal Law of PRC), 77
Asia Watch, 6, 187n, 192n
Aśoka Maurya, 33n

Association of Tibetan People of the Three Provinces (*chol gsum bod mi'i mthun tshog*), 129, 154
Atisha, 62n
autonomous prefectures and counties, 10, 205, 213n
Avalokiteśvara (*spyan ras gzigs*), 33n, 226, 245n
Avedon, John, 12n, 99n, 126n

Bai Nanfeng, 199–202, 199n, 208, 213n
Banakshöl hotel, 169
Barkhor: 22, 23–5, 26–7, 29–33, 35, 36, 62n, 74, 80–2, 97, 110, 139–42, 143, 157, 159, 171, 185; alleged massacre, 165n; displays of posters, 129, 131, 132, 138, 154, 155; and Nobel Peace Prize celebrations, 172–3, 215; parade of Maitreya statue, 79; patrols by troops, 109, 110–11, 112, 160; *see also* demonstrations
Basang (Party official), 113
Beall, Cynthia, 13n, 196n, 198n, 226–7, 227n
Beijing, 11, 18, 19, 54, 68, 133, 148; commitment to reforms, 209; demonstration by Tibetan students in, 143; imposes martial law, 160; plans to shoot demonstrators, 142–3; and screening and investigation, 175; Tiananmen Square demonstration, 179n; *see also* Communist Party of China, People's Republic of China
Beijing University, Institute of Sociology, 135
bod chen mo ("great Tibet"), 10
Bodhisattva, 33n
bourgeois liberalization, 177, 196
bsangs (incense), 23, 28, 172–3
Buddha Śākyamuni, 33

251